The Bedside,
Bathtub & Armchair
Companion to
Shakespeare

Also by Dick Riley and Pam McAllister

The New Bedside, Bathtub & Armchair Companion to Agatha Christie

The Bedside, Bathtub & Armchair Companion to Sherlock Holmes

The Bedside, Bathtub & Armchair Companion to Shakespeare

Dick Riley & Pam McAllister

CONTINUUM • NEW YORK • LONDON

2002
The Continuum International Publishing Group Inc
370 Lexington Avenue, New York, NY 10017

The Continuum International Publishing Group Ltd
The Tower Building, 11 York Road, London SE1 7NX

Design by Stefan Killen Design
Printed in the United States of America
Library of Congress Cataloging-in-Publication Data

Riley, Dick.
       The bedside, bathtub & armchair companion to Shakespeare / Dick Riley &
Pam McAllister.
       p.   cm.
       ISBN: 0-8264-1249-1 (alk. paper) – ISBN 0-8264-1250-5 (pbk. : alk. paper)
       1. Shakespeare, William 1564-1616 – Handbooks, manuals, etc. I. Title:
Bedside, bathtub and armchair companion to Shakespeare. II. McAllister, Pam. III.
Title.
       PR28951.R5   2001
       822.3'3–dc21   2001017332

Contents

Contents

Preface

Man of the Millennium

At the turn of the century, Shakespeare was named "Man of the Millennium" in a British poll. In the States that year, sexy and smart *Shakespeare in Love* won seven Academy Awards, including "Best Picture."

The calendar pages turned, and now it's a new century, a new millennium, but still, on stages around the globe, Will's characters strut their stuff—raging at storms, swooning in balcony scenes, pinching each other's bottoms, poking fun, dying. Shakespeare is as hot as ever.

His world was vastly different from ours. He used a quill pen, not a computer. He never heard of AIDS, though thousands perished outside his London home from the plague. In his day, there was no Elizabeth Taylor to play Cleopatra or Gwyneth Paltrow to play Viola; all the female roles were played by men and boys in pretty dresses. Long before rolling brown-outs and power shortages, his plays had to be performed in daylight for lack of not-yet-invented electricity; there were no foot-lights, nor did his fans go to the local video store to check out his latest productions.

Why is Shakespeare still such a dominant figure on the world's stage? It is the timeless stuff of life and death in his writing that we recognize as familiar. Shakespeare's aging, raging fathers and weeping, strong-willed mothers are not unlike our own. His rebellious daughters and despondent sons are very like the ones who bewilder us today. His uninterested, jealous, or cheating lovers are like the ones who broke our hearts just yesterday. His swaggering braggarts remind us of the wearisome windbags we had to endure this morning at the office. We know these people and realize, with a start, that Shakespeare knows us.

Sitters, Standers, and the Rest of Us

Before modern fire regulations, 3,000 people would sometimes cram into a play-house, like Shakespeare's Globe Theatre, for an afternoon of high drama. Those who paid only a penny *stood* for the full time, generally two or three hours, in a pit so close to the stage they were within spitting distance of the actors. These hearty groundlings were the lifeblood of the theater. For a few pennies more, an audience member could have a seat in one of the three tiers of galleries. Shakespeare had something for everyone—bawdy jokes and plenty of action for the bloke whose blood was still pumping from the execution he'd seen earlier in the day, to subtle poetry for the ruff-wearing gallant seated in the second tier.

It used to be said that no home was complete without a Bible and the collected works of William Shakespeare. In fact, the complete works have been published into more than thirty languages. Individual editions of the plays and poems have been translated into over eighty languages, including Yakut and Zulu.

Today, though academics try mightily to claim him for their own, Shakespeare still has something for everyone—the groundlings, the gallants, and the rest of us.

This is a book for those who, like the groundlings of Shakespeare's time, want more out of life than a TV sitcom when we come home from a long day at school or at work. It is also for the gallants among us, who want nothing more than to sit in our armchairs or soak in our tubs or rest on a cloud of pillows as we read.

Is Shakespeare Worth the Effort?

Yes. Shakespeare is hard work, but the good news is that his plays get easier—and more rewarding — with each reading. His poetry will stay with you forever, his characters will enrich your life. Read a play, not once, but three times. The first time may be difficult. The second time, all the major themes and famous speeches will feel familiar. The third time around, you'll fall in love with the poetry, the majestic manipulation of words that has had scholars and readers and playgoers talking for four hundred years.

Use this book to help you sort out the details, lay the groundwork. (The capsule summaries of each play are presented in the order used in the earliest published collection of Shakespeare's plays, the 1623 *First Folio*.) Next, since the plays were written to be seen and heard rather than read, visit your local library and take out a BBC video or movie of the play you want to read. Better yet, go to the theater and see a play performed on stage. Before long, you'll know what the fuss is about.

Acknowledgments

In addition to the works themselves, we found a number of books to be useful in illuminating Shakespeare's world and its issues. *The Oxford History of Britain*, edited by Kenneth O. Morgan (1984, Oxford University Press), is a good overall guide to the history of the nation; *Shakespeare's Kings*, by John Julius Norwich (1999, Scribner, NY) is a well-written account of the period covered by the history plays; Peter Thomson's *Shakespeare's Professional Career* (1992, Cambridge University Press) offers a good deal of information about Elizabethan theater and Shakespeare's place in it. Samuel Johnson's introduction to his edition of Shakespeare, now more than two centuries old, retains both its freshness and its telling insights.

Two books were particularly helpful in terms of Shakespeare's language: *English, Its Life and Times* (1994, Times Books, NY) by Robert Claiborne, and *The Mother Tongue* (1990, Avon Books, NY), by Bill Bryson

A full list of potentially useful books and articles on Shakespeare would itself consume a good part of this volume. Anyone with a desire to explore further many of the issues covered here would also be well advised to consult either *Shakespeare A to Z* by Charles Boyce (1990, Bantam Doubleday Dell Publishing Group, Inc., NY) or *The Reader's Encyclopedia of Shakespeare* (Campbell and Quinn, eds., Crowell, 1966), an exhaustive and informative compendium of articles on a wide variety of matters Shakespearean.

Two books which will be useful for those just beginning to delve into the works are *Stories from Shakespeare* by Marchette Chute (1976, 1987, Penguin Books USA, NY) and *The Friendly Shakespeare: A Thoroughly Painless Guide to the Best of the Bard*, by Norrie Epstein (1993, Penguin Books, NY).

Many individuals were helpful during the process of researching, writing, and producing this volume. Prominent among them were our editor, Evander Lomke, who set us on this path, and designer Stefan Killen, who helped translate our ideas into book form. We'd also like to thank Terry Geesken of the Museum of Modern Art/Film Stills Archive.

On a personal note, Dick would like to thank Marcia, for her longtime loving support and inspiration, and Ian and Jessa for their patience, particularly in being subjected to impromptu and unrequested renditions of some of Shakespeare's great speeches.

Pam thanks her family for their love and enthusiastic support, with special thanks to her brother-in-law, Gregory Baum, for his help researching Shakespearean gardens. Pam is especially indebted to her friend and neighbor, Edward Nathan, for his critical review of a large portion of the manuscript, his well-seasoned insights, and his encouragement.

Finally, our thanks to the best kept secret in New York City, a little gem of a place in Soho called "Housing Works Used Book Cafe," site of many an editorial conference.

A sketch of the Globe Theatre

All the World's a Stage
—Elizabethan Drama

lizabethan theater took the form of its venues from medieval inns. It competed for its audience with public executions and battles between packs of dogs and bears or bulls. As a group, players had the same status as "vagabonds...and sturdy beggars," meaning that they were automatically suspected of being a drain on the public purse and a threat to public order.

Even "serious" drama of the day included much of what we would now find crude clowning and vulgar displays. Women were not allowed on the stage until after 1660, so such classic female parts as Juliet, Cleopatra, and Lady Macbeth were played by boys. Although in modern theaters the least expensive seats are farthest from the action, in the typical Elizabethan theater the cheap seats were not seats at all, but the roofless standing room before the stage. This was generally occupied by the "groundlings," an often noisy mob of

> *"All the world's a stage,*
> *And all the men and*
> *women merely players."*
> *—As You Like It*

lower artisans, common laborers, and prostitutes from the brothels that shared the theater district.

The players themselves came from a variety of social backgrounds, the only requirement being an ability to remember lines and please the crowd; meanwhile, like the modern movie business, the writers were often hired hands toiling alone or in groups in ill-paid anonymity,.

But whatever its shortcomings, the Elizabethan theater spawned a new and often wildly popular public entertainment; it offered the opportunity for riches and fame for men from a variety of trades and backgrounds; and in the process it created—amid much that was forgettable—art that has delighted and uplifted generations.

Not the least of these were the plays of William Shakespeare.

Origins of the Drama

In the middle ages and the early

1 3

Renaissance, entertainment at fairs and festivals included acrobats and tumblers, balls and pageant-like masques, and mystery and morality plays, where actors portrayed biblical characters or figures such as Vice and Virtue. But in morality plays these were archetypes, and one distinguishing characteristic of Elizabethan drama was the evolution of archetypes into individual characters recognizable as real people.

Innyards and Great Halls

It would not have occurred to anyone at the beginning of this period to have a structure specially built for dramatic performances. While acting companies could set up a stage in any open space, the most profitable places were the yards of inns, which were often designed around a hollow square, the interior being an enclosed yard and the walls consisting of several floors of rooms reached by galleries that looked into the square. The plays were staged in daylight.

For indoor performances actors relied on the great halls—large open spaces—in private mansions or the homes of medieval guilds, lit by candles when necessary. The Inns of Court, effectively the schools for lawyers in London, were often the site of plays.

Staying Ahead of the Authorities

Since the outdoor plays in particular tended to excite the unwelcome interest of the municipal authorities, theaters when they became economically feasible were often built outside the city

walls. London's were first constructed to the north, then later on the south bank of the Thames, in an "entertainment" district already featuring brothels and arenas where bulls and bears were set upon by dogs.

The northern venues included the building known as The Theatre, erected in 1576 by speculators including James Burbage (his son Richard was to head the acting company to which Shakespeare later belonged). In the next year a second theater was in operation nearby.

A number of special-purpose theaters in the London area eventually evolved to serve the interests of Shakespeare's and rival companies, including the Curtain and then the Fortune north of London proper, and the Rose, the Swan and the Globe on the south side of the Thames (the Globe, or more properly its wooden beams, actually were the timbers of the Theatre, first constructed north of the city, then disassembled, transported across the frozen Thames, rebuilt and renamed.)

Although size was not uniform, the open area where the groundlings stood was a rough circle or polygon perhaps fifty to as much as eighty feet across at its widest point; the stage itself forty feet wide, taking up much of one end of the arena and jutting out twenty feet or more, and standing three to five feet off the ground. The vertical walls were stacked with galleries reached by staircases.

Counting both the groundlings and the occupants of the galleries, the theaters are thought to have contained 2,500 to 3,500 persons (a tight fit, but

Elizabethan theater. Folger Shakespeare Library

the Elizabethans were physically smaller than modern audiences).

Indoor theaters like the Blackfriars —at first home to troupes of the boy actors who provided much of the competition to the adult companies—were a good deal smaller. Shakespeare's company eventually took over the Blackfriars, in addition to the Globe, and many experts believe that his later and more contemplative works were composed for these smaller theaters that had a richer and more sophisticated clientele.

In the Middle of the Audience

We have grown used to the "proscenium" stage, in effect a room with one wall removed through which we observe the action. In Shakespeare's day, for both the open-air and enclosed theaters,

the stage jutted out toward the audience, which surrounded it on three sides. Elizabethan stages had no curtains and little or no stage machinery or even scenery.

Dialogue established location and time, entrances and exits were through two doorways to the "tiring house" or backstage area (the dead are ceremoniously carried off in Shakespeare less for dramatic than logistical purposes— there was no other way to clear the stage). A curtained alcove at the back of the stage made do for scenes such as the smothering of the Duke of Gloucester in his bed in *Henry VI, Part Two*. A kind of open gallery high in the back wall provided the balcony outside Juliet's bedroom to which Romeo could climb, or the castle wall from which Richard II could descend to surrender to the usurping Bolingbroke. A roof surmounted the stage, its underside sometimes painted with sky or moon and stars ("the heavens") and a trapdoor in the stage provided entrance and exit for demons and ghosts, or space for the gravedigger in *Hamlet*.

"Costume" Drama

What Shakespeare's theater lacked in stage machinery it made up in costumes. Most English people who could afford it loved rich dress (the Queen as much as anyone), and contemporary observers repeatedly mention the silks and finery of the players—not to mention the audience.

Costumes were of course much more portable than stage machinery, making touring much easier, and the outfits themselves were as likely to belong to the individual players as to the theater company, and to be passed on to their heirs or needy actors.

Whatever the period or setting of the plays—ancient Rome, Egypt, northern Italy, or Prospero's Island—Elizabethans knew the drama was about their own lives, and had no problem with costumes that were historically inaccurate or completely anomalous. One contemporary drawing of the staging of *Titus Andronicus* shows the players in an eclectic mix of modern and Roman armor, along with Renaissance dress.

There was smoke and the noise of cannon for battle scenes, the sounding of trumpets to start battles and to announce the arrival of important figures. Music was also part of most performances, from the trumpet call from the roof of the theater to songs in the plays. There was also incidental music before and during the performance, along with jigs and clowning that often followed even the serious and tragic plays. (see Music, pages 201–9)

The Search for Novelty

Acting companies were under constant pressure to provide new entertainment to their audiences, and it appears that a successful play was performed perhaps half a dozen times in one season. Actors in modern repertory companies may have to keep parts for two or three plays in their heads at one time, but Elizabethan actors probably had to keep many more, and often had several parts in each production. At the same time, they were constantly learning new ones.

Whereas plays performed at court, country manors, or great halls could start at any time, those performed in outdoor venues and theaters began at two or three o'clock in the afternoon, and lasted between two and three hours. Since act-and-scene changes were few or nonexistent, the action was continuous, unlike modern plays. (Even under these conditions, a few plays like *Hamlet* would have taken longer if performed in the form that has come down to us.)

Given their proximity to the audience and the general tenor of Elizabethan crowds, feedback from the audience was immediate, and we can presume shouts of encouragement and applause for convincing scenes, boos and pelting missiles for those that left the audience unconvinced. Groundlings would have paid a penny, the better part of day's pay for a common laborer, and would have expected value for their money.

The Writer's Life

Like most modern popular drama and films, actors rather than authors were the major draw (the modern role of director or auteur as we know it in film did not exist). As in the modern movie business, writers could come up with an idea that they would then propose to a company, be commissioned to write a summary and short version (a "treatment" in modern parlance) and, if approved, to write a complete piece. Like today's movie studios or producers, the company itself could conceive of an idea and approach a dramatist of reputation to put it in shape.

It was not unheard of—once again like the modern movie business—for a company to commission more than one writer for a particular work, and combine their efforts into one play, or to ask a writer to rewrite or revise another's work. The finished product was paid for—two pounds was apparently a not uncommon sum—and became the property of the company, not the playwright. However, it appears that well-known or valued playwrights could receive additional payments if the play had a number of successful performances.

Copyrights as we know them did not exist, and playwrights felt free to take plots and dialogue from other sources. For example, some experts trace a good deal of the *Henry VI* trilogy to earlier plays, and much of the dialogue for Shakespeare's Roman plays comes

directly from an English translation of Plutarch's *Lives of the Noble Greeks and Romans*.

Companies had every reason to avoid publishing successful plays to keep them out of the hands of competing troupes, although plays no longer in the repertory or about to be released in unauthorized versions could be sold to printers.

Such printings were generally in the portable form known as *quartos*, and a number of Shakespeare plays—drawn from play books, actors' reminiscences and other sources—were first published in this form, some with his name on the title page and others without it.

He appears to have had little or no role in such productions, and it was not until his peer and competitor Ben Jonson oversaw the publication of his own plays that dramas were treated with the same care in publication as literature. Shakespeare was, however, careful with the publication of his long poems.

The Advantages of Companies

Municipal authorities, particularly in London, generally treated acting companies with a combination of contempt and suspicion, and whenever the plague swept through London, as it did with regularity, the companies were forced into the uncomfortable and often unprofitable position of touring the provinces looking for audiences.

Because of official hostility, players found their best protection in seeking the patronage of nobles or high officials, who sponsored their appearances at court and smoothed their way in both London appearances and on tour. The leading companies of Shakespeare's day included the Lord Admiral's Men and Shakespeare's own Lord Chamberlain's (later the King's) Men. Although the size of these troupes no doubt varied, it appears most included twelve to sixteen regular players, with day players also available as needed. Most Shakespeare plays can be performed with fifteen or sixteen actors, given doubling of parts.

The companies were organized as partnerships, with some number of the players sharing in the profit or loss of the company. It was presumably as a sharer in the company and its theater, rather than writer and actor, that Shakespeare found financial success. The economics of the new theater business could be compelling. In addition to the groundlings at a penny a head, seats in the highest gallery went for two pennies, and the lower galleries more. Companies that attracted crowds with popular actors and performances could establish a substantial revenue stream, and by some calculations sharers in Shakespeare's company could have received as much as 150 pounds a year in revenues—when five pounds a year could have kept a workingman's family and ten pounds a year was the salary of a university educated schoolmaster in the country.

Richard Burbage, the leading figure in Shakespeare's company and its star tragedian, made, like Shakespeare, a comfortable fortune. His leading rival in the Lord Admiral's Men, Edward Alleyn, married the daughter of the theatrical impresario Philip Henslowe, retired to the life of the country gentry and endowed a school. They were, of course, the exception rather than the rule. Unsuccessful actors and writers ended up in poverty or other lines of work.

The Persistence of Shakespeare's Writing

A number of Elizabethan dramatists loom large in the history of the period, notably Christopher Marlowe and Ben Jonson, whose reputations at the time may have exceeded Shakespeare's.

But while their works are now for students and scholars and rarely performed, Shakespeare's, even after 400 years, have attained the status of classics. It is a measure of his achievement that no such claim can be made for any other artist of his period—in literature, painting, architecture, or music. The poetry of Spenser, the art of Hilliard, the architecture of Inigo Jones, the songs of John Dowland, can still be enjoyed today. But their artistic achievements, however considerable, do not continue to live for us the way Shakespeare's plays continue to invigorate the modern stage.

> "I don't know what it means and I don't care because it's Shakespeare and it's like having jewels in my mouth when I say the words."
> —Frank McCourt, *Angela's Ashes*

THE TEMPEST

DUKE USES MAGIC TO CONJURE STORM AT SEA: STRANDS OLD ENEMIES

Period

Three hours one enchanted afternoon

Setting

A magic-filled island in a distant sea

Shakespeare may have been contemplating his art as conjurer/storyteller when he created this fairytale of a powerful magician. Here are all the elements expected in the tradition of a romance—troubled nobles suffering separation and exile in some exotic, fantastical place abounding with allegorical creatures. After a series of improbable coincidences, families will be reunited and love will triumph.

As the play begins, twelve years have passed since Prospero, the rightful Duke of Milan, was overthrown by his evil brother Antonio, who got some help from Alonso, the King of Naples. Prospero and his three-year-old daughter Miranda were put in a little boat and set adrift on the ocean. It was assumed they would die of exposure. It was their good fortune, however, to be helped by the compassionate counselor, Gonzalo, who smuggled food and water on board as well as books of magic from Prospero's own library.

Though Prospero now admits that he had neglected his worldly responsibilities as duke for his "secret studies," his passion for magic has come in handy on the enchanted island where he and little Miranda washed ashore.

On this island, they encountered two beings. Caliban, whose name is an anagram of "cannibal," is the son of a deceased witch. He is earthy, bound to indulge his crudest emotions, a creature of Nature with a capital N. Prospero, a man of art with a colonizer's zeal, taught him to speak and had hoped Caliban would adapt "civilized" behaviors. That hope was dashed when Caliban attempted to rape Miranda, who is now fifteen. He's been relegated to the status of slave ever since.

The other being on the enchanted island is Ariel, a spirit of the air, indebted to Prospero for freeing him from the witch's curse. Like the resentful

Caliban, the grateful Ariel wishes to be set free. For now, however, he remains a servant to the great magician.

Prospero longs to regain his rightful place as the Duke of Milan. To this end, he creates a great storm at sea, a "tempest," which capsizes a ship carrying his evil brother Antonio and the brother's old cohort Alonso. Also on board are the loving old counselor, Gonzalo, and the king's handsome son Ferdinand. The magic storm terrifies everyone, but no one dies. Each is washed ashore the bewitched island.

With Prospero's magic and Ariel's haunting siren songs, the various characters pass through a series of adventures and enchantments. Handsome young Ferdinand, who for a long time believes he's the only survivor of the shipwreck, and innocent Miranda see each other. It's love at first sight for both of them. The only human Miranda has seen for the past twelve years is her father. She's overwhelmed by the sight of Ferdinand and, eventually, the others, and says, "O wonder! How many goodly creatures are there here, / How beauteous mankind is. O brave new world / That has such people in it!"

Elsewhere on the island, there is injury and discontent, inspiring malicious conspiracies. Caliban has thrown himself at the feet of two drunks, a servant and a jester, and urges them to help him kill Prospero. The jester muses, "Misery acquaints a man with strange bedfellows." Antonio, the evil brother, is once again plotting an overthrow. This time his cohort is Sebastian, Alonso's

greedy brother. Assuming that young Ferdinand is dead and not wanting the throne to be inherited by the king's daughter Claribel, the two plot to kill the king and put Sebastian on the throne.

All make their way to Prospero's door. The generous magician tests and tries them. His spell transforms them and the characters undergo a "sea change." Old wrongs are righted, forgiveness and reconciliation abound. They gather at a wedding masque given by Prospero for Miranda and Ferdinand, whose love hints at new life and moral regeneration, the healing of old wounds. The audience is reminded that, just as the magician manipulated nature, so the playwright and his actors manipulated us. Like the play, (this "insubstantial pageant"), life itself is transient. Prospero speaks:

> "We are such stuff as dreams are made on."
> —*The Tempest*

Our revels now are ended. These our
  actors,
As I foretold you, were all spirits, and
Are melted into air, into thin air...
We are such stuff
As dreams are made on; and our little
  life
Is rounded with a sleep.

Before he sails for home to reclaim his title, abandoning the magical for the ordinary, Prospero keeps his promise and frees Ariel, who sings, "Merrily, merrily shall I live now / Under the blossom that hangs on the bough." Perhaps more significantly, Prospero gives the island back to Caliban and claims a kinship of sorts, saying, "...this thing of darkness / I acknowledge mine."

Likely Source of the Plot

Shipwrecked seamen washing a-shore on a magical island was the theme of several Italian commedia dell'arte plays. Tales of explorers to the "new world" thrilled and intrigued the Elizabethans, and these may have kin-

Notable Productions and Performances

First performed privately at the court of King James I in 1611 and then two years later at the wedding of Princess Elizabeth, the public had to wait. A number of adaptations became popular throughout the seventeenth century, including one called *The Enchanted Island* by Dryden and

dled Shakespeare's imagination. He may also have been influenced by Mont-aigne's optimistic essay "Of the Cannibals," about the utopian potential of newly discovered native societies.

Notable Features

Though written near the end of Shakespeare's career, *The Tempest* was placed first in the earliest published collection of his plays, the 1623 *First Folio*.

Davenant. There was a 1674 opera by Thomas Shadwell and a score for *The Enchanted Island* was composed by Henry Purcell in 1690. Another operatic version, *The Tempest*, was produced in 1756 by David Garrick featuring sixty dancing children.

An 1821 perfomance of *The Enchanted Island*, produced by Frederic Reynolds, included music by seven composers, including Purcell, Mozart, and Rossini. In the mid-1800s, the original Shakespearean text was taken out of mothballs and tried anew, with some success.

In the 20th century, John Gielgud played Prospero in four productions, including one staged by Peter Brook in 1957.

In 1962, James Earl Jones starred as Caliban in the New York Shakespeare Festival presentation by Joseph Papp. And in 1995, after a performance directed by George C. Wolfe at New York City's Delacorte Theater in Central Park, actor Carrie Preston wrote:

One night when we were performing in the Delacorte, we had an experience where theater and nature intersected in an absolutely amazing way. Patrick [Stewart—in the role of Prospero] was doing his "All our revels now are ended" speech at the end of the play, and out of nowhere the wind started whipping through the theater. Patrick's robe billowed around him. "Our spirits now are air." The rose petals we had scattered during the wedding scene started swirling around him. "Our little lives are rounded by a sleep." Suddenly the wind stopped and the petals settled. You couldn't get an effect like that with any amount of technology.

Other Use of Basic Plot

The 1956, opera, *Der Sturm*, by Swiss composer Frank Martin. Others have also composed music inspired by this play including Hector Berlioz (1830), Arthur Sullivan (1872), and Tchaikovsky (1873).

The 1956 film, *Forbidden Planet*, directed by Fred McLeod Wilcox—In this fifties sci-fi treatment, the enchanted island becomes planet Altair-4 where a reclusive mad scientist, Dr. Morbius, (Walter Pidgeon) is aided by Robby the Robot, a computerized Ariel. Morbius is intent on protecting his mini-skirted daughter (played by Anne Francis) who, in turn, is busy flirting with Commander Adams (Leslie Nielsen) who has just arrived from Earth.

USA film, *The Tempest*, 1960, directed by George Schaefer—In this Hallmark treatment for television, Richard Burton played Caliban and Lee Remick was Miranda.

USA film, *Tempest*, 1982, directed by Paul Mazursky—in which a bored urban architect named Philip (John Cassavetes) moves to a deserted Greek island with daughter Miranda (Molly Ringwald) and takes up with a free spirit (Susan Sarandon). Kalibanos (Raul Julia) lurks about, teasing and tempting his prey. In the end, Philip makes the decision to return to Manhattan and to his responsibilities as a family man.

UK film, *Prospero's Books*, 1991, directed by Peter Greenaway. John Gielgud plays Prospero in this avant-garde adaptation of the play, which is about the process of creating. The film explores the themes of Prospero's twenty-four books from which his magical powers are drawn: water, pornography, hell, music. Pages of the books, with their calligraphy and illustrations, whirl over and around Prospero, the creator of the story, as he walks through an abundance of naked flesh in a series of overlapping images, flashbacks, and dream sequences.

USA NBC-TV production, 1998, *The Tempest*—filmed in Charleston, South Carolina, with Peter Fonda as Gideon Prosper, this story is about a father who has moved with his daughter to a secluded island to get away from the Civil War. When a Union soldier comes ashore, Prosper is forced to deal with the world and its agonies.

UK, *Toufann*, a 1999 Mauritian drama in Creole, written by Dev Virahsawmy. Based on *The Tempest*, this play portrays Prospero as a computer genius who develops his science to have total control over nature and people. All his plans begin to fall apart, however, when his beloved daughter states her intention to marry Kalibann, the son of a slave.

The Tempest is the basis for W. H. Auden's poem sequence *The Sea and the Mirror*.

THE TWO GENTLEMEN
OF VERONA

MAN BETRAYS FRIEND OVER
WOMAN WHO SCORNS HIM

Period

Renaissance

Setting

Northern Italy

This is the story of a young man who turns his back on a girl who loves him, finding himself entranced by a young woman who is already engaged to his friend. The plot is driven by a sense of duality of character and roles: two young men of Verona, Proteus and Valentine; two young women, Julia and Silvia; two young servants who serve as comic foils, Launce and Speed; two authority figures, Antonio and the Duke of Milan.

Valentine has decided to seek "the wonders of the world abroad," and is bound for the emperor's court, but his friend Proteus remains at home where, as Valentine notes, "affection chains thy tender days." The object of Proteus's affection is Julia, who, pretending a lack of interest, at first tears up a letter

Proteus has sent her, then picks up and tries to read the pieces.

Antonio, Proteus's father, determines that his son's education must include some time at court, and determines to send him—despite his lack of enthusiasm—to join his friend Valentine.

At court (not the emperor's it turns out, but that of the Duke of Milan) Valentine himself has fallen prey to love, in his case for Silvia, the daughter of the duke, who like Julia is reluctant to make her attraction for Valentine obvious. Instead, she has set him the task of composing a love letter on her behalf to an unnamed person—and then ordering him to keep it himself (the servant Speed has to explain her strategy to Valentine).

Proteus takes a painful leave of Julia, pledging "my true constancy" and exchanging rings with her. But one look at Silvia when he arrives in Milan drives thoughts of Julia from his mind. Valentine tells him that he and Silvia are in love, and because her father plans to

24

marry her to a rich suitor, the lovers are planning to flee.

Wanting Silvia for himself, and sure that he can woo her away from the duke's choice if Valentine is out of the picture, Proteus tells the duke in confidence of Valentine's plans to use a rope ladder to climb to Silvia's window and escape with her. The duke finds the rope ladder under Valentine's cloak, along with a letter to Silvia pleading his love and telling her "this night I will enfranchise thee."

Outraged, he banishes Valentine under pain of death. "What light is light, if Silvia not be seen?" asks Valentine to himself. "What joy is joy, if Silvia be not by?" But while Silvia is confined by her father, Valentine leaves Milan, after Proteus promises that he will see his friend's letters delivered "even in the milk-white bosom of thy love."

In her current "heavy, melancholy" state at Valentine's banishment, Silvia is deaf to the virtues of the duke's choice for her, Thurio. The duke and Thurio therefore prevail upon Proteus, who volunteers to help Thurio's suit by telling Silvia of the faults he knows in Valentine's character. He also urges Thurio to compose a sonnet for Silvia, and to bring musicians to play beneath her window.

Valentine and Speed, meanwhile, in a forest outside Mantua, are set upon by

a band of outlaws. Valentine tells them he has been banished for killing a man, and the outlaws, quite taken with him, offer him the choice of either becoming their captain or of dying. He elects the former.

Back in Milan Proteus mulls his fascination with Silvia ("the more she spurns my love, the more it grows"), then joins Thurio and the musicians in a song at Silvia's window. Among the audience on the street is Julia, who has come from Verona disguised as a boy to find Proteus, and she is overwhelmed to find him paying court to another woman.

She places herself (still in disguise) as a servant to Proteus under the name Sebastian. Proteus gives her the ring that she had given him in Verona, tells her it came from another woman, and orders her to give it to Silvia. Silvia refuses it, knowing that it came from Julia, and Julia (still in her Sebastian disguise) thanks her, saying of Julia "to think upon her woes, I do protest that I have wept a hundred several times."

Silvia, assisted by the gentlemanly Eglamore, makes her escape from Milan, pursued by her father and Thurio. Proteus and Sebastian/Julia have also taken up the chase. They catch up with Silvia as they are all captured by the outlaws, who bring them before Valentine. Despite Silvia's urging that Proteus "read over Julia's heart, thy first best love," Proteus threatens to "force thee to yield to my desire." At this point Valentine confronts him with his treachery.

"My shame and guilt confounds me," a chastened Proteus says. Valentine, moved by his repentance, offers "all that was mine in Silvia I give thee." Julia then gives Proteus a ring, saying it was the ring that Proteus had meant to go to Silvia. However, Proteus recognizes it for the one he gave to Julia in Verona, and Julia reveals her true identity.

Proteus's love of her is immediately restored ("What is in Silvia's face, but I may spy more fresh in Julia's with a constant eye?"). The duke and Thurio appear, and Valentine threatens Thurio if he "but to breathe upon my love." Says Thurio "I hold him for a fool that will endanger his body for a girl that loves him not," and abandons his suit. The duke then embraces Valentine, who insists that the outlaws share in his pardon, and all return to Milan for the planned double wedding of Julia and Proteus, Silvia and Valentine.

Likely Source of the Plot

A similar story about characters named Felix and Felismena (or Philomena) was in circulation during Shakespeare's time, in the form of a story by a Portuguese author and an anonymous contemporary play.

Notable Features

There are two characters who qualify as almost purely comic—the servants Speed and Launce. Speed specializes in rapid-fire observations and wordplay. He tells his master that he knows he has fallen in love because Valentine has learned "to wreathe your arms like a malcontent, to relish a love song like a robin redbreast, to walk alone like one that had the pestilence...to sigh like a schoolboy...to weep like a young wench.... " Launce, on the other hand, spends much of his time talking either to himself or to his dog, Crab. Says Launce of his dog, "I have sat in the stocks for puddings he hath stolen, otherwise he had been executed. I have stood on the pillory for geese he hath killed, otherwise he had suffered for't."

> **"Who is Silvia? What is she, That all our swains commend her?"**
> —*The Two Gentlemen of Verona*

The play is one of the shortest in the canon, with only about 2,300 lines. Based on a variety of internal and external evidence, it is thought to be among Shakespeare's earliest works. There is some speculation that the version that was printed in the *First Folio* (no quarto editions survive) represents the remains of a longer original that had been abbreviated for performance on some special occasion.

If true, that would explain certain inconsistencies, such as the first letter that Julia (as Sebastian) delivers to Silvia, then immediately reclaims, without explanation, as the wrong letter. Other problems of sloppy editing include the fact that the young men are sent to the emperor's court, but end up at that of the duke; and that the constant references to the sea and travel by ship are inconsistent with the fact that Verona is a city in the interior.

More troubling still for modern audiences is the moment near the end of the play when Valentine, after he has prevented Proteus from taking Silvia by force and witnessed Proteus's repentance, offers Silvia to him. (Silvia's views of this generosity are unknown, since she has no lines past this point.) The deep bond between men—a relationship of more import than that between men and their female lovers—was something of a staple of Renaissance drama, including the sources from which Shakespeare drew the story.

Other Notable Uses of the Plot

Valentine agrees to become the leader of the outlaws after they promise him they will "do no outrages" on women or the poor. He describes them to the duke as "reformed, civil, full of good," as he asks for them to be pardoned and readmitted to society. The device of the wronged young gentlemen taking up a life of harmless crime was also a convenient one for Gilbert and Sullivan in *The Pirates of Penzance*.

Notable Productions and Performances

The perceived shortcomings of *Two Gentlemen* have meant that it has a relatively scant production history over the centuries. The *Time-Life*/BBC production, starring Tyler Butterworth and John Hudson as Proteus and Valentine respectively, includes a good performance by Tessa Peake-Jones as Julia and Tony Hagarth as Launce.

The "Chandos Portrait" of William Shakespeare. National Portrait Gallery

The Glover's Boy from Stratford

owever remarkable the literary achievements of William Shakespeare, there is little question but that his life itself was in many ways unremarkable, particularly for a man credited with creating the largest, most varied and most influential body of literary work in English. Although students and historians often complain that his life is ill-documented, we do have a patchwork of records of family events, court cases, critical opinions, and personal recollections of Shakespeare that certainly surpass that of the average glover's boy from an English market town of the latter 16th century. But those documents alone constitute the record of a somewhat ordinary life. He was born into a middle-class family in central England, married young (though his wife was older), got himself both to London and into the theater in a variety of occupations, eventually made a comfortable living, and retired to the life of a prominent citizen in his hometown, where he died at age 53.

Stratford-on-Avon

In the year of Shakespeare's birth, Stratford was a town of some 1,500 people. Before the Industrial Revolution in both farming and transportation, villages were limited in size by the productivity of the surrounding countryside and the ability of streams and rivers to bring necessities in and ship out local products like wool, cloth and cheese. While a village by today's standards, in comparison to the London of its day, Shakespeare's Stratford would have been the equivalent of a small city.

His father, John Shakespeare, was of yeoman stock, meaning that his family may have been reasonably well off, but rented their farms and worked them themselves. His mother's maiden name was Arden, and her family had been part of the gentry. As such they were landlords rather than tenants, and lived off the income from their properties rather than their own work. In fact, Mary Arden's father had been the landlord of John Shakespeare's father. In his youth John

Shakespeare had been a rising young man, and, in addition to the properties his wife brought to their marriage, had a business as a glover and tanner (very respectable crafts at the time) and was also active in buying and selling grain.

This small-town entrepreneur and his wife had eight children. William was the third, born in 1564—his birthday of April 23 is a calculation based on his christening several days later. In William's youth his father was an active player in the town's civic life, and was appointed to a series of local posts of increasing responsibility, culminating in his election as bailiff or mayor.

Early Education

Mandatory public schooling was of course unknown, but there was an excellent "grammar" school in Stratford for the sons of important or well-off families. The grammar involved was that of Latin, and after a few years training in basic English literacy in the local "petty" school, boys of better family spent the remainder of their years in school learning to read, recite and speak Latin, the language in which most scholarly works were still written. The Latin that Shakespeare learned is evident in much of his work, and Latin authors such as Ovid and Terence were an important source for the plays.

The instructors had university degrees, and the best students from a school like Stratford's would often go on with their education. But even if Shakespeare's academic record and interests justified such a move, his family's financial circumstances would not permit it. For reasons that are unclear, his family fortunes began a significant decline during his teenage years, and public records indicate the mortgaging of their property and his father being pursued for unpaid debts.

A Youthful Marriage

In November of 1582, with the special permission of the local bishop (because the ceremony went forward without the usual three readings of the banns), William Shakespeare of Stratford married Anne Hathaway of the neighboring village of Shottery. He was 18, she 26. Their daughter, Susanna was born six months later. Their twins, Hamnet and Judith, were born in 1585. (Hamnet died in 1596).

For the next seven years, Shakespeare's life is something of a mystery. There are few records and a number of traditions. One—that he fled Stratford after being caught poaching deer on a nobleman's estate and ended up holding horses outside a London theater—may be about as reliable as George Washington's destruction of the cherry tree. Another tradition has him serving as a schoolmaster in some country town or in the household of a gentry family.

London Theater

We do know that by 1592, Shakespeare's name was already somewhat established in the world of the London theater. A contemporary writer, Robert Greene, was resentful of the success of an actor-playwright like Shakespeare, particularly since Shakespeare, unlike Greene, had not had a university education. Greene described "an upstart crow" with "his tiger's heart

An Elizabethan schoolroom. Hulton Deutsch Collection

wrapt in a player's hide, supposes he is as well able to bombast out blank verse as the best of you...in his own conceit the only Shake-scene in a country." (The "tiger's heart..." reference is to a line in an early Shakespeare play, *Henry VI, Part Three*.

In 1592 the plague, which broke out periodically in European cities, struck London again, and authorities closed the theaters because of the risk of infections in the crowds. In an attempt to forge a literary career (poetry at that time being more highly valued than drama), Shakespeare used 1592 and 1593 to write and oversee the publication of his two major lyric poems— "Venus and Adonis" and "The Rape of Lucrece." There were multiple editions of the lyric poems, particularly the latter, but Shakespeare returned shortly thereafter to the theater. (His sonnets were not written for publication, and their dating is a matter of dispute).

As part of his professional growth, Shakespeare became associated with an acting company. Acting had a somewhat unsavory reputation and, to increase their respectability and ease their way with various authorities, actors formed groups and sought the patronage of important people. The acting company to which Shakespeare belonged, led by Richard Burbage, eventually took the name of the Lord Chamberlain's Men (the Chamberlain was a key royal official).

The company prospered, in no small part due to the plays that their house dramatist produced. Several times a year they acted before Queen Elizabeth. The company also put on productions in the courtyards of inns, at the law school/professional society halls known as the Inns of Court, and at theaters such as the Swan, built on the south side of the Thames in part to escape the jurisdiction of the London authorities, who were unenthusiastic about the crowds and unrest associated with the theaters.

In 1599 the company built its own theater, the Globe, in the same neighborhood as the Swan. It held an estimated 3,000 people, at rates that varied from a penny for standees, to several cents for a cushioned seat in the equivalent of a box. Most of the great tragedies—from *Hamlet* to *Antony and Cleopatra*, are believed to have been written for and performed in this theater.

> *"He was not of an age, but for all time!"*
> —Ben Jonson

We know that Shakespeare was an actor, although we have no reliable indication of the kind of parts he played. Tradition has him in "featured" roles such as the ghost in *Hamlet* and Chorus in *Henry V*.

After Queen Elizabeth died in 1603, she was succeeded by King James I, who took Burbage and Shakespeare's company under his own patronage, and they became known as the King's Men. Their appearances at court became even more frequent, and they were firmly established as the leading theatrical company of their day.

In 1608, while the company continued to own and operate the Globe, the members also leased an indoor theater in a building known as Blackfriars, giv-

James I

ing them the ability to offer plays year-round and at higher prices. Late plays such as *The Winter's Tale* and *The Tempest* are thought to have been written for the more sophisticated audiences attracted to this venue.

While he spent his professional life in London, over the years Shakespeare had made substantial investments in and around Stratford, where his wife and children always lived. In 1607 his daughter Susanna married a prominent Stratford physician, Dr. John Hall, and settled into a house not far from her parents' home. By 1610 or 1611 Shakespeare is thought to have taken up more or less full-time residence back in Stratford, although there are records of occasional appearances in London, and his last credited play, *Henry VIII* was

produced in 1613 (although many authorities believe it was actually a collaboration between Shakespeare and one of the new dramatists with the King's Men, John Fletcher.)

On April 23, 1616, a few months after the marriage of his second daughter, Shakespeare died in Stratford. He was buried in the church in which he had been christened.

Shakespeare as a Professional

Although we have internalized the 19th century myth of the artist as tortured genius, his life a creative, emotional, and even political struggle, Shakespeare shows us a model of moderation. In a time of considerable public tumult, while hot-tempered actors and writers engaged in everything from public insults to brawls and fatal duels, Shakespeare was known for his civil disposition and genial nature. Careful with money, he earned fees from writing plays, acted in his own and other works, and profited as an owner in the Company and its theaters. He invested his profits in land and buildings, generally in his hometown but also in London.

So expertly did he conceive his works and so facile was his pen that "we scarce received from a him a blot in his papers," his fellow actors and editors recalled after his death. (The same is said to have been true of Mozart.) Shakespeare is credited with writing two or sometimes three plays annually for the better part of twenty years, providing his acting company with a stream of the new material that audiences demanded.

Although he wrote plays about kings

and political subjects, politics always takes second place to character, and his stated political views are completely mainstream for his time. On the great struggle between Catholicism and Protestantism that racked both England and Europe in his time, he is all but silent, and whatever his private beliefs he did not publicly stray from approved Protestant practice.

What We Don't Know

Enormous sections of Shakespeare's life are blank to us, helping to feed the question of whether he in fact was the author of the works credited to his name. We have no real proof that he went to Stratford's school, although it is hard to imagine, given the material in the plays, that he had no formal schooling.

Although he could have seen a good deal of England when his troupe of players toured the country, there is no real evidence that he traveled abroad. Thus there is no easy explanation—other than wide reading and talking to travelers— for his apparent knowledge of other countries. He wrote convincingly of the lives of royalty (admittedly of periods and places not his own), and there are records of occasions when he and his fellow actors were featured at the court of their sovereign (Elizabeth I and then James I). It is not unnatural to assume that he had at least a nodding acquaintance with many of the leading political and social figures of his time. But to the extent that we can determine, his society was that of his fellow actors when he was in London, and his fellow townsmen in retirement.

He had some hopes of literary fame, based on his longer poems (which he oversaw through publication). His poetry was well-received, but failed to ignite the reading public. His work in the theater was no doubt exceedingly interesting, and his involvement as an actor and shareholder made it lucrative. But we might infer from the fact that he made no attempt to preserve his plays that he thought that the future would find them of little interest. Yet for four centuries his plays have dominated our stage, his dramatic images and characterizations have illuminated our literature. It is hard not to think that he would find these facts the most remarkable of all.

The Secret of Psalm 46

uman beings seem endlessly intrigued by possibilities of secret codes and hidden messages. In the 20th century, we played record albums backward and thought we heard buried messages, and we read much into a photograph of four musicians crossing a street, one shoeless. Shakespearean lore has its share of puzzles too. The most fascinating concerns the Bible and the number 46.

The year 1610, when Will Shakespeare of Stratford would have turned forty-six, was a busy one for the committee of scholars employed

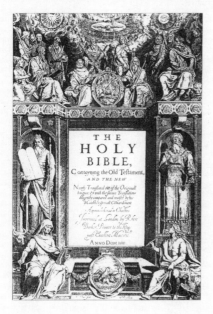

Title page for the King James Bible, 1611. British Library

by King James to translate the holy Scriptures. In that last year before publication of the King James Bible, many revisions were made. The scholars did a good job. Although no longer considered accurate by biblical scholars, this translation is still popularly cherished as the most lyrical and poetic. Did the scholars leave a secret code in Psalm 46? You decide.

Count 46 words from the beginning of the Psalm. You will find the word "shake." Now, count 46 words from the end of the Psalm, not including the punctuating "selahs" (a Hebrew word that indicates a pause in the music of the psalm) sprinkled throughout, and discover the word "spear."

*God is our refuge and strength, a very
  present help in trouble.
Therefore will not we fear, though
  the earth be removed,
and though the mountains be carried
  into the midst of the sea;
Though the waters thereof roar and
  be troubled,
though the mountains **shake** with
  the swelling thereof. [Selah]
There is a river, the streams whereof
  shall make glad the city of God,
the holy place of the tabernacles of
  the most High.
God is in the midst of her; she shall
  not be moved: God shall help her,
  and that right early.*

*The heathen raged, the kingdoms
were moved: he uttered his voice,
the earth melted.
The Lord of hosts is with us; the God
of Jacob is our refuge. [Selah]
Come, behold the works of the Lord,
what desolations he hath made
in the earth.
He maketh wars to cease unto the
end of the earth; he breaketh
the bow,
and cutteth the* **spear** *in sunder; he
burneth the chariot in the fire.
Be still, and know that I am God: I
will be exalted among the heathen,
I will be exalted in the earth.
The Lord of hosts is with us; the God
of Jacob is our refuge. [Selah]*

Did James I ask his star wordsmith to lend a hand in shaping a psalm or two? If so, could Shakespeare have buried a split signature in the text? Did he carve his initials on the sacred writings, to say "I was here," a marker to stand through the ages? Or did scholars honor the Bard with the cryptogram, presenting it as a gift on his 46th birthday? Or have we imagined the whole thing?

THE MERRY WIVES
OF WINDSOR

KNIGHT GETS COMEUPPANCE
AFTER PROPOSITIONING TWO WOMEN
WITH SAME LOVE LETTER

Period

16th century

Settings

Windsor and environs

This is a sitcom, minus commercials, in which two women (think Lucy and Ethel of 1950s television) do a slapstick routine at the expense of a popular buffoon and to the delight of the audience—no laugh track needed. Sir John Falstaff, a fat, lecherous, and greedy knight borrowed from *Henry IV*, has arrived in town with a get-rich-quick scheme. To accomplish his goal, he has turned a leering eye on two attractive, prosperous married women, Mistress Ford and Mistress Page. Falstaff doesn't want either woman, only access to their husbands' money. He writes two love letters, identical "letter for letter, but that the name of Page and Ford differs." Mistress Page says in disgust, "I warrant he hath a thousand of these letters, writ

with blank space for different names." The women are deeply insulted and immediately begin to plot their revenge. They decide to flirt and play along until Falstaff's efforts at seduction lead him into bankruptcy.

The two husbands are tipped off to the knight's intentions. Page doesn't doubt his wife for a moment and finds the whole prospect of her seduction by Falstaff comical, saying, "If he should intend this voyage toward my wife, I would turn her loose to him: and what he gets more of her than sharp words, let it lie on my head." Ford, on the other hand, worries, "A man may be too confident," and decides to spy on his wife to see if she will remain faithful. He soon learns that his wife and her friend are not only unwavering in their marriage vows, they are probably the wittiest, most sensible people in all of Windsor.

The two feisty women remain true to their husbands, but make great sport of toying with the unsuspecting would-be gigolo. Three times the merry wives make a fool of Falstaff. The first time

James Henry Hackett (1800-1871), the leading American Falstaff of his time

they stuff him into a basket of dirty linen and dump him in a ditch. The second time they trick him into disguising himself as an old woman. Finally, they humiliate him as he unwittingly plays the part of Herne the Hunter at a midnight gathering 'round an ancient sacred oak tree. Wearing a buck's head, he is mobbed by children dressed as hobgoblins and fairies who make him their scapegoat for the evening. In the end, he is graciously allowed to laugh at himself.

In a secondary plot, young Anne Page makes her way through a minefield of unappealing suitors (including the choleric French doctor favored by her mother and Slender, the little "whey-faced" idiot favored by her father). She triumphs, through the use of an elaborate deception, and marries Fenton, who "speaks holiday" and "smells April and May."

Likely Source of the Plot

Similar plots appear throughout medieval and classical literature and were especially popular in Renaissance Italian novellas. The story also follows in the tradition of the medieval morality plays satirizing human weaknesses, such as Falstaff's greed.

Notable Features

This work—almost completely in prose—is the only play Shakespeare set in the England of his day. It is also unusual since its main characters are of the middle class, not the nobility. A popular account holds that, after seeing a performance of *Henry IV* at court, Queen Elizabeth proclaimed that she would like to see a whole play about Falstaff in love, and so the play was written in only two weeks.

Notable Productions and Performances

Although it was probably performed for Elizabeth in 1597, the first record of a performance dates from the court of King James I in 1604. Before the Puritans closed the theaters, this play was very popular and when the theaters were reopened, it was one of the first to be staged for the drama-starved population.

BBC 1982, production in which Ben Kingsley played the frantic Mr. Page; Richard Griffith was Falstaff; Judy Davis and Prunella Scales played the two merry wives.

Royal Shakespeare Company production at Stratford, 1985, directed by Terry Hands. Reminiscent of a TV sitcom, the play was set in a 1950s' style suburbia with beehive hairdos and poodle skirts, and effectively revealed the playwright's attitudes toward middle-class pomposity.

Production at the Shakespeare Theatre at the Folger, 1990, directed by Michael Kahn. The actress Pat Carroll played Falstaff.

Other Use of Basic Plot

Otto Nicolai turned the play into an opera in 1849, as did Giuseppe Verdi in 1893 with *Falstaff*. The play also inspired a musical adaptation by Frederick Reynolds in 1824, *Sir John in Love* by Ralph Vaughan Williams in 1929 and a symphonic study, *Falstaff*, by British composer Edward Elgar in 1913.

MEASURE FOR MEASURE

DUKE GOES UNDERCOVER; FANATICAL AGENT OF LAW AND ORDER EXPOSED AS FRAUD

Period

16th century

Setting

Vienna

Fundamentalists, fascists, and rigid authoritarians have something in common: they adhere to the letter of the law, not the spirit of it. With their inflexible moral stance, they often miss the point, stomping about in heavy boots, destroying what they claim to value.

As this play opens, everyone agrees that something must be done: Vienna is out of control. It is a city of vice, booming with bordellos and enduring a tsunami-sized crime wave. The duke, having ruled unsuccessfully from the top down, realizes he has lost control of the situation. He decides to dress in disguise and see the city from the bottom up to discern what can be done. To this end, he announces his departure and appoints Angelo as chief deputy.

Chief Deputy Angelo is rigidly obsessed with law and order, a stickler for detail. He decides to make an example of someone and, in a city teeming with con men and crooks, Angelo turns his vengeful eye on young Claudio. When Claudio and his sweetheart, Juliet, had premarital sex, two things happened that complicated their young lives: Juliet got pregnant, and the families postponed the wedding in a feud over the dowry. Awaiting their wedding day, the young lovers have been living together as husband and wife, like hundreds of other casual couples in the city. Technically, however, such an arrangement is an offense punishable by death. Angelo brings the entire letter of the law down on the head of young Claudio. While thieves, gamblers, and bordello owners look on, Claudio is paraded through the streets as an example of immorality. In three days, he will be executed.

Desperate, for a reprieve, Claudio decides to ask his sister Isabella for help. Just a rosary bead away from entering a convent, she judges her brother's sin harshly, but decides to go to the chief deputy to beg for Claudio's life. Cold-hearted Angelo takes one look at Isabella and melts. Telling her to return the next day, he thinks up a plan. If Isabella will surrender her virginity to him, he will spare her brother.

Angelo pitches his idea to Isabella the next day, saying, "redeem thy brother by yielding up thy body to my will." In short, the self-righteous deputy who rules with an iron fist demands illicit sex in exchange for pardoning a man condemned for having illicit sex. Isabella is appalled at the hypocrisy and refuses the deal. She's told to go away and think about it for one day. If she won't change her mind, Claudio will be tortured to death.

Isabella visits her brother in his prison cell and tells him about Angelo's insulting proposition. On the one hand, Claudio is outraged; on the other hand, he really wants to live. He contemplates his death and concludes:

The weariest and most loathed
  worldly life
That age, ache, penury and
  imprisonment
Can lay on nature, is a paradise
To what we fear of death.

Maybe, he suggests, Isabella could sleep with Angelo just this once. "Sweet sister, let me live." But it's not so easy. Isabella can't imagine being defiled by Angelo, the filthy fraud, even for a good cause.

The duke, exploring his city disguised as a friar, has overheard the whole sibling conversation. He tells the brother-sister duo something that may help them. There is a woman named Mariana who is in love with Angelo, even though he dropped her when she lost her dowry. The friar/duke suggests they pull a "bed-trick" on self-righteous Angelo. Maybe Mariana would be willing to pretend to be Isabella for a night in Angelo's bed. And willing she is. Isabella tells Mariana about the rendezvous with Angelo planned for that night. When Mariana shows up in the garden, Angelo doesn't know the difference between one woman and another. He thinks he's with Isabella.

After the tryst, his lust sated, this world-class hypocrite goes back on his word and, instead of freeing Claudio, secretly orders his beheading that night. When the friar/duke learns of this, he tries to find someone who might substitute for Claudio. This proves to be easier said than done. A condemned convict named Barnardine is asked if he'd mind losing his head, but the man protests that he's too drunk to die. He's spared. Luckily, a pirate died in the prison just that morning, and it is his head that's chopped off and sent to Angelo. Although her brother's head is intact, Isabella is told he's been beheaded on the order of Angelo.

The duke decides he has seen enough and ceremoniously returns. He is met at the city gates by Isabella, who publicly accuses Angelo of his crimes. The chief deputy isn't worried; after all, it is her word against his. Then, Mariana steps forward to tell her part in the scheme. The duke once again puts on his disguise as friar to further the suspense. At an opportune moment, he pulls off the disguise and reveals that he

never left the city, but has been there all along, observing the corruption of his chief deputy.

The final scene is a frenzy of forgiveness. Judgments are passed and mercy granted. In a famously ambiguous ending, the duke asks long-suffering Isabella (who, remember, really wanted to be a nun) to be his wife. To the monumental consternation of directors and audiences alike, Isabella exits without giving her answer, and we are left wondering.

Likely Source of the Plot

This bitter little comedy about judgment and mercy, takes its title from the Sermon on the Mount in which Jesus said:

Do not judge others, and God will not judge you; do not condemn others, and God will not condemn you; forgive others, and God will forgive you. Give to others, and God will give to you. Indeed, you will receive a full measure, a generous help-

*ing, poured into your hands—all that you
can hold. The measure you use for others
is the one that God will use for you. (Luke
6:37–38)*

Shakespeare also took inspiration
from an actual scandal. In Italy in 1547,
a judge promised mercy for a murderer
sentenced to death in exchange for sex
with the man's wife. After the judge had
his fun, he went back on his promise
and executed the man anyway. This
story was retold many times. Cinthio, an
Italian writer and professor of philosophy, based a novella on the incident, and
it is believed Shakespeare read this work
in the original Italian in a collection of
Cinthio's work titled *Hecatommithi*
(1565). Cinthio reworked the novella as
a drama, *Epitia*, in 1583. Another
dramatist, George Whetstone, inspired
by Cinthio's novella, also wrote a play
about the scandal, *Promos and
Cassandra* (1578). The Italian scandal
also inspired *Too Good to Be True*, written in 1581 by Thomas Lupton, who
was primarily known as the English
author of a popular health manual.

Tales of rulers exploring their
domain in disguise have fascinated people for centuries and were especially
popular in 16th century England.

Notable Feature

Measure for Measure, in which innocence is tested and hypocrisy revealed,
is considered one of Shakespeare's three
"problem plays." Labeled a comedy, it is
nevertheless a grim and cynical satire
filled with unpleasant characters and
disturbing points of view and thus falls
into a categorical limbo. The term
problem play was first applied to
Shakespeare's dramas by the scholar
Frederick S. Boas in 1896 and specifically refers to three works: *Measure for
Measure, All's Well That Ends Well*, and
Troilus and Cressida.

Notable Productions
and Performances

First performed at court in 1604, the
play did not become popular until the
early 18th century. It fell out of favor
again during the Victorian era when
audiences were scandalized by the "bed
trick."

Peter Brook's 1950 Stratford production starring John Gielgud as Angelo was
famous for the exceedingly long pause
(sometimes up to two minutes) which
preceded Isabella's appeal for her brother's life.

Was Shakespeare Really Shakespeare? The "Authorship Question"

ho wrote Shakespeare's plays? This is not a trick question. It is, in fact, what *Life* magazine once called "history's biggest literary whodunnit."

To be honest, it is hard to imagine that any mere human penned the words we love so well. The range of expression and exquisite rendering of the language seem almost to have come from the hand of God or to have always existed—like the sky, the stars, the air we breathe. It's hard to imagine our lives without *King Lear* or *Romeo and Juliet*, *Othello* or *Hamlet*.

Someone did write the words, however, and that someone was rooted in a specific time and place. The question is who? The answer is not self-evident. The greatest wordsmith of all time left behind no letters to friends; no diary; no early drafts of plays or poems (or late drafts, either) despite the fierce longings of all the planet. This literary Void with a capital V is at the core of the mystery. It is so complete an absence that many believe it must be deliberate. But why?

To make matters worse—or better, if you like a mystery—the shape of what we think we know of Shakespeare's life doesn't seem to fit the scope of the literature he left the world. His life was simply too little and limited. As Ralph Waldo Emerson put it, "I cannot marry the life to the work."

From the late 1700s to the present, there have been those who have thought that Will the glover's son, our Will of Stratford (1564–1616), wrote nary a word, but was, instead, a rather ordinary actor well rewarded for fronting for a mysterious "Other." Henry James, pondering the mystery, said, "I am...haunted by the conviction that the divine William is the biggest and most successful fraud ever practiced on a patient world." There have been many famous names among the doubters, including: John Greenleaf Whittier, Walt Whitman, Mark Twain, Sigmund Freud, Helen Keller, Orson Welles, Muriel Spark, Malcolm X, and Supreme Court Justice Harry A. Blackmun.

"I'm confused now. Was Shakespeare somebody else or was somebody else Shakespeare?"

Sir Derek Jacobi put his doubts this way: "I am highly suspicious of that gentleman from Stratford-on-Avon....I'm pretty convinced our playwright wasn't that fellow. This opinion is very unpopular with the good burghers of Stratford, I realize, but they also make their living on the legend of Shakespeare's local origins. I don't think it was him."

A Brief History of the Authorship Question

Before the publication of the collected plays (*First Folio*) in 1623, there was little link between the Stratford actor and the dramatist. The *Folio* was vague on details about Shakespeare's life, but readers were left with the impression that he was a self-made man from a rural background who had little knowledge of Latin or Greek, (an odd claim for the dramatist whose plays contain hundreds of references to classical names and who drew from many Latin authors).

Legends about Shakespeare's life began to emerge in the mid–1600s. One writer, who was only eight years old when Will of Stratford died in 1616, later claimed to have witnessed Shakespeare in "wit-combats" with Ben Jonson at the Mermaid Tavern. Other similarly doubtful anecdotes were promoted to fill in the blank pages of biography for a curious world.

In 1769, David Garrick staged a Shakespeare Jubilee at Stratford and, from that time on, the Shakespeare industry was firmly established and Stratford became a mecca for pilgrims worshiping the Bard.

Doubts about Shakespeare's true identity began festering in the 1780s when a retired minister, James Wilmot, a friend of Samuel Johnson, moved to Stratford with the intention of writing a biography of Shakespeare. He searched the town and its surrounding area high and low for anything linking the Stratford man to the works by Shakespeare and found nothing. He reluctantly came to the conclusion that Shakespeare was not Shakespeare, but confided this only to a close friend, presumably not wanting to burst the world's bubble.

In the 1850s, an American eccentric, Delia Bacon, loudly raised doubts and opened a can of worms. Suddenly there were many doubters, each with a different idea of Shakespeare's real identity. Over the years, claims have been made for Francis Bacon, Christopher Marlowe, Elizabeth I, and even Anne Hathaway. In all, over sixty different candidates have been proposed.

Why do people doubt that Will of Stratford-on-Avon was the author of the plays and poems attributed to him? Here are some of the reasons:

Reasonable Doubts about Will

Life Documents

What is actually known about the life of Shakespeare could easily fit in the back pocket of a stage hand. The books written about his life are 99.9 percent conjecture.

A few facts have been established with the help of parish records, all of them discovered almost one hundred years after Will's death, but no one knows what happened to Will for the seven years after he turned twenty-one. It is assumed he had a basic grammar school education. It is known he had a wife and three children. Yet, just seven winters later, after what the biographers have dubbed his "lost years," he surfaced in London with lightning speed, became a published poet, immensely successful, on publicly intimate terms with the Earl of Southampton. Scholar Richard Whalen, wrote, "If Will

Shakspere was the author, his initial learning curve was not just steep, it was vertical."

While Shakespeare's name was becoming the stuff of legend in London, Will's name continued to appear on mundane business and legal records in Stratford. He was accused of hoarding grain during a famine and cited for tax evasion. He sued people for small sums owed him.

Documents exist that reflect the comings and goings of his life as a businessman, acquiring property, selling grain. He seems to have retired from London abruptly in 1604, at the very height of his creativity.

There is nothing strange here, if one is considering the paper trail of an ordinary fellow, an actor and businessman making his way in a life split between Stratford and London. It is, on the other hand, a very odd paper trail if one assumes it belongs to the world's greatest writer.

A Question of Class

Those who defend Will from Stratford as the author of the sonnets, poems and plays, say he was a genius and that genius knows no bounds of class, race, or gender and that those who believe he was an unlettered yokel are elitist snobs.

Others argue that the question of class can cut two ways and that it is elitist to blithely dismiss the barriers imposed by the kind of rigid class system which was in place in Elizabethan England. Working-class Will would not have had easy access, if any, to the exclusive world of the nobility who were the subjects of all Shakespeare's plays except

one. Only *The Merry Wives of Windsor* features working-class characters. This play is also regarded as Shakespeare's most artificial and contrived. Imagination must feed on raw material. How could the young man who grew up three days' horseback ride from London manage the subtleties of court life with such familiarity and skill over and over again? When was he exposed to the sports of the nobility such as falconry? When did he find the time and resources to study horticulture and music in the depth reflected in the plays? He knew classical history and mythology in detail and was able to use legal terminology with ease. His numerous references to Italy revealed detailed knowledge of the peculiarities of Venetian law, obscure Italian artists and comic allusions to regional accents. He drew on Italian texts which had not yet been translated into English. How did Will of Stratford gain this degree of expertise? Italian was not taught in Elizabethan grammar schools. His references to law, music, classical mythology, and so on were specific, not general. Could working-class Will have found that much time to study and write while learning his way around London, making theater contacts, and performing on stage?

Charlie Chaplin, whose "little tramp" became a working-class hero in the era of silent films, once said, "In the work of the greatest geniuses, humble beginnings will reveal themselves somewhere but one cannot trace the slightest sign of them in Shakespeare.... Whoever wrote [Shakespeare] had an aristocratic attitude."

Walt Whitman, too, known as the "poet of the common man," contemplating Shakespeare's history plays concluded that whoever wrote the plays attributed to Shakespeare must have been "one of the 'wolfish earls' so plenteous in the plays themselves."

Could Shakespeare Spell His Own Name?

Shakespeare lived in the days before computerized spell-checkers or dictionaries for that matter. Spelling was arbitrary, based on oral tradition. Not only the spelling of common words, but family names as well, varied from document to document, depending on what the person with the pen heard.

Stratford legal documents, almost without exception, spelled Will's last name so that it reflected the pronunciation "shack spur." This is how his name was spelled when legal records were required for momentous life occasions:

- baptism   *Shakspere*
- betrothal   *Shaxpere*
- marriage bond   *Shagspere*
- baptism of daughter *Shakespeare*
- baptism of twins   *Shakespeare*
- body of will   *Shackspeare*
- burial record   *Shakspere*

We could assume that the folks in Stratford had relaxed criteria for spelling, but how did he spell his own name when a document required a signature? There are six known signatures by Will from Stratford. None of them uses the spelling Shakespeare. On his will he signed his name *Shakspere*, twice, and *Shakspeare*, once. The three signatures found on other legal documents have him spelling his name *Shakspe*, twice, and then *Shaksp*.

What raises eyebrows, however, is not the inconsistent spelling of these phonetic variations of the Stratford pronunciation "shack spur," but the remarkable consistency of the London poet/ playwright's name which was uniformly spelled *Shakespeare* or was hyphenated to *Shake-speare*. On the title pages of his published works and in his dedications on the two narrative poems and on the published sonnets and in the vast majority of printed comments by his contemporaries—the name is spelled *Shakespeare*. The conclusion some people draw is that the "shack spur" spelling belongs to a real person, our Will of Stratford. The "Shakespeare" spelling was a pseudonym used by the author of the plays and poems.

Could Will of Stratford spell his own name? All the legible signatures made by Will are unsure and quavering. Scholar Tom Bethell fantasized "a bailiff helpfully at his elbow: 'Keep goin', Will, now an S. That's *good*.' " Each time, he scribbled his name differently, spelled it differently. Surely the great Bard of Avon, who spent so many hours writing with his quill pen, would have developed a signature uniquely and consistently his own in practiced penmanship.

Lack of References to the Stratford Man as Author

Although it is true that you can't go home again, it is exceedingly strange that the people of Stratford-on-Avon didn't seem to realize that their Will had written anything. There are no diary entries or letters by the literate people of his hometown proudly acknowledging their native son. Even his diary-keeping son-in-law, Dr. John Hall, who kept notes about his patients, with an occasional reference to writers of the day, never mentioned his father-in-law. In other words, there is no evidence that, while he was alive, anyone referred to the man from Stratford as an author of anything.

Shortly before his death, Will of Stratford made out a very detailed will, giving specific instruction on the disposal of everything from a silver bowl and plate to his sword and clothing. Much has been made of the fact that he left his "second best bed" to his wife. What is far more remarkable is what he did not leave: he left no manuscripts and no instructions on what was to be done

Chained library, 16th century, Hereford Cathedral, England

with the almost twenty plays which were as yet unpublished. Nor was there mention of a library or any of the books the dramatist had used as references so many times—books by Ovid and Chaucer, the Geneva Bible, Holingshed's *Chronicles*, Plutarch's *Lives*. Books were scarce and cherished in Elizabethan England, often chained to shelves or desks. They were never incidental. If Will of Stratford was the great "Shakespeare," where were all his books?

In his will, he remembered three of his fellow actors by name, but not one poet or playwright, not even the great Ben Jonson, who, it was later claimed, had been a personal friend.

Though the works of Shakespeare were well-known and his name celebrated far and wide, no one painted a portrait of the great writer while he was alive. The few portraits we have were rendered after his death, and the most famous, the engraving on the cover of the *First Folio*, was done by Martin Droeshout who was just 15 years old when Will of Stratford died.

Deafening Silence at Will's Death

By the time Will of Stratford died in 1616, the works of William Shakespeare were famous, yet no one said a word at his death. There was not a single eulogy, though this was an era known for effusive eulogizing.

Mark Twain summarized this odd detail in his last published work, a 1909 pamphlet titled "Is Shakespeare Dead?"

When Shakespeare died in Stratford it was not an event. It made no more stir in

THE BEDSIDE, BATHTUB AND ARMCHAIR COMPANION TO SHAKESPEARE

England than the death of any other for-gotten theatre-actor would have made. Nobody came down from London; there were no lamenting poems, no eulogies, no national tears—there was merely silence, and nothing more. A striking contrast with what happened when Ben Jonson and Francis Bacon and Spenser and Raleigh and the other distinguished liter-ary folk of Shakespeare's time passed from life! No praiseful voice was lifted for the lost Bard of Avon; even Ben Jonson wait-ed seven years before he lifted his.

Hundreds of eulogies were written for the less renowned playwright Francis Beaumont, who died a month before Will of Stratford. Richard Burbage, a popular actor of the day, was eulogized at his death. The year Will died, Ben Jonson wrote a poem praising John Donne, but wrote nothing about the man he would eventually consecrate as "the swan on Avon."

Will was buried in an unmarked grave at Trinity Church in Stratford-on-Avon. His gravestone, absent any family name, included only a strange, rather low-brow verse:

Good friend for Jesus sake forebear,
To dig the dust enclosed here:
Blest be the man that spares these stones,
And curst be he that moves my bones.

Mysteriously, seven years later, the eulogies came, along with a monument bearing a name spelled Shakspeare. Several of the most memorable eulogies that finally emerged from the long silence were unusually dismissive of the monument or the body buried there.

Ben Jonson wrote,

Soule of the Age!
The applause! delight! the wonder of
    our Stage!
My Shakespeare, rise; I will not
    lodge thee by
Chaucer, or Spenser, or bid
    Beaumont lye
A little further, to make thee a roome:
Thou art a Moniment, without a tombe,
And art alive still, while thy Booke
    doth live,
And we have wits to read, and praise
    to give.

John Milton, too, seems preoccu-pied with dismissing the significance of a burial place.

What neede my Shakespeare for his
    honour'd bones,
The labour of an Age in piled stones
Or that his hallow'd Reliques should
    be hid
Under a starrey-pointing Pyramid?
Deare sonne of Memory, great
    Heir of Fame,
What needst thou such dull witnesse
    of thy Name?
Thou in our wonder and astonishment
Hast built thy selfe a lasting
    Monument.

If the Stratford Fellow Wasn't Shakespeare, Who Was?

In 1920, a schoolmaster from north-ern England with the lamentable name of Thomas Looney, published a book titled "Shakespeare" Identified in Edward de Vere, the Seventeenth Earl of Oxford. Today, Edward de Vere (Oxford) is the leading contender as the likely author behind the name Shakespeare.

Edward de Vere, Seventeenth Earl of Oxford. National Portrait Gallery

The Case for Edward de Vere, Seventeenth Earl of Oxford

In brief, here are some arguments scholars have set forth in defense of the claim that Edward de Vere (Oxford) used the name of Shakespeare as a pseudonym and wrote the plays, poems, and sonnets associated with that name.

• *Easy Access to Books and Education*

Born to a life of privilege, Edward was surrounded, from the beginning, by people who cherished the arts. His father, John, loved theater and kept a troupe of actors. Edward began studying at Cambridge when he was only nine and earned a bachelor's degree by age fourteen. One of his tutors was his mother's brother, Arthur Golding, a noted translator of Ovid from whom "Shakespeare" drew many stories. He and Edward were said to have a close literary friendship and he dedicated two books to his nephew. By age sixteen, Edward (by now called Oxford) earned his master's degree from Oxford University and was admitted to Gray's Inn in London to study law. Throughout his youth, he had access to a large fortune. Surviving receipts show that he spent his money lavishly on books by

5 1

Chaucer, Plutarch, Cicero, Plato, the Geneva Bible, and volumes in Italian.

• *A Hidden Name*

The author of the sonnets is someone in pain both physically and spiritually. In his personal correspondence from the 1590s, Oxford complained of his aging and his poor health, and he made specific references to lameness. At age 45, he referred to himself as being lame in a letter to his father-in-law, "I will attend your Lordship as well as a lame man may.... " In Sonnet 37, the poet writes:

As a decrepit father takes delight
To see his active child do deeds of youth,
So I, made lame by Fortune's dearest
    spite,
Take all my comfort of thy worth and
    truth.

Whoever wrote the sonnets was a man who had known disgrace and shame, whose name must be hidden. He had loved a young man and a woman to whom he was not married. We know that Oxford, a great favorite of Queen Elizabeth, (she affectionately called him "my Turk" and bestowed many favors on him), disgraced himself numerous times. He abandoned his wife for a period of four years and had an affair with one of the queen's maids-in-waiting, and was punished with a short stay in the Tower of London. Around this time he was publicly accused of "buggering" several young boys and was called "womanish" by one detractor. He lost most of his fortune on lavish spending, only to be rescued by the queen's gift of an annual

pension. In the sonnets, the poet refers numerous times to his "shame" and to his "outcast state," and prays that his "name be buried where my body is."

Gentlemen of the court thought it undignified to put their names to verse or plays, especially to any writing published for access to common readers. It was generally considered gauche and it simply wasn't done. If one had scandal attached to one's name, that was an additional reason for disguise. Oxford was both a member of the gentry and someone associated with scandal. Those who propose his name as the true author of the Bard's work suggest that shortly after 1590, when he was forty and suffering the consequences of his earlier bad-boy behavior, Oxford stopped putting his own name on his poems and plays. At about this time the name "Shakespeare" first appeared as the author of poems and plays. Coincidently, Will of Stratford moved to London and became an actor in 1592. Within five years he was able to buy the second largest house in Stratford, although acting paid little.

Perhaps, one theory goes, Oxford saw a notice about the actor, Will Shakspere of Stratford, and saw an opportunity to hide behind a borrowed name and persona. The name alone would have sparked his imagination. After all, Pallas Athena, the Greek goddess who was the patroness of the theater, was frequently depicted carrying a spear and was known as the "spear-shaker." And, as a youth, Oxford's crest had been a lion shaking a spear. Did he pay Will of Stratford for the use of his name and persona? If so, it is believed that Oxford's use of the name

Pallas Athena, spear-shaker

"Shakespeare" would have been a respected and open secret, discussed in coded language and protected by the literary and royal elites, from Ben Jonson to the queen.

• *Life Experiences Reflected in the Plays*

The plays of Shakespeare, taken as a whole, reflect the life experiences of Oxford—from his love of everything Italian, to his accomplishments as a musician. They are about the world he knows best, and are often about the underside of that world. *Hamlet*, in particular, is held up by advocates of Oxford as having details, large and small, that echo his life experience.

In 1583, Oxford's brother-in-law was sent on a diplomatic mission to Denmark and returned with tales of life at the royal court at Elsinore, the setting of *Hamlet*.

Oxford's mother, like Hamlet's, remarried quickly after his father's untimely death when Oxford was twelve. He became a royal ward under the supervision of Sir William Cecil, later named Lord Burghley, widely believed to be the model for Polonius. Lord Burghley expressed contempt for Oxford's "lewd friends" just as Polonius has disdain for Hamlet's players. Hamlet identified Polonius as a "fishmonger." Burghley was known for his efforts in Parliament to promote the interests of fishermen.

Oxford, like Hamlet, was an outcast and pariah in the royal court.

• *When Did Shakespeare Die?*

Oxford died of the plague in 1604. Around this time, it is believed that Will, the glover's son, retired from London at the height of what should have been a brilliant literary career. Will died in Stratford twelve years later, in 1616, on his birthday.

Is there evidence that "Shakespeare" was dead before 1616?

In a poem by William Barkstead, published in 1607, Shakespeare is referred to in the past tense, "His Song was worthie merrit" (note the word "*was*"), and the passage ends with, "Cypress thy brow will fit." Cypress was a symbol of mourning in Elizabethan times (see page 187).

In 1609, the Sonnets were published for the first time. The publisher was Thomas Thorpe. He titled the volume *Shake–speare's Sonnets*. Why? A book of poems by a living author would normally have carried a byline underneath a title—such as *Sonnets* by William Shakespeare. Furthermore, the preface carried a dedication, not by Shakespeare, but by the publisher. Why? Lastly, the publisher referred to Shakespeare as "our ever-living poet." Why? This is an odd dedication for someone still alive and kicking. It seems instead to suggest that the poet lives on in memory, not in flesh.

Perhaps the biggest argument against Oxford as the true Shakespeare is the belief, held by traditional "Stratfordian" scholars, that many of the

"late" plays were written after 1604. Advocates for Oxford, however, question the conventional dating of the plays and claim that no play of Shakespeare's is based on a source written after 1603. Half the plays were not published until

1623, years after the deaths of both men. Establishing when they were actually written has always been a matter of conjecture for scholars, as it continues to be.

Conclusion

The authorship question has itself become an industry. Libraries, bookstores, and Internet sites abound with writings about this puzzle, yet the true Shakespeare continues to elude us. Al Austin, producer of "The Shakespeare Mystery" summarized the debate this way, "Those who believe in de Vere must believe in a giant conspiracy. Those who believe in Shakespeare of Stratford must believe in miracles."

Like so many of the king's men trying to put Humpty Dumpty together again, we search for little pieces to make it all fit perfectly. So far, no one has managed to accomplish the feat. Many who love the work scratch their heads at the effort and ask if it matters who wrote the plays. As Charles Dickens said, "The life of Shakespeare is a fine mystery, and I tremble every day lest something should turn up."

THE COMEDY OF ERRORS

CITY TURNS CIRCUS AS FATHER ARRIVES IN SEARCH OF MISSING TWINS

Period

One day in the 1st century B.C.E.

Setting

Ephesus, Greece

This fast-paced farce opens with the misery of old Aegeon of Syracuse. Life has not been going well for him, and things are about to get worse. He is the father of identical twins who, at birth, had been given identical twin servants. When the boys were still infants, the whole family was in a shipwreck. Missing after the disaster at sea were Aegeon's wife, one son and one servant. Years passed and, when his remaining son turned eighteen, the boy had set out with his servant beside him, to find his long lost brother. He had never returned, and Aegeon has been alone and miserable ever since, his entire family missing in action. He is so desperate, he doesn't even care that his search has brought him to the Greek port of Ephesus, a city at war with his home

city of Syracuse. According to the laws of Ephesus, old Aegeon must be put to death at sundown, just for setting foot on enemy soil, unless he can pay a huge ransom. He doesn't care. He's lost hope of ever finding his sons.

One more thing: both of his sons are named Antipholus, and both of his sons' servants are named Dromio.

As it happens, Antipholus of Syracuse (Antipholus/S) and his trusty servant Dromio (Dromio/S) have also just arrived in town in their long search for their lost brothers. They won't know it until the end of the story, but they have arrived in the right place. The long-lost Antipholus (Antipholus/E) is established in Ephesus. He has a house, a wife named Adriana, a sister-in-law named Luciana, and a fat and greasy kitchen maid named Nell. His trusty servant Dromio (Dromio/E) lives there too.

It is a madcap day in the busy city, and misunderstandings abound with these look-alikes on the loose. Antipholus/S sends Dromio/S back to the inn where they will be lodging to deposit the bag of gold they've brought with them. It's best not to carry it around town. Meanwhile, Dromio/E has been sent to look for his master and tell him it's time for dinner. Instead of finding his master, however, he finds the look-alike who has come ashore. He's bewildered when the man he thinks is his master denies having a wife and peppers him with questions about a bag of gold.

Dromio/E returns to his mistress with the news that her husband won't come home and that he seems obsessed with a bag of gold. Adriana jumps to the conclusion that her Antipholus/E must be cheating on her. She tells Dromio/E to go back and drag her husband home. Then, after talking it over with her sister, the two women decide to go themselves and get the errant husband. The man they find is, of course, the wrong twin, a bachelor, who is bewildered at being accosted by a woman who claims to be his wife. Adriana is so persistent, that the bachelor brother gives in and goes home with her. His servant goes too, for protection.

No sooner are they inside than the real husband arrives home with his servant, his goldsmith Angelo, and a business friend, Balthasar. Imagine his surprise when he's denied entrance to his own house and to the dinner he is expecting!

Inside, Antipholus/S has gotten himself into hot water. He's fallen head over heels in love with Luciana, a proper lady who's outraged that the man she thinks is her sister's husband is suddenly flirting with her. Dromio/S is in trouble too. Nell, the corpulent kitchenwench, "all grease," has mistaken him for her lover-boy, Dromio/E, and is demanding he

marry her. He tells his master, "She is spherical, like a globe. I could find out countries in her." Amused, Antipholus/S asks about the location of one country after another on this globe called Nell. The bawdy banter ends when he asks, "Where stood Belgia, the Netherlands?" to which Dromio/S replies, "O, sir, I did not look so low."

Still standing at the gate is Antipholus/E, humiliated at being locked out of his own house. He swears to get even with Adriana. He'll dine with a courtesan and give her the gold chain he had intended to give his wife. That will teach his wife a lesson! There's one small problem. The chain has been delivered to the wrong Antipholus, and now the goldsmith is demanding payment. Antipholus/E refuses to pay for merchandise he has not received, and the goldsmith has him arrested. The wrong Dromio is sent to fetch bail money which is, of course, turned over to the wrong Antipholus. At the jail, Dr. Pinch, a hungry and "hollow-eyed" exorcist, is called in to judge the sanity of the beleaguered Antipholus/E. He pronounces both master and servant possessed. His prescription: both men must be bound and laid in a dark room, standard treatment of the insane in Elizabethan England.

Now, even though he has been unbelievably lucky—he's been fed, given the gold chain and the bag of bail money, all unbidden—Antipholus/S is ready to leave this crazy town. He's baffled by the Courtesan who accosts him demanding the gold chain she was promised and then by the goldsmith who appears and demands payment. A crowd of confused characters assembles just as tempers flare and swords are drawn. The set of twins from Syracuse flees and seeks refuge in the local convent where the Abbess takes the two under her protective wing.

The duke wanders into the crowd, on his way to the execution of poor old Aegeon, who has not been able to come up with the ransom money. Antipholus/E and Dromio/E show up, too, having escaped the creepy Dr. Pinch. The Courtesan and the goldsmith get into the mix, as does Adriana, the disgruntled wife. The duke is overwhelmed by the chaos and sends for the Abbess. When she appears, she has with her the other set of twins. Everyone stops cold. The two sets of twins are finally in the same place at the same time. Suddenly, all the confusion is resolved into one great moment of clarity.

The final surprise is that the Abbess turns out to be Aegeon's long lost wife, the mother of the twin Antipholuses. She invites the whole town over to her abbey for a celebration. Everyone is happy, as the story ends—especially Antipholus/S who realizes he is now free to court Luciana and the twin Dromios, who exit, hand in hand.

Likely Source of the Plot

Shakespeare's primary source for this story was *The Menaechmi*, a play written by the Roman playwright Plautus (ca. 254 B.C.E.–184 B.C.E.). Shakespeare may have read it in Latin, because the play was not translated into English until 1595, sometime after the first performance of *The Comedy of Errors*. The idea to add a second set of confused twins may have come from *Amphitryon*, another play by Plautus.

Notable Features

Shakespeare's shortest play, *The Comedy of Errors* contains several errors of its own in the form of anachronisms. Though set in a pre–Christian era, two characters seek refuge in a Christian convent and are sheltered by the abbess. Also, Shakespeare imposed an Elizabethan sensibility on ancient times with Doctor Pinch's diagnosis and treatment of lunacy.

Notable Productions and Performances

The play was first performed on December 28, 1594, at The Gray's Inn. In the 17th and 18th centuries, the play was rearranged almost beyond recognition. It was restored to its original form in 1855 with a production by Samuel Phelps.

Other Use of Basic Plot

Operatic arrangement produced by Frederick Reynolds, 1819, lawyer-turned-theatrical entrepreneur and playwright, whose libretto included a hodge-podge of songs from other Shakespearean plays.

Musical comedy, 1938, *The Boys from Syracuse* by Richard Rodgers and Lorenz Hart.

Trevor Nunn's 1976 film *The Comedy of Errors*, with Judi Dench as Adriana.

New York City, 1999, *The Bomb-itty of Errors: An Add-RAP-tation of Willy Shakespeare's Comedy*, written by Jordan Allen-Dutton, Jason Catalano, GQ, and Erik Weiner. In this Off-Broadway hit, Shakespeare's story is set to a new text delivered in rap to the beat of a hip-hop DJ.

MUCH ADO
ABOUT NOTHING

EAVESDROPPERS SUCCUMB
TO MATCHMAKING CONSPIRACY;
GOVERNOR'S DAUGHTER SLANDERED

Period

13th century

Setting

Messina, Italy

Sparkling wit takes center stage and plays matchmaker to a confirmed free spirit and an equally marriage-resistant bachelor in this tale of two sassy singles. Gossip plays a more complicated role. In the hands of friends, it nurtures affection; in the hands of a sinister troublemaker, it almost destroys a life.

As the play begins, two brothers, one sweet, one sour, are welcomed to the house of Leonato, Governor of Messina, where there is an air of excitement and festivity. The two brothers are Don Pedro, the Prince of Arragon, and his "bastard brother," Don John. The former has quelled a rebellion headed by the later, who is now "reconciled" if sulky.

With these brothers are two gallant fellows. Benedick is a committed bach-

elor with sparkling eyes and ready wit. As soon as he hits town he's engaged in a "merry war" with Beatrice, the governor's niece. Like Benedick, Beatrice is adept at verbal sparring, loves to laugh, and is in no hurry at all to give up her independence. Her father says of her, "She is never sad but when she sleeps: and not ever sad then, for I have heard my daughter say, she hath often dreamed of unhappiness and wakes herself with laughing." Beatrice enjoys being single, but, even more than that, she enjoys exchanging insults with Benedick.

The other gallant fellow arriving with the prince is Claudio, a Florentine lord, who has his eye on the governor's daughter, Hero. The prince fancies himself a matchmaker, and he offers to help Claudio win Hero's heart. He has a plan; he will disguise himself as Claudio that evening at a masked ball, flirt with Hero, and coax her into marrying Claudio.

The sulky Don John, proud of his bad boy persona, has too much time on his hands. When he overhears his brother's plan to court Hero for Claudio, he can't resist trying to spoil the fun but his meddling is quickly cleared up. The prince finds Claudio and tells him the good news: his marriage to Hero has been arranged, to everyone's delight.

Having successfully played matchmaker to Claudio and Hero, the prince is eager for another challenge. He decides he'll trick Benedick and Beatrice into falling in love with each other and will orchestrate the trick himself. To pull off this mammoth and unlikely undertaking, he secures the cooperation of the governor, Claudio, and Hero. The four merry conspirators set out to accomplish their goal. First, when they know that Benedick is eavesdropping, the governor alleges that Beatrice loves Benedick with "an enraged affection." He claims that Beatrice stays up at nights writing love letters which she then rips to shreds rather than deliver for fear of being laughed at. The gossipers gush about the virtues of Beatrice, describing her as sweet and wise, but adding that they fear for her health. They say flattering things about Benedick too, who eventually emerges from his hiding place, convinced that what he has overheard is true.

Next, the matchmaking conspirators work their magic on the unsuspecting Beatrice, who hides in the honeysuckle to eavesdrop on Hero and her gentlewoman. Sure that Beatrice is listening, the women report that Benedick loves Beatrice "entirely" but is afraid of being

> "Speak low, if you speak love."
> —*Much Ado about Nothing*

rejected by her. They describe, in the most sympathetic terms, the dilemma of poor, lovesick Benedick. The ploy works. When the others depart, Beatrice emerges from the honeysuckle, marveling at what she has overheard.

While this sweet plot is unfolding under Don Pedro's guidance, so is a sinister one under the direction of his "bastard brother" Don John who is set on undoing the wedding plans of Hero and Claudio. Don John and Borachio, a partner in crime, devise a plan to make Claudio doubt his beloved's faithfulness. The night before the wedding, Margaret, an attendant, will disguise herself as Hero, stand before her bedroom window and welcome a lover. Don Pedro and the gullible Claudio will be lured to the scene where they are bound to draw the obvious conclusion.

The evil plot is foiled by an over zealous, bumbling, word-scrambling constable named Dogberry, his elderly sidekick named Verges, and two watchmen. Though they turn everything logical upside-down in confusion, they do so in a most orderly way. The result, in the end, is the discovery of the evil plot against Hero's good name, but this conclusion is long in coming. Before it does, disaster befalls poor Hero.

During the wedding ceremony at the church the following morning, Claudio surprises everyone by refusing to be married, claiming that he and the prince caught Hero with a lover the night before. Don Pedro backs up Claudio's outrageous claim. Hero is publicly

Denzel Washington as Don Pedro in Much Ado about Nothing.
Courtesy Museum of Modern Art/Film Stills Archive

accused and rejected by her husband-to-be who is so convincing that even the governor father suspects her of infidelity. Hero faints dead away.

In the chaos that follows, the friar performing the ceremony defends Hero's innocence, as do Beatrice and Benedick who take this odd moment to confess their love for each other. Then, Beatrice demands that Benedick kill Claudio as a villain who has slandered her dear cousin. When Benedick balks, she laments, "O God, that I were a man! I would eat his heart in the marketplace." Benedick is swept up in the intensity of Beatrice's passion and goes off to challenge Claudio to a duel. By this time, the governor has reviewed the situation, changed his mind about his daughter's guilt, and also challenged Claudio to a duel. Adding to his vehe-

mence is the report that his maligned daughter did not just faint; she is dead.

Before anyone can draw their swords, Dogberry, the clumsy constable, and his pals appear with Don John's servants who have confessed to the evil plot against the wrongly accused Hero. She has been framed and slandered and the ugly scheme is now fully exposed. Claudio, deeply ashamed of ever doubting his good woman, is not told that she is still alive. He's instructed to publicly mourn her, as he once publicly shamed her, and then to marry her cousin. He agrees. At the family crypt, an epitaph is read for Hero:

Done to death by slanderous tongues
Was the Hero that here lies;
Death, in guerdon of her wrongs,
Gives her fame which never dies.

Claudio promises to perform this mourning rite yearly. Then everyone returns to the governor's house where Claudio learns that Hero is indeed alive. Benedick and Beatrice discover that they were tricked into their love, but all is forgiven. Benedick stops Beatrice's mouth with a kiss and teases the prince that he looks sad and should find a wife. With two loving couples present, a double wedding is called for. Everyone is about to begin a dance when word comes that the malevolent Don John has been apprehended.

Likely Source of the Plot

The verbal sparring of the play's witty free spirits, Beatrice and Benedick, was probably inspired by the debates between a fictional man and a woman invented by the Italian Renaissance writer Baldassare Castiglione in his 1528 *The Book of the Courtier*. The Hero-Claudio plot was based primarily on a 1532 Italian poem, *Orlando Furioso*, by Ludovico Ariosto. Shakespeare may have read the English translation by Sir John Harington, published in 1591. The character of Dogberry, the comical constable, a staple on the stage and an echo of Constable Dull of *Love's Labour's Lost*, is thought to be a Shakespearean original.

Notable Productions and Performances

This play was popular from the very beginning. Shakespeare's contemporary,

Leonard Digges, wrote, "let but Beatrice and Benedick be seen, lo, in a trice the Cockpit, Galleries, Boxes, all are full."

In the 20th century, the part of Beatrice was played to great acclaim by Maggie Smith (1965), Judi Dench (1976) and Emma Thompson (1993). In 1988, Judi Dench directed a production at the Renaissance Theatre Company in Birmingham.

A 1988 production by the New York Shakespeare Festival, starring Kevin Kline and Blythe Danner, was especially popular, and, in 1989, Elijah Moshinsky's production at the Strand featured Alan Bates and Felicity Kendal as a Beatrice and Benedick well up in years, with failing eyesight.

Other Use of Basic Plot

1862, opera, *Beatrice et Benedict*, by Hector Berlioz, omitted the Claudio-Hero plot.

Film directed by Kenneth Branagh, 1993, starring Branagh as Benedick, Emma Thompson as Beatrice, Denzel Washington as Don Pedro, and Keanu Reeves as Don John. This is high-spirited Shakespeare, filmed in the lush landscape of Tuscany, with a fast-paced story that unfolds through a series of picnics, dances and feasts.

What to Do about Nothing, 1998 play by Judy Sheehan. Shakespeare's story, in which gossip and eavesdropping are central, is fittingly retold in the context of the Red Scare in America during the days of McCarthyism.

The Fair Youth, a Rival Poet,
and the Dark Lady—
The Sonnets as Soap Opera

hall I compare thee to a summer's day? Shakespeare wrote.

This is poetry for poets, who look here and find universal themes of love, jealousy, beauty, and death written in the most exquisite language.

It is wine and roses for romantics and greeting-card manufacturers, who quote—and misquote—borrowing the words for personal use or monetary gain.

This poetry is a marvel to linguistic scholars, who study the ornate words, fit so neatly into the strict and unforgiving structure of the sonnet. A form devised by the Italians in the 13th century and perfected in the next century by Petrarch, sonnet cycles did not catch on in England until 1590, when, suddenly, everyone, especially in the aristocracy, seemed to be writing them. While Edmund Spenser belabored his six-volume (yet ultimately unfinished) epic poem *The Faerie Queene* (1590–96), an allegorical work celebrating the moral values of Christian chivalry, Shakespeare joined the sonneteering craze

and fit his secular and sexual expressions into the poetic straitjacket: fourteen lines, ten syllables each, English rhyme scheme: *abab cdcd efef gg*.

Shakespeare's sonnets are no less grist for the rumor mill. Some scholars believe the sonnets are not to be taken literally. They are artifice, meditations on universal themes. They are represen-

Petrarch

tative of the genre, a wordsmith's playground.

Others, however, believe the sonnets are a peek inside the poet's diary, the closest thing we have to Shakespeare's autobiography. And what a story we find! Historians toss and turn in their sleep, dreaming of this drama of love and jealousy and its odd cast of characters. Of the sonnets, William Wordsworth wrote, "With this key, Shakespeare unlocked his heart," but imagine our surprise when we learn that "Shall I compare thee to a summer's day?" was written for a young man. This is where our story begins.

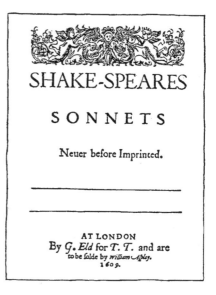

The Fair Youth Sonnets

The starkly numbered sonnets tell a sad story. The first 126 sonnets are addressed to a Fair Youth. The poet is smitten and in anguish; the "sweet boy" is a young, handsome nobleman, decadent and naughty.

Sonnets 1–17 are sometimes called the "procreation poems," or, more crudely, the "breed sonnets." In them, the poet urges his "sweet boy" to get married and make babies. "Look in thy glass [mirror], and tell the face thou viewest / Now is the time that face should form another" (Sonnet 3). In sonnet after sonnet, the poet argues that the Fair Youth owes the world some offspring, for it would be a shame if such human beauty was not passed on in the blood. "Is it for fear to wet a widow's eye / That thou consumest thyself in single life?...The world will be thy widow and still weep, / That thou no form of thee hast left behind" (Sonnet 9). The poet vows to immortalize the Fair Youth in

poetry so that all will not be lost if offspring are not forthcoming and age wreak havoc with the beloved's face. "Yet do thy worst, old Time: despite thy wrong, / My love shall in my verse ever live young" (Sonnet 19). The poet, imagining himself alone, an outcast and self-despising, counts himself among the lucky to be the recipient of the Fair Youth's favor. "For thy sweet love rememb'red such wealth brings/ That then I scorn to change my state with kings" (Sonnet 29).

Sonnet 33 introduces a touch of foreboding. In this and in several of the following poems we learn that the Fair Youth has evidently expressed remorse for some misdeed, which is readily forgiven by the poet. "No more be grieved at that which thou hast done: / Roses have thorns, and silver fountains mud" (Sonnet 35). But this is just the beginning of a love gone wrong. The poet continues to shape his words of love and all is forgiven until Sonnets 40–42 in which "straying youth" proves false, and the Fair Youth cavorts with a woman. It would appear that the bad boy has had an affair with the poet's own mistress. Evidently, the mistress is no great loss; it is for the love of the straying youth that the poet grieves.

The crisis passes and the words of love continue to flow. He returns to the theme of immortalizing his love in verse. Poems will, he promises, last longer than statues of stone. "Not marble nor the gilded monuments / Of princes shall outlive this pow'rful rhyme" (Sonnet 55). The poems will even serve to defeat the inevitability of death and decay. "His beauty shall in these black lines be seen, / And they shall live and he in them still green [young]" (Sonnet 63).

The poet is sick with love, and can think of little else. His life is not his own. The Internet's "Leather Online!" once featured Shakespeare's "slave sonnets"—numbers 57 and 58, which seem to come from a masochist's pen. "Being your slave, what should I do but tend / Upon the hours and times of your desire? / I have no precious time at all to spend, / Nor services to do till you require" (Sonnet 57). "Oh, let me suffer, being at your beck, / The imprisoned absence of your liberty: / And, patience tame to sufferance, bide each check / Without accusing you of injury" (Sonnet 58).

Lacking all self-confidence at this point, the poet is miserably obsessed with aging. Looking in his mirror, he finds himself to be "beated and chopped with tanned antiquity" (Sonnet 62), and like a "decrepit father" (Sonnet 37). In Sonnet 73, the poet finds numerous metaphors from nature for his advanced age, which he compares to autumn, a time "when yellow leaves, or none, or few, do hang / Upon those boughs which shake against the cold, / Bare, ruined choirs where late the sweet birds sang."

Shakespeare is depressed, bitter, and filled with self-contempt. Things are about to get worse.

The Rival Poet Sonnets

Suddenly, in Sonnets 78–86, we learn that the Fair Youth is being courted by another man, a rival poet of a "worthier pen"—worthier than Shakespeare's? The Rival Poet is more successful, his verses more beautiful and effective in expressing love. "Oh, how I faint when I of you do write, / Knowing a better spirit doth use your name" (Sonnet 80). Jealousy now becomes the theme, though the love is never dimmed. Indeed, the words of two poets, rivals in pen and in matters of the heart, are not enough to do justice to the Fair Youth. "There lives more life in one of your fair eyes, / Than both your poets can in praise devise" (Sonnet 83). In all humility, the poet concedes that his own words may be inferior to the verses created by the Rival Poet, but no one can come close to loving the Fair Youth more.

Sonnet 87 leads us to the inevitable—a separation. The love is lost,

> "Scorn not the Sonnet; Critic, you have frowned, Mindless of its honors; with this key Shakespeare unlocked his heart."
> —William Wordsworth

the heart is fully broken. "Farewell: thou art too dear for my possessing." The melancholy poet's self-loathing is nowhere more apparent than in these verses. He has concluded that he's not worthy of the Fair Youth's love or attention and that he deserves to be unloved, abandoned, forlorn.

In Sonnet 90 we learn that his heartbreak is not the only thing going wrong in the poet's life. In fact, nothing is going right. The whole world seems to be against him. The poet has hit bottom, but the only thing that matters is the loss of his beloved Fair Youth who is right to abandon such a lowly miserable worm: "Then hate me when thou wilt— if ever, now—/ Now, while the world is bent my deeds to cross." The poet feels, he writes, like "a deceived husband."

In Sonnet 94 there is, at last, some hint of disgust at the Fair Youth's callous nature. He may look pretty, but he is bad news and the poet knows it. "For sweetest things turn sourest by their deeds;/ Lilies that fester smell far worse than weeds." The misery continues. In Sonnet 97, the poet writes about the period of absence from the Fair Youth; "What freezings have I felt, what dark days seen! / What old December's bareness everywhere!"

In Sonnet 109, the poet still pledges undying love; "For nothing this wide universe I call / Save thou, my rose; in it thou art my all." But this is followed by a confession—that the poet, under the strain of unrequited love, has himself "strayed" a little. "Alas! 'Tis true I have gone here and there..." (Sonnet 110).

Sonnet 116 is perhaps the most well-known of the sonnets. In it, the poet writes that true love is as constant as the North Star, unchanging. This poem, however, is followed by a string of apologies for the poet's failure to adequately stand by his man. Guilt-ridden, the poet nevertheless finds a benefit to having lost and then regained the relationship with his beloved. In Sonnet 119 he writes, "ruined love, when it is built anew, / Grows fairer than at first, more strong, far greater."

In Sonnet 121, the poet curses those "frailer spies," men with "adulterate eyes" who dare to judge and criticize his "sportive blood." In his own version of "let he who is without sin cast the first stone," the poet concludes the sonnet: "By their rank [licentious] thoughts my deeds must not be shown,/ Unless this general evil they maintain: / All men are bad and in their badness reign."

The saga of erotic misadventure progresses to reconciliation and more protestations of love. Sonnet 126, addressed to "my lovely boy," is another on the theme of beauty and the inevitable damage to be done by Time.

The Dark Lady Sonnets

Sonnet 127 takes us by surprise. Obsessed as the poet has been with his, "lovely boy " he is now equally obsessed by a beautiful woman with sad, black eyes. As if grown tired of the soap opera of his life, the poet has abruptly turned to other arms for physical affection. In Sonnet 130, the woman is described as having dun-colored breasts, wiry hair, and breath that "reeks," and so has been identified as the "Dark Lady" by scholars.

In one sonnet after another, the poet professes love and adoration despite the Dark Lady's cruel disdain and torment of the poet. Once again the poet is enmeshed in a lover's triangle, though the Rival Poet seems to have dropped out of the picture. This time the triangle involves the Fair Youth and the Dark Lady. In Sonnet 134 he writes, "Him have I lost, thou hast both him and me."

A 1640 execution of a bishop for the crime of "buggery"

In Sonnet 144, the poet articulates the homosexual sensibility (if not homosexuality outright) made famous by the Greeks and echoed repeatedly by men of the English Renaissance, in which male friendship was exalted and juicy adjectives were exuded honoring male beauty. In the words of another 16th century playwright, John Lyly; "The love of men to women is a thing common

and of course; the friendship of man to man infinite and immortal." Considering his two loves, Shakespeare wrote, "The better angel is a man right fair, / The worser spirit a woman colored ill. / To win me soon to hell, my female evil / Tempteth my better angel from my side...."

It is a matter of debate whether our poet's homoeroticism actually found its expression in physical sex. Men could sometimes express their love for each other physically, but they had to be cautious because, in 1533, Protestant-leaning England had officially taken the sin of "sodomy" (a Bible-based term) away from the church and made it a matter of civil law. The "Vice of Buggery" was punishable by death. Noting wryly that, "If Shakespeare were to apply for an NEA grant on the basis of the Sonnets, he would probably be denied one," Norrie Epstein, author of *The Friendly Shakespeare*, points out:

Viewed as a whole, the entire [sonnet] sequence is a full expression of the diverse ways human beings can love—homosexual, heterosexual, intellectual, companionable, paternal, the purely idealistic as well as the purely carnal.... To classify the Sonnets as either heterosexual or homosexual would be to oversimplify them, ignoring Shakespeare's great achievement.

In the later sonnets, the poet, once again a lovesick mess, is most often obsessing about his Dark Lady, as in Sonnet 147, "My love is as a fever..." and "Past cure I am, now reason is past care, And frantic-mad with evermore unrest.... " "For I have sworn thee fair, and thought thee bright, / Who are as black as hell, as dark as night." Lamenting the woman's cruelty and his response of uncontrolled lust, the poet writes in Sonnet 148, "O cunning love, with tears thou keepst me blind, / Lest eyes well seeing thy foul faults should find."

Thinly disguised genital imagery rises and falls throughout Sonnet 151, as the poet decries his bondage to physical passion, though, by this time the poet's tone is both weary and affectionate. As one who has indulged in unwholesome behavior, he is almost tolerant of his partner-in-sin, calling her "gentle cheater."

The sonnet series ends with a reference to a Roman myth in which a nymph attempts to put out Cupid's "love-kindling fire" by dropping his torch in a well. The attempt fails; the well water becomes like a medicinal bath, retaining "heat perpetual." Thus the sonnet series ends with this truism; "Love's fire heats water; water cools not love." This sentiment also echos a verse from the Bible's "Song of Solomon" (chapter 8, verse 7); "Many waters cannot quench love, neither can floods drown it."

This is where the saga ends, but the mystery is just beginning.

Who Are These People?

As can be imagined, biographers have had a field day (albeit one lasting 400 years) hypothesizing the identities of Fair Youth, the Rival Poet, and the Dark Lady.

The mystery is confounded by the fact that *Shake-spear's Sonnets* was first published, most likely without the author's permission, in 1609, certainly after the sonneteering craze had abated in England and probably long after the sonnets were written. (That some of the sonnets had been circulated at an earlier time we know from a 1598 printed reference to Shakespeare's "sugred sonnets among his private friends.") The 1609 collection was published with this dedication: "To the onlie [only] begetter of these ensuing sonnets. Mr. W.H."

First there is the question of who provided the dedication. Was it Thomas Thorpe, the book's publisher, acknowledging a patron? Some have suggested that Thorpe intended to thank "William Himself" as the "only begetter." Or perhaps the H. was a typo and he meant to type S. for Shakespeare. Still others claim W.H. was the manuscript buyer William Hall, who may have acquired copies of the poems and passed them on to the publisher, thus being logically acknowledged as the "only begetter" by Thorpe.

Most scholars, however, have assumed that the poet penned the dedication and that W.H., and the Fair Youth, are one and the same. This has led to some fascinating theories.

At the close of the 18th century, Edmund Malone (considered the first of the serious Shakespearian scholars) posited the theory that W.H. stood for William Hues or Hughes—based on one line in Sonnet 20: "A man in hue, all hues in his controlling." It's a stretch. In the late 19th century, Oscar Wilde picked up Malone's theory as the basis for his story "The Portrait of Mr. W.H." and ran with it. Wilde developed the idea that W.H. was William (Willie) Hughes, a boy actor on the Shakespearean stage, adept at playing women's roles. We can imagine a rosy-cheeked young lad with full lips and sparkling eyes, a beautiful boy not yet grown out of his adolescent androgyny, dressed as fair Juliet, who "steals men's eyes and women's souls amazeth."

Another scholar has proposed that W.H. was one William Hatliffe, who acted at Gray's Inn. The four Inns of Court were not taverns or bed-and-breakfast lodgings, but resident law schools located west of London. Gray's Inn was one specifically known for its young and lively gentlemen who excelled in dramatics. *The Comedy of Errors* was first performed at Gray's Inn, in December 1594. Could the poet have fallen in love with a young actor there?

Still others have proposed the notion that, damn the initials!, the Fair Youth was none other than Queen Elizabeth—who was often "considered a man."

Others have theorized that W. H. stood for William Herbert, third Earl of Pembroke (and thus also sometimes called "Pembroke"). The collection of Shakespeare's plays published in 1623 under the title the *First Folio* was dedicated to William Herbert, who was acknowledged to be a supporter of the theater in general and of Shakespeare in particular. Could he have been the W.H. of the Sonnets' title page? If we assume the "procreation poems" were written about 1595, he would certainly have been young—only fifteen years old, in fact, to Shakespeare's age of 31. It was well-known that his mother, the Countess of Pembroke, began pushing the earl to marry at about that time and that he was unwilling. But then, this was also apparently the case for the other prime contender.

Henry Wriothesley (pronounced "Risley"), third Earl of Southampton, is believed by many to be the name behind the Fair Youth. Shakespeare had dedicated his earlier published poems to Southampton, a patron of the arts who was, by all accounts, beautiful. Men drooled over him with obsequious flattery. Tom Nashe, author of satirical pamphlets, pledged to the young nobleman, "A new brain, a new wit, a new style, a new soul will I get me, to canonize your name to posterity." Another writer, John Florio, oozed, "To me and many more, the glorious and gracious sunshine of your Honor hath infused light and life." Southampton was younger than Shakespeare, being 22 in 1595, and he was resistant to marriage. Why his initials would have been reversed from H.W. to W.H. no one can say. It is also unlikely that he would have been addressed as "Mr." Nevertheless, there are many who believe he was the Fair Youth of the sonnets.

Who was the Dark Lady? Again, theories abound. Some say she was likely a lady-in-waiting. Mary Fitton joined the court in 1595 as maid of honor to the queen. It is known that she became pregnant in 1600 by William Herbert. She was banished from the court for her sexual indiscretions and, when Herbert refused to marry his pregnant mistress, he was jailed. The baby died in infancy. Mary Fitton might have been Shakespeare's Dark Lady—except that in two portraits she is depicted as a blond with a fair complexion.

Another contender is Emilia Bassano, the teenaged mistress of Lord Hunsdon, a patron of the Chamberlain's Men, the theatrical company of which

Christopher Marlowe, possible contender for the Rival Poet. Unknown artist, 1585.
© *The Master and Fellows of Corpus Christi College, Cambridge*

Shakespeare was a member. When Bassano became pregnant in 1593, Hunsdon married her off to Alphonse Lanier, a musician in the queen's court. She later wrote a book-length poem about women of the Bible, which was published but not well received, and opened a school, which ultimately failed. Gifted but unlucky, she lived much of her life in poverty. We know about Emilia Lanier, née Bassano, primarily from the private journals of the astrologer Simon Forman, who was a confidant of a number of women who turned to him for advice about private matters.

There were many "dark women" in London's brothels as evidenced in letters of the time. One author referred to "his Moor," another to "his negress." It is said a woman known as "Lucy Negro, Abbess de Clerkenwell" came to the Christmas revels of Gray's Inn in 1594. Was this Lucy Morgan, nicknamed "Black Luce"—a notorious brothel-keeper in London? Could she have been Shakespeare's Dark Lady?

Who was the Rival Poet? Some have speculated that it was Christopher Marlowe, the popular poet and playwright, born the same year as William Shakespeare. His plays included *Dr.*

Faustus and *Tamburlaine*, and it is believed that his use of dramatic blank verse and rich language influenced Shakespeare. A free-thinker, he was known as a homosexual and atheist, at odds with church teachings, and accused of making disrespectful remarks about the Holy Ghost. His genius ended when he was stabbed to death in a barroom brawl in 1593. Others have postulated that the Rival Poet might have been George Chapman. A melancholy man with many enemies, Chapman nevertheless was celebrated as a poet and a playwright of popular comedies set in contemporary London. He was known for his perceptive insights into the Elizabethan psyche. Samuel Daniel, considered a major literary figure in England by 1595, was known for his immensely popular sonnet sequence, *Delia* (1592) and for *The Complaint of Rosamund* (also published in 1592)—a very popular love story set in verse. He was a tutor to William Herbert. Could he have been the Rival Poet? Another contender is Barnabe Barnes, a noted sonnet writer who eulogized the Earl of Southampton whose "gracious eyes," according to Barnes, were "heavenly lamps which give the Muses light." Was Shakespeare referring to metaphysical poet John Donne (an intimate of Pembroke's) when he wrote in Sonnet 76: "Why, with the time, do I not glance aside / To new-found methods and to compounds strange?"

We may never know the identities of these people, but there is no mistaking the sheer beauty and power of the poems themselves. In the acknowledgments to her book *The Art of Shakespeare's Sonnets*, Helen Vendler writes:

My mother was the first person to introduce me to Shakespeare's sonnets. She quoted them often, and had memorized many of them. Her last pieces of writing (which we found after Alzheimer's disease had robbed her of memory) were fragments of the Sonnets *which, either from fear of forgetting or as a means of self-reassurance, she had written down on scraps of paper. It is no mean tribute to the* Sonnets *that they, of the hundreds of poems she knew by heart, were the last to fade.*

LOVE'S LABOUR'S LOST

VISITING PRINCESS AND ENTOURAGE DENIED ENTRY TO PALACE; KING FEARS DISCIPLINE ON THE DECLINE

Period

16th century

Setting

Navarre, Spain

Shakespeare was the prince of punsters but this play takes the prize, being remarkable for having over two hundred puns, topical allusions, and Elizabethan in-jokes. Geared to savvy Renaissance spectators, much of the wordplay is lost on a 21st century audience, but this doesn't diminish our delight.

King Ferdinand and his idealistic young lords (Berowne, Longaville, and Dumaine) have the best intentions. After some quibbling from Berowne, they swear an oath to spend three years studying and fasting and sleeping only three hours a night. One more thing—they vow to abstain from the company of women. You know what they say about good intentions. When the Princess of France arrives on a diplomatic mission with her smart, vibrant and lovely ladies-in-waiting, the men struggle mightily with their pledge. Because of his oath, the king denies the princess entry to the palace, but negotiates with her in a park outside the gates. Almost at once, he and his companions are smitten with their visitors.

Meanwhile, Costard, the illiterate, clownish local yokel, has been jailed for his roll in the hay with Jaquenetta, an earthy country wench. A pompous knight, Don Armado, has had his own leering eye on Jaquenetta, and he gets Costard out of jail with the assignment to deliver a love letter to her, though she can't read. On his way, Costard is also commissioned by one of the king's companions to deliver a love letter to one of the princess's maids-in-waiting. This proves to be one love letter too many for poor Costard, who promptly delivers the wrong letter to the wrong woman.

Suddenly, the hills are alive with versifying men sending secret love letters and with maids in waiting tittering at the miss-matched missives.

On the edge of the action is Holofernes, a pretentious academic and his deferential follower Nathaniel. They impress themselves with their learned Latin, in language so convoluted that it's comical. Holofernes will eventually get his comeuppance.

In the end, the derailed oath-takers learn two important lessons—that women are "the books, the arts, the academes, that show, contain and nourish all the world," and that "the tongues of mocking wenches are as keen as is the razor's edge invisible." The latter is a painful lesson for the men. Thinking to deceive the women by dressing as Muscovites (Russians), the men are themselves deceived into wooing the wrong women and looking foolish.

The giddy comedy is abruptly interrupted by the news of the death of the princess's father. As the women prepare to leave Navarre, (this is, after all, Love's Labour's LOST, not found), they gently assign mock penance to the vow-breaking king and his men, and promise to give answers to their proposals of marriage in a year and a day.

Likely Source of the Plot

There is no known literary source for this comedy, though the play was informed by contemporary events in Anglo-French diplomatic relations. English troops had only recently fought beside Henri, King of Navarre, a Protestant rebel who had founded an academy based on Italian Renaissance models. This play may also have been penned as an answer to George Chapman, whose long poem, "Shadow of Night" (1594) denigrated pleasure.

Notable Feature

Most of the comedies about love end with a wedding or two or three. This play

does not. It does, however, have Shakespeare's longest word. In act 4, scene 1, Costard, the clown, and Moth, the page, comment on the highfalutin speech of Holofernes and Nathaniel. The clown says, "I marvel thy master hath not eaten thee for a word, for thou are not so long by the head as *honorificabilitudinitatibus*; thou art easier swallowed than a flap-dragon."

Notable Productions and Performances

It is believed that this play was performed at the court of Queen Elizabeth during the Christmas festivities of 1597; with a repeat performance the same time of year in 1604. As far as anyone knows, that was the last performance until the year 1839, when an elaborate production was staged at Covent Garden in London.

In a book of memoirs, *Blessings in Disguise*, Sir Alec Guinness wrote about hearing the closing lines of this play spoken by Ernest Milton at the Old Vic in 1936, "The words of Mercury are harsh after the songs of Apollo. You that way, we this way." Guinness wrote:

The small hairs on the back of my neck stirred. He had put, with sweetness and regret, a great gulf between audience and players; a gulf which would widen as the curtain fell, the lights went out, and stage and auditorium would be empty even of ghosts.

Other Uses of Basic Plot

Love's Labour's Lost, 2000, a film directed by Kenneth Branagh, inspired by old Hollywood musicals.

A MIDSUMMER NIGHT'S DREAM

THREE COUPLES TO WED AT PALACE AFTER NIGHT OF STRANGE HAPPENINGS IN THE WOODS

Period

Antiquity

Setting

Athens and a nearby forest

Here is a fairy tale of upscale young lovers tried and tested by all the powers that be (and a few powers that "don't be") before its happy ending.

As the play opens, law, order and patriarchy prevail with such solidity, it is hard to believe we are about to be turned upside down and inside out in a blink of a fairy's eye. Theseus, Duke of Athens, has battled the Amazon queen, Hippolyta, and won. Now he plans to wed her. Suddenly, old Egeus appears at the duke's palace with a problem. He wants his daughter Hermia to marry Demetrius, but she's in love with Lysander. When it looks like all the authority of state and family will prevail, Lysander reminds Hermia, "The course of true love never did run smooth." Madly in love, the two conspire to

elope. Their first step: meet in the woods.

As it happens, there will be three groups of beings romping through the enchanted woods that night. First are the young paramours—not two, but four. Lovely but loveless Helena follows the eloping lovers into the woods, as does the object of her affection, Demetrius, who is, of course, set on marrying Hermia.

Also in the woods is a small ensemble of amateur actors, sweet, bumbling, nervous and sincere. These working men, called "Mechanicals"—a carpenter, joiner, weaver, bellows-mender, tinker, and tailor—are looking for enough space and privacy to rehearse a theatrical piece to present at the duke's wedding. It is a short play with a long, nonsensical title: *The most Lamentable Comedy and most Cruel Death of Pyramus and Thisby*.

The third group in the woods, and the most at home there, are the fairies. Titania, queen of the fairies, is attended by Peaseblossom, Cobweb, Moth, and Mustardseed. Oberon, the imposing fairy king, is attended by the mischievous Puck (a.k.a. Robin Goodfellow). They are engaged in a quarrel over custody of the little changeling boy Titania adopted. Oberon devises a plan to trick his queen.

As sometimes happens, one trick leads to another, and soon the woods are filled with comic confusion. Oberon orders Puck to fetch a certain flowering herb called "Love-in-idleness." Then, he squeezes the juice of the flower into sleeping Titania's eyes knowing that its magic will cause her to become infatuated with the first live creature she sees when she opens her eyes. She is awakened by Bottom, the most cocky of the bumbling actors, who is singing to comfort himself. He's been "translated" by Puck who has put an ass's head on him. Bottom takes the vigorously amorous attentions of the fairy queen in stride, saying philosophically, "Reason and love keep little company together nowadays."

Oberon observes the plight of the young lovers in his woods and instructs Puck to put the magic flower juice into Demetrius's eyes, assuming the reluctant youth will awaken to lonely, lovestruck Helena. Puck, however, can't tell one Athenian lad from another, and so the wrong boy gets the juice. Oberon tries to correct the mistake, and suddenly both lads are in love with Helena and no one is in love with the once cherished Hermia. Each woman takes offense at this sudden turn, feeling variously mocked and betrayed. More turmoil ensues, which amuses Puck no end. He shakes his head and mutters, "Lord, what fools these mortals be."

When dawn comes to the moonstruck woods, there is a return to order, of sorts. The fairy quarrel ends in a dance and the song of a lark. The four seemingly interchangeable human lovers are awakened by the duke on his morning hunt, and they too find happiness and order. Paired into loving couples, they are invited to be married at the duke's own wedding ceremony.

Finally, Bottom awakens, minus the ass's head, and returns to his astonished friends. Hired to entertain the wedding guests, the Mechanicals put on a play about young lovers, who, like Romeo and Juliet, kill themselves after a series of unfortunate accidents and misunderstandings. The acting is so bad, however, that the tragedy leaves everyone laughing and in good humor.

It is midnight ("almost fairy time") when the three happy couples walk away from the day's festivities arm-in-arm toward their marriage beds. Once more, the fairies appear, this time to bless the three human couples with a song, a dance and some pretty words. Finally, Puck addresses Shakespeare's audience, begging forgiveness for any offense, and suggesting that the whole drama was nothing more than a dream from which we will now awaken.

Likely Source of the Plot

One of the few plays thought to have come almost entirely from Shakespeare's own imagination, elements in it were inspired by several sources. *The Golden Ass*, a classic text written by Apuleius in the 2nd century C.E. and available in an English translation in Shakespeare's day, tells the story of a man turned into an ass. Theseus and Hippolyta were borrowed from Chaucer's "The Knight's Tale" while the fairy king and queen, quarreling over a human, were mooched from "The Merchant's Tale." The legend of "Pyramus and Thisbe" came from Ovid's *Metamorphoses,* said to be one of Shakespeare's favorite books, translated into English in 1567 by Arthur Golding. Oberon, king of the fairies, was a familiar figure in Elizabethan folklore, as was Puck.

Notable Features

This play was probably written to be performed at an aristocratic wedding, perhaps the February 1596 marriage of Elizabeth Carey, the granddaughter of a patron of the theater troupe in which Shakespeare was a partner.

Notable Productions and Performances

Between 1642 and 1660, an abridged version of the play was performed surreptitiously and was eventually published as *The Merry Conceits of Bottom the Weaver.* Samuel Pepys, who saw a rare performance of *A Midsummer Night's Dream* in 1662, said it was, "The most insipid ridiculous play that ever I saw in my life."

The play was rarely performed until 1840 when Shakespeare's text was restored by Madame Vestris (who also played Oberon!) at Covent Garden, with music by Felix Mendelssohn. An 1856 production by Charles Kean featured nine-year-old Ellen Terry as Puck. Terry would have a long career as a Shakespearian actress, retiring in her seventies after playing the Nurse in *Romeo and Juliet.*

Throughout the 20th century, *Dream* was one of the most frequently performed Shakespearean plays. In 1900, a spectacular presentation by Beerbohm Tree at London's Haymarket Theatre featured live rabbits and birds. In 1914, Harley Granville-Barker's avant-garde production featured minimalist slate-gray canvas flats behind robotlike fairies painted gold.

In the Royal Shakespeare Company's 1970 production, directed by Peter Brook and dubbed "Brook's Dream," the enchanted forest was replaced by a white box, designed by Sally Jacobs. Titania and Puck observe the human follies from above, while swinging on trapezes.

The 1989 production directed by John Caird featured a whimsical scrapyard stage set designed by Sue Blane and gum-chewing fairies dressed in big boots and tutus.

The Royal Shakespeare Company's 2000 production by Michael Boyd was remarkable for its attention to the emotional landscape, if not a geographic one. The opening scene takes place in a stark, black-and-white setting in which law and order prevail. The actors, all dressed in heavy, Soviet–style winter coats and hats, were severe and grim as they heard those in authority dictate who could marry and who couldn't. Then, the barren winter scene was transformed when two actors helped shed each other's heavy clothing to reveal an earthy Puck and a barely corseted, lip-licking Peaseblossom. Red poppies sprouted from the bare, white stage floor. Inhibitions were removed as the young lovers bounced from the heavy-handed rule of civilized patriarchs to the arbitrary magic of the slightly mad, self-centered fairies.

Other Use of Basic Plot

Silent film made in Germany, 1913, directed by Hans Neumann. It came with a censorship rating "Forbidden for Juveniles." That Oberon and Puck were changed into femmes fatales gives us a clue to its exotic and erotic interpretation.

USA, 1935 film, directed by Max Reinhardt and William Dieterle. Set to Mendelssohn's score and featuring Mickey Rooney as Puck, Olivia de Havilland as Hermia, and James Cagney as Bottom, this extravaganza was lush and chaotic. Tots dressed as blond fairies offset a sinister, manic Puck.

UK, 1968 film, directed by Peter Hall. Some said this was Shakespeare "on acid." Dominated by the 1960s' attitude of "do your own thing," Judi Dench plays Titania in nothing but green body paint, while other heroines (Diana Rigg is Helena) sport miniskirts and long hair. The heroes have long hair too, Beatles' style, and wear Nehru jackets.

USA 1982 film, A Midsummer Night's Sex Comedy, directed by Woody Allen, starring Mia Farrow, Tony Roberts, Jose Ferrer, Mary Steenburgen, and Julie Hagerty. In this farce, set in 1900, three mismatched couples romp through a moonlit forest.

USA 1999 film, directed by Michael Hoffman. In this dusky fairy kingdom, complete with digital butterflies, lovers and would-be lovers come and go on bicycles and frolic in the nude (albeit discreetly). Critics were lukewarm despite the big stars: Kevin Kline as Bottom, Michelle Pfeiffer as Titania, and television's "Ally McBeal," Calista Flockhart, as Helena.

Adaptation conceived and co-direct-

James Cagney as Bottom. Courtesy Museum of Modern Art/Film Stills Archive

ed, 1999, by Diane Paulus and Randy Winer, *The Donkey Show: A Midsummer Night's Disco*, in which Titania is a 1970s go-go dancer, Oberon is a night-club owner, and Puck is a roller-skating drug-dealer.

Other

Henry Purcell's musical version, 1692, *The Fairy Queen*, had characters and creatures not in Shakespeare's version, including the Four Seasons, Sleep, six dancing monkeys, and, in the finale, a chorus of Chinese men and women. *A Comic Masque of Pyramus and Thisby* was an operetta composed by Richard Leveridge in 1716. The play has inspired operas by Carl Orff and Benjamin Britten as well as a 1939 jazz version, *Swinging the Dream*, featuring the Benny Goodman Sextet and Louis Armstrong as Bottom, and a ballet choreographed by George Balachine to the music of Felix Mendelssohn. The composer's mid-19th century score is the source of the ever-loved "Wedding March," still used for the bride and groom's traditional recessional.

Puck:
Shakespeare's Shape-Shifter

ometimes he was an old man, other times a child. Sometimes he was a bird or a beast, an eagle or an ass. Other times he was a goblin or an imp. A thousand years ago, he was the devil himself. Sometimes he was Puki (Old Norse) or Pooka (Irish) or Pwca (Welsh). To the Germans he was Puks, to the Latvians, Pukis. By whatever name, in whatever shape, for over a thousand years he has been a mischief-maker. To be "pouk-ledden" meant to be misled by Puck, who might, for example, appear before uncertain travelers with a lantern and then blow out the light just as they approached a cliff. Later, "pouk-led-den" became "pixy-led."

In *A Midsummer Night's Dream*, Puck is the fairy king's acolyte who summons the fog, circles the earth to fetch a flower, and, later, having made a mistake with his magic, finds the resulting chaos amusing. He delights in disarray, and says, "those things do best please me That befall prepost'rously." He knows who he is. He tells one of the fairies:

I am that merry wanderer of the night.
I jest to Oberon, and make him smile
When I a fat and bean-fed horse
*   beguile,*
Neighing in likeness of a filly foal.

Indifferent to human suffering, Shakespeare's Puck is nevertheless more naughty elf than demon, though there is a hint of malice in his pranks.

The wisest aunt, telling the saddest
*   tale,*
Sometimes for three-foot stool
*   mistaketh me;*
Then slip I from her bum, down
*   topples she.*

Shakespeare did something unusual with Puck; he combined him with another shape-shifter known to the Elizabethan audience—Robin Good-fellow. In *Dream*, Robin and Puck are the same, but this is the first known linking of the two.

Traditionally, Robin Goodfellow was the original hobgoblin. "Hob" is a variation of Robin, and Robin was a medieval name for the devil. Good-fellow was often a bad fellow, misleading travelers, pulling pranks, laughing with a marked "Ho, Ho, Ho." On the other hand, he could be helpful and would occasionally clean houses.

Once the subject of numerous ballads, in modern times Puck is rarely found outside of Shakespeare's *Dream*, though there are exceptions. Most notably, Puck was delightfully brought to life in Rudyard Kipling's *Puck of Pook's Hill*

(1906). In this story, two children, Dan and Una, spend Midsummer's Eve in a meadow on a circle of dark grass known as a "fairy ring," where they act out a shortened version of *A Midsummer Night's Dream*. They enjoy it so much, they do the whole thing three times. As it turns out, this is the secret formula which awakens Puck—"the oldest Old Thing in England." He appears to the children in his "bare, hairy feet," wearing a dark blue cap and saying, "What hempen homespuns have we swaggering here, So near the cradle of the Fairy Queen?"—just as he does in the play. Soon, the two children are sharing their hard-boiled eggs and biscuits with Puck, who can remember when Stonehenge was new. He reminisces:

> **"Lord, what fools these mortals be!"**
> **—*A Midsummer Night's Dream***

The People of the Hills have all left. I saw them come into Old England and I saw them go. Giants, trolls, kelpies, brownies, goblins, imps; wood, tree, mound, and water spirits; heath-people, hill-watchers, treasure-guards, good people, little people, pishogues, leprechauns, night-riders, pixies, nixies, gnomes, and the rest—gone, all gone! I came into England with Oak, Ash and Thorn, and when Oak, Ash and Thorn are gone I shall go too.

The other notable appearance of Puck was in the movie classic *Harvey* (1950), starring James Stewart as Elwood P. Dowd. Dowd is a lovable lush with an invisible friend named Harvey, a rabbit who stands over six feet. Harvey is said to be a "Pooka."

A Lamentable Comedy

t the end of *A Mid-summer Night's Dream*, Bottom, and the other Mechanicals stumble their way through an amateur performance for the entertainment of guests at a wedding. Even before their play, *Pyramus and Thisby*, is begun, the wedding guests are murmuring their criticisms. When Peter Quince completely botches the prologue, the Duke of Athens winces and whispers to his bride, "His speech was like a tangled chain; nothing impaired, but all disordered." The melodrama continues, with bits of exaggerated speech and over-acting, forgotten entrances, and missed cues.

Amateurish skits like this one were often performed at noble weddings in the context of a *masque*. The tradition of the masque began when members of the court entertained themselves by donning masks and costumes to dance the night away. Eventually the masque evolved into a more formal theatrical production staged at royal weddings, birthdays, and holiday celebrations. A masque often included acrobats, mimes, professional musicians and dancers, and amateur actors who performed allegorical skits. The sets and costumes could be elaborate, and some of the short dramas were by notable writers such as Ben Jonson. Queen Elizabeth enjoyed masques, but

King James I had a real penchant for the form. Under his reign, masques became increasingly decadent, and their expense became a political issue.

Shakespeare peppered his plays with masques. In *Timon of Athens*, a boy playing Cupid escorts a "Masque of Ladies" dressed as Amazons into the banquet hall. The Ladies play their lutes and dance with the guests. In *Romeo and Juliet*, Romeo is accompanied to the Capulet banquet by a group of masquers, and in *Henry VIII*, there is a masque to entertain the court in the first act. At the end of *As You Like It*, as the tangle of exiled lovers gets sorted out, the Roman god of marriage appears to lead a masque and bring the comedy to a dignified close.

Sometimes at a masque, the excessively moralizing dramas were acted and sung by choirboys with at least one alliterative lament sung in a treble voice.

In *A Midsummer Night's Dream*, long before we get to the pitiful performance by the well-meaning working men for the wedding guests, we understand that Shakespeare is poking fun at something. The earliest hint of this is the silly title of the botched little play-within-a-play: *The most Lamentable Comedy and most Cruel Death of Pyramus and Thisby*. Beyond parodying a popular and overrated genre, Shakespeare was specifically mocking a melodramatic piece of theatrical tripe by Thomas Preston, the vice-chancellor of Cambridge University. Written in 1569, its full title was, *A Lamentable Tragedy, Mixed Full of Pleasant Mirth, Containing the Life of Cambyses, King of Persia, from the beginning of his kingdom unto his death, his one good deed of execution, after that many wicked deeds and tyrannous murders committed by and through him, and last of all his odious death by God's justice appointed.*

Not surprisingly, the play was usually called *Cambyses* for short.

The Canon, the *First Folio*, and the Apocrypha

ther than Authorship itself, few Shakespearean subjects attract as much attention as the question of which dramas Shakespeare really wrote. The dispute is complicated by the fact that the official compilation of the plays, the *First Folio*, includes works that most authorities believe are collaborations; other contemporary publications, including later *Folios*, have additional plays credited to Shakespeare that almost surely are not his; and there are a few other short works or fragments that bear his stamp if not his name.

Elizabethan Drama Factories

In Shakespeare's time the drama was still an emerging form, and its emergence depended in large part on the demands of the marketplace. Like the modern movie business, the stories themselves were usually subordinate to the major actors whose presence drew audiences, and to the theater owners and acting companies that financed the productions.

Plays came from many sources, including books, legends and previous plays. They could represent the efforts of one writer, or of several, either working together or consecutively, and they

The First Folio. *Courtesy The Folger Shakespeare Library*

were often revised between productions, to make them more stageworthy or to tailor roles to individual performers. Once approved by the theater owner or company, the parts would often be written out by professional scribes to be memorized by the actors, while the prompter would retain an overall edition marked with stage directions and entrances and exits. Because successful plays were valuable properties, companies tried to keep them for themselves, and would generally license publication only when their stage life was thought to be over.

A business did emerge, however, in one-volume editions designed for reading rather than watching (the Elizabethans actually referred to "hearing" a play rather than seeing it.) Some of these were licensed by the companies that owned them, others were obtained by other means and published without the permission of the playwright or company (there was little of the modern sense of copyright).

Size Matters

The one-volume editions of the plays, whether authorized or not, were generally in the form of quartos, about the size of a slim modern trade paperback. The term refers to the number of times the printers' sheets were folded (quarto two times, folio once), and hence directly to the dimensions of the book. A number of such approximately seven-by-nine-inch volumes survive, and students of the canon generally divide them into "good" quartos, meaning they were printed from a relatively complete text, or "bad," meaning they were

An early print shop

patched together from various sources, including early drafts and actors' or even audience members' memories.

Ben Jonson was the first playwright to pull together, edit, and oversee the publication of his plays, a task he finished in 1616. (Shakespeare had provided this kind of editorial oversight only for his long poems, published in the 1590s). The compendium was published not in quarto form, by in the folio format. This format was more impressive, more expensive, and presumably more suitable for a gentleman's library, where Jonson believed his work belonged. The success of this volume was no doubt an inspiration for two colleagues from the King's Men, John Heminges and Henry Condell. Presumably relying on the contents of the company's library of scripts, they collected 36 plays and contracted to produce *Mr.*

William Shakespeare's Comedies, Histories and Tragedies in 1623.

Fourteen of the total were listed as comedies, from *The Tempest* to *The Winter's Tale*, and including the *Merchant of Venice*. The histories were printed in historical order, from *The Life and Death of King John* to *The Life of King Henry the Eighth*, and the remaining eleven plays were listed as tragedies, from *Macbeth*, *Hamlet*, and *Lear* to *Coriolanus* and *Cymbeline*.

New Publications, and New Versions of the Old

The editors included eighteen plays that had never been published in quar-

Frontispiece of a 1709 publication of Pericles

to. Plays that had appeared in quarto were represented by presumably more authoritative texts, in many cases very different from what had been public before. Ben Jonson contributed an introductory poem that includes many of the complimentary lines still used for Shakespeare ("Soul of the age!.... Sweet swan of Avon!"). The *Folio* title page carries what has become the most famous image of Shakespeare, the high fore-headed visage that looks out from the Droeshout portrait. It also includes a list of the members of his acting company, including the editors of the *Folio*, Shakespeare himself, Richard Burbage and the comic players William Kempe and Robert Armin.

About 1,000 copies were printed, priced at one pound, a respectable sum at the time. Several hundred copies of the book survive, in various states of repair. In 1632 the *Second Folio* was printed, and a *Third Folio* in 1663 and 1664.

Pericles, Prince of Tyre

The *Third Folio* included *Pericles*, available previously only in a 1609 quarto. The Pericles of the title comes to the court of Antioch, where he perceives the guilty secret of the incest between King Antiochus and his daughter. While he keeps the secret to himself, he flees, pursued by an assassin. He ends up going from his home in Tyre to Tarsus and eventually to Pentapolis, where he wins the heart of Thaisa, daughter of the local king.

He tries to return to Tyre, along with his wife, who gives birth at sea to their daughter, and then drowns in a storm. He leaves his daughter in the hands of friends in Tarsus and returns to Tyre. His daughter Marina grows to womanhood in Tarsus, but her beauty makes the queen there so jealous she sells the girl to a brothel-keeper in Mytilene. Her refusal to take part in the trade leads her to be placed in an honest household.

Pericles is eventually reunited with not only his daughter, but also his wife, whose body was cast off the ship by sailors and who was revived by a physician in Ephesus and has become a priestess at the temple of Diana.

Most authorities believe that even if Shakespeare wrote some of this play, someone else wrote a good deal of it, particularly the early sections.

The Two Noble Kinsmen

When first printed in 1634, this play was credited to John Fletcher and William Shakespeare, and its tentative dating to 1613 would make it possible for Shakespeare to have written some of it. Like the other play attributed to the Shakespeare/Fletcher collaboration, *King Henry VIII*, it has numerous opportunities for pageantry.

The story tells of noble cousins of the Greek city of Thebes, Arcite and Palamon. Wounded and captured in battle with the forces of Athens, the two both fall in love with Emilia, the daughter of their jailer. They eventually end up fighting for her hand, with the loser facing death.

Other Contenders for the Canon

An anonymous play called *Edward III* was one of many in the 17th century

attributed at least in part to Shakespeare. As part of the canon, it would fit very neatly into the historical framework that now begins with *Richard II*. Some editions now list it as part of the canon, while other authorities strongly resist, on the grounds of the quality of the writing.

The *Third Folio* attributed to Shakespeare a number of plays that virtually no one now credits to him, from *The London Prodigal* to *Locrine*.

Fragments and Lost Plays

Sir Thomas More was a play—apparently never produced—that included sections by a number of Elizabethan authors. Some three pages that have survived are not only credited to Shakespeare, but some authorities believe may be in his hand.

Two other plays theoretically by Shakespeare are mentioned in contemporary records. They are *Cardenio* and *Love's Labour's Won*.

There are no copies of *Cardenio*, but an 18th century editor claimed that a manuscript he discovered of a play called *Double Falsehood* was the missing drama, which apparently had not been seen since it was performed by the King's Men in 1613. Since by that time John Fletcher is thought to have supplanted Shakespeare as the company's principal playwright, many authorities that do accept its authenticity credit it to Fletcher. *Love's Labour's Won* is believed to be an alternate title to one of the other comedies, speculation running from *Taming of the Shrew* to *Much Ado about Nothing* or *All's Well That Ends Well* (among others).

THE MERCHANT OF VENICE

MONEYLENDER MISCALCULATES, LOSES FORTUNE AND DAUGHTER

Period

Renaissance

Setting

Italy

The Merchant of Venice tells two connected stories. The first is the trial of a young man's love, in which he must choose among three chests, winning his true love only if he chooses correctly. The second major story line is that of Antonio, who borrows 3,000 ducats from the usurer Shylock, promising to give him a pound of his flesh if the loan is not repaid on time. Bassanio is the young man in love, and Antonio is the source of the money he needs to pursue the lovely Portia ("a lady richly left"), who has been constrained by the requirements of her dead father's will to subject each of her suitors to a trial in which they must choose among chests of gold, silver, and lead to find the one that holds her portrait. Two more love

stories are tied into this first, those of Bassanio's friend, Gratiano, and his lover Nerissa (Portia's maid), and of Lorenzo and Jessica, the daughter of Shylock.

The Prince of Morocco arrives at Belmont, Portia's home. "All that glitters is not gold," is the message in the golden chest when the prince opens it. The Prince of Aragon later chooses the silver chest, and discovers the portrait of an idiot.

After their departure Bassanio, using the money he has borrowed on Antonio's surety, arrives in Belmont. After a good deal of pondering, he chooses the chest of lead, and finds in it "fair Portia's counterfeit." Portia, in her joy at his victory, gives him a ring, and the happiness of the scene is increased by the announcement that Bassanio's companion, Gratiano, and Portia's maid, Nerissa, are also getting married.

But the happiness of their wedding day is constrained by news from Venice. Antonio had taken out the loan from Shylock in the certainty that one of his

An eighteenth-century Shylock. Shakespeare Centre Library, Stratford-upon-Avon

many ships would come successfully back to Venice before the loan fell due. Unfortunately, all his expeditions have foundered ("Hath all his ventures failed...not one hit?" asks Bassanio) and Shylock is demanding his pound of flesh. Antonio has sent a message asking only that he be able to see his friend before what amounts to a death sentence is carried out. Bassanio and Gratiano leave for Venice immediately, and Portia and Nerissa announce that they are going into a nunnery for the duration of their husbands' absence.

At the trial in Venice, despite Bassanio's offer to use his new wife's resources to pay twice the amount of Antonio's debt, Shylock insists on his pound of flesh. The court relies on the good offices of Balthasar, a youthful lawyer who comes to them on the highest recommendation. Balthasar, who is Portia in disguise, tries to persuade Shylock to show mercy to Antonio ("The quality of mercy is not strained) but Shylock refuses ("My deeds upon my head. I crave the law, the penalty and forfeit of my bond").

After warning Antonio that he must be prepared to pay the debt, as Shylock approaches him with a knife Balthasar reminds him that he may have a pound of flesh, but not one drop of blood, or he will forfeit his property and his life.

Shylock then is willing to settle for the 3,000 ducats, but he is charged with an attack on the life of a Venetian citizen; in the end he agrees to pass on his wealth to his daughter Jessica, who has eloped with the Christian Lorenzo.

Balthasar's pay, provided with some reluctance, is Bassanio's ring, the one given him by Portia before their marriage. Gratiano gives up his ring to Balthasar's clerk, who is Nerissa in disguise. The ring theme is concluded at the end of the play, when Portia and Nerissa, back in Belmont and no longer in disguise, first chide their husbands on the loss of the rings, then reveal their deception.

Likely Source of the Plot

The casket plot and the pound of flesh story were used in other tales available to Shakespeare, though not in the combined form he employed. There seems little question that this play also owes something to Christopher Marlowe's popular *The Jew of Malta.* (An alternative title for *The Merchant of Venice* was *The Jew of Venice*, although in fact the merchant of the title was Antonio, not Shylock.)

Notable Feature

The play is unapologetically anti–Semitic, no doubt reflecting popular Elizabethan sentiment, particularly toward moneylenders. What makes it different from similar revenge dramas is its insistence on providing Shylock not only with a racial/religious animosity toward Christians ("he hates our sacred nation," says Shylock of Antonio), but

personal emotions based on personal incidents. "You call me misbeliever, cut-throat dog, and spit upon my Jewish gabardine," Shylock reminds him. "Hath not a Jew eyes?" Shylock asks in his famous speech. "If you prick us, do we not bleed?"

Although Shylock is by far the most clearly drawn and the most memorable character in the play, the court scene is not the play's climax. *Merchant* is a comedy, and the three love stories (Bassanio/Portia, Gratiano/Nerissa, and Lorenzo/Jessica) are in some way the focus of the drama and continue well past the court scene. In addition, there is a heavy comic element in Launcelot Gobbo, first Shylock's servant and then Bassanio's.

Notable Productions and Performances

The first Shylock may have been Shakespeare's colleague Richard Burbage. In the 19th century, American actor Edwin Booth often played the role. The strong role of Portia has attracted the attention of prominent actresses, including Ellen Terry in the 19th century and Peggy Ashcroft in the 20th. George C. Scott's 1962 performance as Shylock for the New York Shakespeare Festival is regarded as a modern landmark. Jonathan Miller directed a 1970 stage version with Laurence Olivier, who also starred in Miller's 1973 film. Joan Plowright played Portia and Jeremy Brett was Bassanio. But because of the anti-Semitic element, in the post-World War II era producers and directors have often trod lightly.

AS YOU LIKE IT

LOVE POEMS GROW ON TREES IN LAND OF EXILE

Period

Middle Ages

Setting

Forest of Arden, France

A magical forest awaits us, where music and romance thrive and love poems seem to grow on trees. Before we arrive at this quirky countryside, however, we must witness discord in the court and turmoil in two dysfunctional families. In this tableau of contrasts and counterparts, there is a little something for everyone—just as the title suggests.

Oliver, eldest son of a noble family, hates his popular brother Orlando. He has withheld the younger brother's inheritance, denied him an education, harassed and humiliated him—verbally and physically. Oliver sincerely hopes his brother will be killed in the wrestling match he has arranged with the death-dealing muscle-man Charles. At the same time, Duke (senior) has been ban-

ished from the court by his younger brother, Duke Frederick, and is living in exile in the Forest of Arden. His daughter, Rosalind, has remained behind with her beloved cousin Celia.

When Rosalind and Celia encounter handsome Orlando, it is love at first sight for Rosalind. She and Celia try to talk Orlando out of the wrestling match but he insists on meeting the challenge. To everyone's surprise and relief, he wins, but then is unfairly refused the prize. He doesn't care; he has fallen desperately in love with Rosalind. He manages to learn her identity before he is warned of danger and forced into hiding.

Shortly after Orlando's exit, Rosalind, too, is banished by the dictatorial duke. Celia decides she would rather have Rosalind's company than stay behind. The two set out to join Rosalind's father in the Forest of Arden. For reasons of safety and freedom, Rosalind decides to disguise herself as a boy and go by the name of Ganymede. Celia changes her dress and pretends she is Ganymede's sister. Touchstone, a court jester, joins them on their venture into the pastoral wilderness.

When Duke Frederick discovers that his daughter is gone, he concludes that she and Rosalind must have joined forces with Orlando. He wants that boy arrested. He questions Oliver about Orlando's whereabouts, and threatens to kill or banish him if he doesn't find Orlando within one year's time. Now Oliver's on the run, too.

As luck would have it, all the likable people in this play wind up in the forest together. Already in the woods with Duke (senior) are his friends Amiens, a singer, and the pessimistic and gloomy Jaques. Soon, Orlando stumbles in with his ailing old servant and traveling companion, Adam. Both are made welcome to this court-in-exile. Before the close of the scene, Jaques gives his famous soliloquy on the phases of human life, which begins:

find that it has been decorated. Orlando has hung love poems to Rosalind on the trees. When they finally find the lovesick poet, Rosalind—as the "saucy lackey" Ganymede—proposes to cure

Audrey and Touchstone, from an 1850 production.
Courtesy Shakespeare Centre Library, Stratford-upon-Avon

All the world's a stage,
And all the men and women merely
players;
They have their exits and their entrances;
And one man in his time plays many
parts,
His acts being seven ages.

Rosalind and Celia, in disguise as brother and sister, enter the forest and

Orlando of his mad infatuation. He is instructed to woo Ganymede as he would Rosalind and to expect changeable behavior in return, frustrating enough to wash away any spot of love. Orlando says he'll try, and he does, dutifully calling Ganymede "Rosalind." With Rosalind's lively intelligence, wit, and hearty sense of humor, the game is a good one. All the while, she falls deeper in love with Orlando, while he seems to be attracted to her despite her boyish disguise.

Orlando and Rosalind are not the only ones wrestling with the most untamable of emotions. The forest is filled with people falling head over heels in love with each other. Touchstone woos a naive and earthy goatherd, Audrey. Although he is condescending in his courting, they decide to get married as soon as possible. Less lucky in love is Silvius, a shepherd. He falls in love with Phebe, a shepherdess, who has fallen madly and badly in love with the pretend boy, Ganymede.

Oliver arrives in the woods, carrying a bloody bandage which he presents to Ganymede. He explains that he is Orlando's brother, once his enemy and now reformed, and says that Orlando saved him from a hungry lion on the loose. The brave boy was injured but is recovering nicely. There is one more thing: Oliver is in love with Celia.

The final act is a riot of weddings as the disguises fall away and true love is revealed. Two sets of couples—Oliver and Celia and Touchstone and Audrey—make plans to wed the next day. Ganymede promises Orlando that Rosalind will appear at the ceremony and will wed him, and then gives the very confused Phebe a riddle that baffles the shepherdess even more but promises an end to the confusion. The next day, Hymen, the Roman god of marriage, appears in the flesh and leads the festivities. A radiant Rosalind emerges as herself, the Ganymede disguise no longer needed or wanted, much to the delight of Orlando and the chagrin of Phebe,

who shrugs good-naturedly and agrees to marry Silvius after all.

As this tipsy-topsy take on pastoral romance comes to a merry close, word comes that the brother of the exiled duke has been reformed by a holy man and has decided to retire to a monastery. Jaques likes the sound of this and decides to do the same thing. The banished duke and his happy friends are free to return to life at the court. The fractured relationships are now all mended; the reconciliation is complete. On that happy note, the four couples begin to dance—a prelude to their wedding ceremony.

Likely Source of the Plot

Shakespeare drew largely on Thomas Lodge's prose romance *Rosalynde* (1590), but he invented Jaques, Touchstone, and Audrey.

Notable Feature

As You Like It has more songs than any other play by Shakespeare.

Notable Productions and Performances

It is believed that *As You Like It* was the first play to be performed at the Globe Theatre, the principal home of Shakespeare's acting company, when it opened in 1599.

Rosalind is one of the prize roles for any actress, and many have found their strength in her. 20th century audiences raved at the performances by Vanessa Redgrave, Katharine Hepburn, and Maggie Smith.

What if Shakespeare Had
Been Born a Girl?
Women in the Queen's England

n *A Room of One's Own*, a slim book published in 1929, Virginia Woolf considered the puzzle of women in Renaissance England. In ballads, sonnets and plays of the era, she noted, extraordinary women seemed to abound. These women were "heroic and mean; splendid and sordid; infinitely beautiful and hideous in the extreme." In real life, however, these women of men's imaginations did not exist. Real daughters, wives, and working women were commonly subject to physical beatings if they challenged the authority of fathers, husbands, or patrons and, except for a handful of silk-stockinged aristocrats, they received meager education. They were expected to marry, bear children, and keep house. In an age "when every other man, it seemed, was capable of song or sonnet," few women wrote diaries or letters, nor were the details of women's lives considered worth recording. Woolf concluded that the woman of Elizabethan fiction was, in fact, fictional:

> She pervades poetry from cover to cover; she is all but absent from history. She dominates the lives of kings and conquerors in fiction; in fact she was the slave of any boy whose parents forced a ring upon her finger. Some of the most inspired words, some of the most profound thoughts in literature fall from her lips; in real life she could hardly read, could scarcely spell, and was the property of her husband.

"She Is within; Where Should She Be?"

Will Shakespeare had two daughters. The oldest, Susanna, must have been not only smart but spirited. She once successfully sued a man for libel when he publicly accused her of adultery, and the epitaph on her gravestone says that she was "witty above her sex." No doubt Shakespeare was proud of her. The fathers in his plays, however, often reflect the Elizabethan attitude that daughters were expected to obey and were considered, by law and by tradition, property to be passed from father to husband.

In *A Midsummer Night's Dream*, Hermia wants to marry Lysander, the man she loves, but her father wants her to marry Demetrius instead. The Duke of Athens, at first, backs the father and warns Hermia:

Be advis'd fair maid,
To you your father should be as a god;
One that compos'd your beauties; yea,
*   and one*
To whom you are but as a form in wax,
By him imprinted, and within his power
To leave the figure, or disfigure it.

In *Romeo and Juliet* we find another daughter, unhappy at her parents' matchmaking efforts. Although she is not yet fourteen, her parents, in the custom of the aristocracy, have arranged for Juliet to marry Paris. Alas, as all the world knows, she's in love with Romeo. When she protests the approaching wedding day, her father calls her "young baggage" and "disobedient wretch," and reminds her that she is his and must obey. There are consequences if she doesn't.

Graze where you will, you shall not
*   house with me....*

An you be mine, I'll give you to my friend;
An you be not, hang, beg, starve, die in
*   the streets,*
For, by my soul, I'll ne'er acknowledge thee,
Nor what is mine shall never do thee good.

In the wedding scene at the end of *The Tempest*, Prospero gives his daughter, Miranda, to young Ferdinand, saying, "Then, as my gift, and thine own acquisition / Worthily purchas'd, take my daughter." He includes this warning:

But if thou dost break her virgin-knot
*   before*
All sanctimonious ceremonies may
With full and holy rite be minist'red,
No sweet aspersion shall the heavens let
*   fall*
To make this contract grow; but barren
*   hate,*
Sour-ey'd disdain, and discord, shall
*   bestrew*
The union of your bed with weeds so
*   loathly*
That you shall hate it both.

In *The Taming of the Shrew*, a spit-fire named Kate struggles with the confines of matrimony. According to tradition and to her wealthy merchant father, Kate must be tamed, wooed, and wed before her coy, manipulative, suitor-laden sister Bianca can be married. To the surprise of one and all, a suitor is found for Kate: he is a hearty young man named Petruchio, whose sole aim is finding a rich wife. He doesn't care that she is known as a shrew. He says:

Be she as foul as was Florentius' love,
As old as Sibyl, and as curst and shrewd
As Socrates' Xanthippe or a worse—

She moves me not, or not removes, at least,
Affection's edge in me, were she as rough
As are the swelling Adriatic seas.
I come to wive it wealthily in Padua;
If wealthily, then happily in Padua.

Father and suitor make a deal, Petruchio asking, "Then tell me, if I get your daughter's love, / What dowry shall I have with her to wife?" and the father responding, "After my death, the one half of my lands / And, in possession, twenty thousand crowns." When Petruchio informs Kate that Sunday will be their wedding day, she responds, "I'll see thee hang'd on Sunday first." The bulk of the comedy, then, is watching how Petruchio manages to conquer Kate's aggressive tendencies and turn her into an obedient wife. By play's end, she exemplifies and, without prompting, articulates the Elizabethan description of a good wife

Thy husband is thy lord, thy life, thy
*   keeper,*
Thy head, thy sovereign; one that cares
*   for thee,*
And for thy maintenance commits his body
To painful labor both by sea and land,
To watch the night in storms, the day in
*   cold,*
Whilst thou liest warm at home, secure
*   and safe;*
And craves no other tribute at thy hands
But love, fair looks, and true obedience—
Too little payment for so great a debt.
Such duty as the subject owes the prince,
Even such a woman oweth to her husband;
And when she is froward, peevish,
*   sullen, sour,*
And not obedient to his honest will,
What is she but a foul contending rebel
And graceless traitor to her loving lord?

Modern directors have treated this ending in various ways. In an adaptation by Charles Marowitz, Kate delivered this speech without expression, as if shell-shocked into submission by her conqueror. In other productions, Kate has been presented as something of a time bomb, ready to go off, who speaks with a thinly veiled hostility which is, nevertheless, unrecognized and thus

Queen Elizabeth I

dismissed by uncomprehending men. In still other productions, the whole thing is played as a farce, a merry romp through the battle of the sexes by two strong-willed people too smart to fit their lives into the little expectations of convention-bound society.

In Shakespeare's plays, as in life, women, regardless of status, ability, age, or appearance, had to deal with the confines of gender expectations dictated by their time in history. In *Romeo and Juliet*, when the Nurse asks where Lady Capulet is, Juliet replies, "Where is my mother! Why, she is within; Where should she be?" That was the question. Where should a woman be? A "pam-

phlet war" was being waged in Renaissance England during Shakespeare's day as people wrangled with all sorts of new ideas, including the appropriate roles for women in a land ruled by one. In 1560, the printer, John Kynge, had put out a number of publications about women, including one by Edward More titled *The Lytle and Bryefe tretyse, called the defence of women*. In 1589, Thomas Nashe attacked women in a pamphlet called *The Anatomie of Absurditie, Contayning a breefe confutation of the slender imputed prayses to feminine perfection*, which was answered in a pamphlet by someone aptly named Jane Anger, claiming to be a woman writing for other women. Her pamphlet was titled *Jane Anger her Protection for Women. To defend them against the scandalous reportes of a late Surfeiting Lover, and all other Venerians that complaine so to bee over cloyed with womens kindnesse*. The nature of the sexes was a hot topic in Elizabeth's England.

That the questions about gender expectations were being asked was at least a step toward human progress, but the fact remained that only some girls were permitted to attend grammar school; none were admitted to universities. With few exceptions, they were expected to focus their primary energies on the domestic duties involved with tending to their husbands and children. Is it any wonder that several of Shakespeare's most adventurous heroines dress themselves in men's clothing in order to move about their world more freely? In *As You Like It*, Rosalind, banished by the duke, masquerades as Ganymede to make her getaway. Once in the Forest of Arden, however, it is not clear why she continues the disguise except to escape the limitations placed on her as a woman.

News! Juliet Was a Boy!

In Shakespeare's plays there are mad women and Amazons, bearded witches and flitting fairies, daughters—both devilish and dear, girlfriends—pursued and pursuing, wives—merry and not, earthy working women and dignified queens. Some of his women are tragic, villainous, or victimized and destroyed. Many heroines are smart, saintly, strong. And all, on England's Renaissance stage, were played by boys or young men.

When Elizabethan audiences watched Romeo kiss Juliet, they were watching two young men kissing—and they knew it. They knew that Lady Macbeth was no lady. Nor were they in denial about Cleopatra, but were able to put aside reality for a few hours and forget that she was played by a teenaged boy who was probably worrying about what would happen to his career when his voice broke. Accustomed to such gender layering and cross-dressing in the context of theater, audience members were adept at embracing illusion. They had to be.

For the literal-minded, things could get very confusing. In *Twelfth Night*, for example, the character of Viola is disguised as a young man and finds herself in strange circumstances when another woman falls in love with her, thinking she's male, not female. From the Elizabethan audience perspective, however, it was even more complex; they were watching a boy playing a girl in love with a boy playing a girl disguised as a boy. Talk about gender confusion!

Why were there no women on stage in England? Scholars can only theorize. Some say there was a single-sex gender system operating in Elizabethan England in which women were regarded as incomplete men. Others point to the homoerotic underpinnings of the culture.

Another explanation is that, in England, as secular theater emerged from the confines of the Mystery, Miracle, and Morality plays of medieval religious drama and the dictates of the male-only world of the church, it immediately got tangled in another male-only domain—the university. Apart from Shakespeare, most playwrights in Renaissance England, including Christopher Marlowe and Thomas Kyd, held degrees from Oxford or Cambridge or Westminster School where Ben Jonson was educated. In addition, their plays drew on the tradition of the Greek and Latin classical theater, another male-only tradition. It was a triple whammy for women, and the exclusion was complete.

By contrast, women on the Continent were allowed on stage. The secular theater just across the English Channel, once free from the limitations of the medieval church, developed in the streets of Italy as the populist theater form commedia dell'arte. From the start, women were players and, all through Europe, working class women were able to add to the family budget by performing on the stage. One woman, Isabella Andreini (1562–1604) even performed in the courts of Ferdinando I and Henri IV.

The commedia dell'arte plays, bawdy and raucous, most often featured a servant who had to outwit a master or who was called on to help a pair of young lovers in their fight against a tyrannical father. The audience always cheered for the servant and the lovers and expected to see the ruling patriarchs humiliated in the end.

Commedia dell'arte did not arrive in England until 1660, and then only as the rude, crude Punch and Judy shows which were about as violent as our Saturday morning cartoons. The hooked nose, hunchbacked Punch and his wife Judy and their abused baby usually whacked each other with "slapsticks" while the audience roared with laughter (see "Wise Enough to Play the Fool," page 265).

The last male actor to play a female character on the English stage was Edward Kynaston (1619–87) who was said to be exquisitely beautiful. In 1662, King Charles II licensed women to act on the English stage:

Whereas the women's parts in plays have hitherto been acted by men in the habits of women, at which some have taken offence, we do permit and give leave for the time to come, that all women's parts be acted by women.

The first English actress on record was Margaret Hughes who played Desdemona in a production of *Othello*. She joined William Davenant's company in 1676 and had a long, successful career. In the days when the play was written, however, women could attend the theater with or without an escort, but not act in it and certainly not write for it.

Shakespeare's Sister

In her exploration of Elizabethan women, Virginia Woolf imagined "what would have happened had Shakespeare had a wonderfully gifted sister, called Judith, let us say." While Will went to school, got married, and went off to seek his fortune in London, Judith, "as adventurous, as imaginative, as agog to see the world" was not sent to school, but, instead, was betrothed to a neighboring son before she was out of her teens. Woolf outlined the probable expectations of a bright and bold Elizabethan girl and concluded, "it would have been impossible, completely and entirely, for any woman to have written the plays of Shakespeare in the age of Shakespeare." With little access to money and no room of her own, Judith, unlike William, could do very little to bring forth her natural gift. The world around her was not merely indifferent to her genius and wit, but was openly hostile. Nor were women allowed on stage. Imagining Judith, Woolf wrote,

She had the quickest fancy, a gift like her brother's, for the tune of words. Like him, she had a taste for the theater. She stood at the stage door; she wanted to act, she said. Men laughed in her face.... She could get no training in her craft. Could she even seek her dinner in a tavern or roam the streets at midnight?

In the end, Woolf's imagined female Shakespeare finds herself pregnant and, in despair, kills herself, never having written a word.

THE TAMING OF
THE SHREW

SWAGGERING SUITOR FOUND
FOR KATE THE CURST,
YOUNGER SISTER FREE TO WED

Period

16th century

Setting

Padua, Italy

This is a tale told to a drunken tinker. Having been thrown out of the ale-house, he is found unconscious by a great lord who decides to have some fun. When the tinker awakens, he is in a castle surrounded by servants who pretend he is their master. A play about the taming of a shrewish woman is then presented for his enjoyment and, turning our attention to the unfolding story, both playwright and audience forget about the tinker and the practical joke.

Baptista, a rich Italian merchant in the city of Padua, has two daughters, Katherina and Bianca. The younger of the two is Bianca, sweet and docile, albeit manipulative and insincere, who wants to get married. She is being energetically courted by, not one, but two

suitors. First, however, a husband must be found for the elder daughter, Katherina, who is anything but docile. Katherina prides herself on having a violent temper. Criticized during a lute lesson, for example, she breaks the musical instrument over her teacher's head. Everyone is afraid of the volatile and unhappy Katherina, it seems, except for a new fellow in town. Petruchio is a vibrant young man, whose sole aim is to find a rich wife. He has decided to tame Katherina.

It is a battle of two strong-willed, equally bright, lively, resourceful people. What tips the balance is that this is Elizabethan England, where an understanding of natural law dictates that husbands must rule their wives and wives must be obedient to their husbands. Petruchio makes a game of wooing "bonny Kate, and sometimes Kate the curst," by turning her world upside-down. He continues the process of taming, even after he carts her off on their wedding day, by starving and humiliating her, all the time pretending

Elizabeth Taylor and Richard Burton in The Taming of the Shrew.
Courtesy Museum of Modern Art/Film Stills Archive

that he is pampering and protecting her.

We know he has won the battle when she confesses that she will call the moon the sun if he tells her to. In the end, the newly married couple returns to Padua for a visit. The whole town turns out to see what has become of Katherina. She has been tamed, and the play ends with her publicly lecturing her spoiled sister on the joys of wifely submission.

Likely Source of the Plot

Shakespeare took an age-old plot, the stuff of common ballads and folk tales, and, with a nip here and a tuck there, fashioned something new. *A*

Merry Jest of a Shrewde and Curste Wyfe, a ballad printed in 1550, contains several elements found in the Bard's play. In this song, as in most of the popular versions of the storyline, the virago is beaten into submission, which, along with the thrashing of servants, was made to seem amusing. In *A Merry Jest*, the woman is bludgeoned to a bloody pulp and then wrapped in the salted skin of an old horse. In Shakespeare's less violent version of the plot, the battle is one of evenly matched wits. The playwright takes for granted the fact that the husband should have authority over his wife, but here the focus is on two vigorous, bold, high-spirited, cunning people, who make peace in a partnership based on mutual respect, if not equality.

Notable Features

The Taming of the Shrew is not to be confused with *The Taming of a Shrew*, published in 1594. In this play, there are three sisters, each one with a suitor. Christopher Sly, the poor drunk who appears at the beginning, is not cut out of the action so abruptly, but appears in several interludes and an epilogue. *A Shrew* may have been an early edition of the play, reconstructed from the faulty memories of actors who rehearsed it. The result was a pirated or stolen play called a Bad Quarto.

Notable Productions and Performances

New York's Delacorte Theater in Central Park, 1978. Meryl Streep, playing opposite Raul Julia, paused in her entrance to do several well-muscled chin-ups on a bar in the doorway.

In the Mediaeval Players production, 1985, both Katherina and Bianca were played by men and several male roles were played by women, all in the commedia style.

At New York's Delacorte Theater in Central Park, 1990, a production directed by A. J. Antoon, starred Morgan Freeman, Helen Hunt, and Tracey Ullman.

Other Uses of Basic Plot

The Woman's Prize, or The Tamer Tamed, 1611—a sequel written by John Fletcher (1579–1625). Petruchio, as widower, remarries a woman who tames him.

The Taming of the Shrew, 1929 (rereleased, 1966), film directed by Sam Taylor, starring Mary Pickford as Kate and Douglas Fairbanks as Petruchio who, at one point, roughhouse with whips.

Kiss Me Kate, 1953, USA film directed by George Sidney, with music by Cole Porter, in which the offstage conflict between the two main stars (once married to each other, now divorced) parallel their on-stage roles.

The Taming of the Shrew, 1966, UK film directed by Franco Zeffirelli, with Elizabeth Taylor as Kate, Richard Burton as Petruchio. This sex romp profited from the offscreen trials and tribulations of its two stars, from Taylor's ample bosom straining against a tightly laced bodice, and from her well-exercised throwing arm.

BBC-TV version, 1980, directed by Jonathan Miller, starring Sarah Badel and Jonathan Cleese.

10 Things I Hate About You, 1999, USA film directed by Gil Junger. Billed as a teen Taming of the Shrew, the story revolves around rebellious, sullen Kat, who spends her time reading the poetry of Sylvia Plath, and her popular but petty younger sister Bianca. Their father won't let the younger sister go to the prom at Padua High unless the older sister has a date too. Local bad boy, Patrick, is persuaded to ask her out, and the teens have a memorable night.

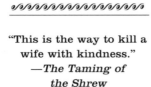

"This is the way to kill a wife with kindness."
—The Taming of the Shrew

ALL'S WELL THAT ENDS WELL

DYING KING CURED; HEALER REWARDED WITH WAYWARD HUSBAND

Period

Sixteenth century

Settings

France and Italy

If this comedy were candy, it would be a sour ball. If you're expecting something sweet, be forewarned.

In a palace in the south of France, young Bertram, the Count of Rousillon, is saying good-bye to his mother, the countess. He and old Lord Lafeu and Parolles, a lowlife companion (albeit one of noble birth), are all on their way to Paris to see the King of France, who is gravely ill.

Standing quietly to one side is Helena, daughter of a famous physician. When he died, Helena became a ward of the court. She is infatuated with Bertram. He barely knows she exists, and why should he? He is of high birth, she is not. Her love for him is futile, unrequited. She bids him farewell, then,

briefly left alone, she muses aloud about her desperate longing for the man she cannot have.

The countess learns that Helena is lovesick for Bertram, and she counsels the girl whom she loves like a daughter. Helena decides to travel to Paris to see the king, whom she hopes to cure with one of her father's old remedies. When she arrives in Paris, Helena cures the dying king and is granted her wish to marry any man in the court. When she chooses the great love of her life, Bertram, he publicly rejects her, saying with utter disdain, "A poor physician's daughter my wife!" The king lectures Bertram about his attitude, pointing out that true nobility of spirit is born in a person and has nothing to do with society's ranking system. Besides, he will grant Helena increased status if that's all Bertram objects to. The king says,

Good alone
Is good without a name.... She is young,
*   wise, fair;*
In these to nature she's immediate heir;

*And these breed honor.... Honors thrive
When rather from our acts we them
    derive
Than our fore-goers....
If thou canst like this creature as a maid,
I can create the rest. Virtue and she
Is her own dower; honor and wealth
    from me.*

Still, Bertram refuses, until the king commands him to marry Helena. The wedding is a hasty one, and then the sulking Bertram refuses to consummate the marriage. He would rather go to war. Without looking back, he heads for the battleground in Italy with Parolles by his side, who cries merrily, "To the wars, my boy, to the wars!" Bertram then writes a few letters. One goes to his mother. He tells her he has married Helena but not bedded her and that he has run away. He signs it "your unfortunate son." Another letter goes to Helena. It presents a set of fairy-tale riddles and challenges. It reads:

When thou canst get the ring upon my finger, which never shall come off, and show me a child begotten of thy body that I am father to, then call me husband.

At first, Helena obsesses that her true love is in danger on the battlefield and that she has driven him there. She resolves to leave the palace and wander as a loveless pilgrim, in the hope that, with her gone, Bertram will come home to his mother and to France.

With all the world before her, it is probably something less than coincidence that Helena, dressed in pilgrim garb, finds her way to Florence. There, she lodges with an old Widow whose daughter, Diana, is warned by friends and neighbors about a French soldier who has been very busy, on the battlefield and off, and about his sidekick, "a filthy officer" named Parolles.

When some French soldiers decide to expose Parolles for the loudmouth coward he is, they trick him into think-

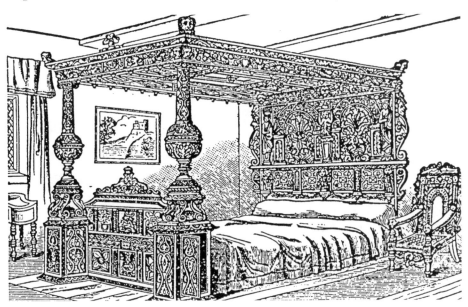

ing he's been captured by the enemy. As Bertram listens, Parolles behaves just as his companions expected he would—by betraying all his companions in order to save himself. As Bertram listens, his buddy Parolles divulges military secrets, then says terrible things about his compatriots, especially Bertram whom he calls "a foolish idle boy" and "dangerous and lascivious." With little provocation, he says Bertram steals, rapes, lies, drinks. Exposed as an opportunistic fraud, the blindfold is removed and he looks into the faces of his disgusted colleagues. They want nothing more to do with him. Now alone, Parolles decides he could put his bluffing ability to good use as a jester or fool, (after all, his name means "words" in French).

Helena has devised her own plan to snare her cheating husband. Bertram has been relentlessly chasing Diana, eager to get her into bed. Helena persuades Diana to say yes to the unwanted advances, coax him into exchanging rings, and promise not to talk when they meet that night. For this "bed trick," Helena takes Diana's place and, in the dark, Bertram doesn't know the difference.

A rumor begins to circulate that Helena has died. With his wife dead and the war over, Bertram goes home to the south of France to see his mother. She is mourning the death of Helena, and Bertram is suddenly repentant. The king comes to visit, and he too mourns Helena's death. Diana arrives full of accusations.

Suddenly, Helena herself shows up, very much alive, and explains everything. Bertram, realizing that his wife has found a way to fulfill the demands made in his letter, has a complete change of heart and accepts her as his wife. Helena, who has never stopped loving Bertram despite all she knows about him, is happy at last. Even Diana is happy because the king offers to pay her dowry for any man of her choice.

Likely Source of the Plot

The basic plot of the story is taken from the *Decameron*, written in 1353 by Giovanni Boccaccio.

Notable Feature

Like *Measure for Measure* and *Troilus and Cressida*, this is one of Shakespeare's so-called problem plays. When the last lines are spoken, the audience is left to wonder what it is that has ended so well. The heroine has valiantly overcome obstacles and gotten her man, but who cares? She's a scheming airhead and he's a genuinely unlikable cad, immature, rude, shallow, lewd.

Notable Productions and Performances

Published in the *First Folio* of 1623, there is no record of a performance until 1740. It was popular for one decade, then disappeared again for a century. The play became palatable again in the second half of the 20th century.

Tyrone Guthrie's productions at Stratford, Ontario, in 1953 and 1959 were popular but controversial for treating the play as a farce.

Mars in Retrograde:
Astrology in the Plays

n *All's Well That Ends Well*, Parolles passes himself off as a noble warrior born under the influence of Mars, the planet named after the god of war. Helena, the play's heroine, isn't impressed. She knows Parolles to be a cowardly braggart. She quips that he might have been born under the influence of Mars, but only if Mars was in retrograde. She believes, as did many in the audience watching the play, that a retrograde Mars would inspire less than worthy personality traits such as dishonesty, weakness, laziness.

In Shakespeare's day, the discernible movements of the sun, moon, and planets were believed to hold great significance, and those who could interpret the signs of the Zodiac were held in esteem. Astrologers and their horoscopes were regularly consulted. Queen Elizabeth used the services of John Dee, the most famous astrologer of the day.

Sometimes, the celestial signs were credited with having a positive effect on a character's personality, as in *Much Ado about Nothing* when Beatrice says, "There was a star danced, and under that was I born." In *Pericles*, when King Antilochus thanks the stars for the sweet and endearing qualities of his daughter, he says. "The senate-house of planets all did sit, / To knit in her their best perfections."

On the other hand, the stars and planets could be blamed for human misfortune. In *The Winter's Tale*, when the faithful Queen Hermione is falsely accused of adultery, she sighs, "There's some ill planet reigns: I must be patient till the heavens look / With an aspect more favorable." Romeo and Juliet are "star-crossed lovers."

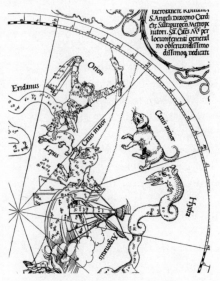

The motions of the planets were especially useful in foretelling disaster. In *Troilus and Cressida*, the Greek commander worries that the planets have begun to wander aimlessly through the sky. He says, "When the planets / In evil mixture to disorder wander, / What plagues and what portents! what mutiny! / What raging of the sea! shaking of earth!"

The moon, too, was believed to have an influence on human emotions and affairs. In *A Midsummer Night's Dream*, Titania, the fairy queen, says, "Therefore the moon, the governess of floods, / Pale in her anger, washes all the air, / That rheumatic diseases do abound." The witches in *Macbeth* prepared some of the ingredients for their cauldron away from the moon's gaze chanting, "Gall of goat, and slips of yew, / Sliver'd in the moon's eclipse." In *Richard II*, a reddish moon portends coming disasters—"The pale-faced moon looks bloody on the earth." In *Romeo and Juliet*, the cherry-lipped lass looks down from her balcony and begs her sweetheart not to swear by the moon, "the inconstant moon, / That monthly changes in her circled orb, / Lest that thy love prove likewise variable."

Elizabethan people held many superstitions about comets, which seemed to play by their own rules. They had heard that the Peloponnesian War between Athens and Sparta, which began in 431 B.C.E., was foretold by an abundance of comets, as was the death of Caesar. At the funeral in the opening scene of *King Henry VI, Part One*, the Duke of Bedford speaks of unusual activity in the sky when he says, "Hung be the heavens with black, yield day to night! / Comets, importing change of times and states, /

Brandish your crystal tresses in the sky, / And with them scourge the bad revolting stars / That have consented unto Henry's death!"

There are those with doubts about the significance of heavenly bodies on human behavior in Shakespeare's plays too. In *Julius Caesar*, Cassius refuses to find excuses in astrological signs when he speaks his famous line, "The fault, dear Brutus, is not in our stars, / But in ourselves, that we are underlings."

In *King Lear*, Edmund, Gloucester's illegitimate son, pooh-poohs astrology in an eloquent soliloquy:

This is the excellent foppery of the world, that, when we are sick in fortune, often the surfeits of our own behavior, we make guilty of our disasters the sun, the moon, and stars; as if we were villains on necessity; fools by heavenly compulsion; knaves, thieves, and treachers by spherical pre-dominance; drunkards, liars, and adulterers by an enforc'd obedience of planetary influence; and all that we are evil in, by a divine thrusting on. An admirable evasion of whore-master man, to lay his goatish disposition to the charge of a star! My father compounded with my mother under the Dragon's Tail, and my nativity was under Ursa Major, so that it follows I am rough and lecherous. Fut! I should have been that I am, had the maidenliest star in the firmament twinkled on my bastardizing.

Elizabethan Holidays and Calendar Confusion

n 1582, when the rest of Europe went along with Pope Gregory XIII and adopted the Gregorian Calendar, the one we use today, the English were so fiercely anti-Catholic that they refused to switch to the pope's plan. They kept the Julian calendar of their old Roman invaders until 1752.

To add to the confusion, the English celebrated New Year's Day on January 1st as did the rest of Europe, but, ulike most of the Continent, they did not change the number of the year until March 25th.

The seasons of the Elizabethan year were punctuated by holy days and holidays. Most of the religious observances had a secular side, and Shakespeare wove references to these special days into his plays.

Twelfth Day

January 6th was the twelfth day of Christmas (calculated by counting the day after Christmas as day number one).

This day was also called Epiphany, the day Christians observed the three kings' journey to see the Christ child. *Twelfth Night* marked the close of the Christmas festivities. and was observed with plays, masques, feasting, and drinking Wassail (a spiced ale). One Twelfth Night ritual was the serving of a special fruitcake containing one dried bean and one dried pea. The man who got the bean was crowned the King of Misrule and the woman who got the pea was the Queen. This couple presided over the night's revels.

Saint Valentine's Day

In 496, the old pagan fertility festival of Lupercalia was renamed Saint Valentine's Day. Celebrated on *February 14th*, the day was named for a Christian priest who was remembered as a defender of romantic love because he performed secret marriage ceremonies for young lovers. Viewed as a rebel-priest, he was beheaded in 270 for refusing to worship Roman gods.

According to legend, birds chose their mates on Valentine's Day, which is why, in *A Midsummer Night's Dream*, Theseus says, "Good morrow, friends. St. Valentine is past; / Begin these wood-birds but to couple now?"

Another tradition held that the first two unmarried people to meet on the morning of February 14th would have a good chance of becoming romantically involved with each other—thus the song, sung by Ophelia in Hamlet:

To-morrow is Saint Valentine's day,
All in the morning betime,
And I a maid at your window,
To be your valentine.

Shrove Tuesday/Shrovetide

This movable day, falling between *February 3rd* and *March 9th*, was the last day before the deprivations of the Lenten season began. Not as wild as the modern Fat Tuesday or Mardi Gras, it was a day for playing football and tormenting roosters in "cock-thrashing." Occasionally it was a day for rioting in protest of various grievances. It was always a day for feasting on fritters and pancakes. In *All's Well that Ends Well*, the clown speaks of "a pancake for Shrove Tuesday." In *Henry IV, Part Two*, Justice Silence sings, "'Tis merry in hall, when beards wag all, / And welcome merry shrove-tide, Be merry, be merry."

Lent

The season of Lent began on the Wednesday (called Ash Wednesday even in Protestant England) before the sixth Sunday before Easter. Throughout her reign, Queen Elizabeth kept the old Catholic restriction on eating meat during the forty days, but she did it primarily to boost England's fishing industry. In *Henry IV, Part Two*, Falstaff says that Hostess Quickly had been indicted "for suffering flesh to be eaten in thy house, contrary to the law, for the which I think thou wilt howl," to which she quips, "all victuallers do so: what's a joint of mutton or two in a whole Lent?"

One Lenten custom in Elizabethan England involved a dummy made of straw and old clothing, called a "Jack-a-Lent." It was a symbol for life's hardships or, some said, for Judas, the disciple who betrayed Jesus. It would be carried through the streets and then pelted with stones or burned. It is mentioned twice in *The Merry Wives of Windsor*. Once, Mistress Page says to Robin, "you little Jack-a-Lent, have you been true to us?" Another time, Falstaff says, "wit may be made a Jack-a-Lent, when 'tis upon ill employment!"

Easter

Using the lunar-based Jewish calendar instead of the solar-based Roman one, Easter was celebrated on the first Sunday after the first full moon on or after March 21, just as it is today. It was customary in Elizabethan England for parishioners to wear a new article of clothing that day as a symbol of resurrection and new life. In *Romeo and Juliet*, Mercutio teases his sweet-tempered friend Benvolio with a list of all the trivial disagreements he's had and asks, "Didst thou not fall out with a tailor for wearing his new doublet before Easter?"

The day after Easter was *Black Monday,* named for the dark day in 1360 when King Edward III and his men were camped outside Paris. Many men died on their horses' backs from the bitter cold. In *The Merchant of Venice,* Launcelot says, "it was not for nothing that my nose fell a-bleeding on Black Monday last at six o'clock i' the morning."

Saint David's Day

March 1st was the day to honor the patron saint of Wales who ordered his Britons to place leeks in their caps in order to distinguish them from the Saxons. In *Henry V,* Fluellen says to the king,

If your Majesties is remembered of it, the Welshmen did good service in a garden where leeks did grow, wearing leeks in their Monmouth caps; which, your majesty know, to this hour is an honorable badge of the service; and I do believe your majesty takes no scorn to wear the leek upon Saint Tavy's day.

In the same play, Pistol says of Fluellen, "Tell him, I'll knock his leek about his pate Upon Saint Davy's day."

Saint George's Day

April 23rd, the feast day of the guardian saint of England, is frequently mentioned in Shakespeare's plays, as in *Henry VI, Part One,* when Bedford speaks of keeping "our great Saint George's feast withal." According to the legend, Saint George rode on horseback and slayed a dragon. His likeness is depicted on dozens of signs in London, hanging over the doorways of pubs and taverns. In Shakespeare's *King John,* Philip refers to one such sign when he speaks of, "Saint George, that swinged the dragon, and e'er since / Sits on his horse back at mine hostess' door." Incidently, Shakespeare's birthday is traditionally celebrated as April 23, 1564, and it is commonly believed that he died on this day in 1616.

May Day

May 1st, which heralded summer in England, often began just after the stroke of midnight, when young people would dance through the streets to the music of pipes and horns, on their way to the woods where they'd collect tree branches and flowers. The revelers would return home by sunrise of May 1st to hang their garlands over their doors and windows. Of course, the flower gathering was also a convenient cover for young lovers to rendezvous for a little shared passion. It is this tradition to which a character designated only as Man refers in *Henry VIII* when he tells the Porter not to be so upset about the noisy commoners who have assembled in the palace yard to witness the christening of the infant Elizabeth. He says, "Pray, sir, be patient; 'tis as much impossible, / Unless we sweep 'em from the door with cannons, / To scatter 'em as 'tis to make 'em sleep / On May-day morning; which will never be."

In *A Midsummer Night's Dream,* Lysander, coaxing Hermia to elope with him, reminds her of an earlier tryst:

If thou lovest me then,
Steal forth thy father's house to-morrow
*   night;*
And in the wood, a league without
*   the town,*
Where I did meet thee once with
*   Helena,*
To do observance to a morn of May,
There will I stay for thee.

May Day festivities often included the raising of a maypole, decorated with flowers, ribbons, and topped with Saint George's red-cross banner. Another common May Day feature was the Morris dance, a ritual dance in which the participants dressed in outlandish costumes and represented specific characters, usually including a hobby horse, a Maid Marian (usually a man dressed as a woman), and a fool and sometimes Robin Hood, Little John and Tom the Piper. There is a long passage, spoken by the schoolmaster in *Two Noble Kinsmen*, describing the Morris Dance to King Theseus.

Whitsuntide (Pentecost)

Celebrated roughly fifty days after Easter (*May 10 to June 13*), this favorite summer festival commemorated the New Testament event of the coming of the Holy Spirit to the apostles. (In Judaism, Shabuoth is celebrated at the same time.) It was a day for Morris dancing, pageants and processions, and folk plays about the Creation, the Fall of Lucifer, the Deluge, or scenes involving that old biblical tyrant, Herod. Julia, disguised as a boy in *Two Gentlemen of Verona*, refers to this tradition when she says, "At Pentecost, / When all our pag-

eants of delight were play'd, / Our youth got me to play the woman's part, And I was trimm'd in Madam Julia's gown."

Another Whitsuntide tradition was the sports competition, not unlike the Olympics, known as the Cotswold games, which featured a range of events usually including wrestling, pitching the bar, handling the pike, and hunting. There are several references to the Cotswold games sprinkled throughout Shakespeare's plays. In *The Merry Wives of Windsor*, Slender asks Page, "How does your fallow greyhound, sir? I heard say he was outrun on Cotsall?"

Sheep-Shearing Festivals

In rural areas, June was the month to shear the sheep and a good excuse to party. Bagpipes played as the countryfolk sang and danced. In *The Winter's Tale*, the Clown made this shopping list in preparation for such a festival:

Let me see: what am I to buy for our sheep-shearing feast? Three pound of sugar, five pound of currants, rice—what will this sister of mine do with rice? But my father hath made her mistress of the feast, and she lays it on. She hath made me four and twenty nosegays for the shearers—three-man song-men all, and very good ones; but they are most of them means and bases; but one Puritan amongst them, and he sings psalms to hornpipes. I must have saffron to colour the warden pies; mace; dates—none, that's out of my note; nutmeg, seven; a race or two of ginger, but that I may beg; four pound of prunes, and as many of raisins 'o the' sun.

Midsummer Eve / Saint John's Eve

June 24th was associated with many superstitions that drove people into the woods in search of roses, St. John's Wort and other herbs and flowers believed to hold magical powers. Young women would set their mix of greens in clay, calling this a "Midsummer man" and look the next morning to see which way the stalks leaned, right or left. According to the tradition, the inclination would reveal whether or not a lover would be faithful. Young men, on the other hand, looked for pieces of coal or dead roots which they placed under their pillows to inspire dream revelations. Morbid folk would sometimes fast on Midsummer Eve then sit near the church where they could see a procession of the spirits of those persons destined to die in the coming year approaching the church doors. On the lighter side, the night was often celebrated with a big bonfire and parades featuring giants, dragons, and fireworks.

Lammas Day

August 1st marked the beginning of the month of harvesting grain. The day was originally a pagan festival honoring the goddess of the grain, and the Saxons celebrated it as Hlaf-mass, the "Feast of Bread." It was also identified with the Celtic midsummer festival of Lugnasad, a holiday marking the death and resurrection of Lug, a grain god. To the Elizabethans it was remembered as a medieval Christian holiday which was believed to have taken its name from "loaf-mass," a day on which people made a loaf of bread from new wheat. The name was also thought to have been a variation of "lamb-mass" for the tradition of bringing a lamb into the church in payment for living on the church's

land. In *Romeo and Juliet*, Nurse is anticipating Juliet's fourteenth birthday when she asks, "How long is it now to Lammas-tide?" to which Lady Capulet replies, "A fortnight and odd days." The Nurse exclaims, "Even or odd, of all days in the year, / Come Lammas-eve at night, shall she be fourteen."

Saint Bartholomew's Day

August 24th was the day of the yearly fair in London which had as its chief attraction the roasting of pigs. In *King Henry IV, Part Two*, Doll teases the fat knight, Falstaff, saying, "Thou whoreson, little, tidy Bartholomew boar-pig."

Saint Crispin's Day

October 25th commemorated two Roman brothers, Crispin and Crispinian, who traveled to France, made shoes to sell to the poor, and converted nonbelievers to their Christian religion. The governor of Soissons had the two beheaded and they became the guardian saints of shoemakers everywhere. In Shakespeare's *King Henry V*, on the eve before the battle of Agincourt, the English troops in France are badly outnumbered. The king addresses his worried nobles in an impassioned speech:

This day is call'd the feast of Crispian.
He that outlives this day, and comes
*   safe home,*
Will stand a tip-toe when this day is nam'd,
And rouse him at the name of Crispian.
He that shall live this day, and see
*   old age,*
Will yearly on the vigil feast his neighbors,
And say "Tomorrow is Saint Crispian."
Then will he strip his sleeve and show
*   his scars,*
And say "These wounds I had on
*   Crispian's day."*
Old men forget; yet all shall be forgot,
But he'll remember, with advantages,
What feats he did that day....
This story shall the good man teach
*   his son;*
And Crispin Crispian shall ne'er go by,
From this day to the ending of the world,
But we in it shall be remembered—
We few, we happy few, we band of brothers:
For he today that sheds his blood with me
Shall be my brother: be he ne'er so vile,
This day shall gentle his condition;
And gentlemen in England now a-bed
Shall think themselves accurs'd they
*   were not here,*
And hold their manhoods cheap
*   whiles any speaks*
That fought with us upon Saint
*   Crispin's day.*

Hallowmas

November 1st was the feast of All-Hallows' or All Souls', a Christian commemoration of the dead and the continuation of the ancient Celtic festival of Samhain named for Samana, the Lord of Death, the "Leveler." It was believed to be a time for the dead to wander, and it was customery to build bonfires, tell fortunes, feast on nuts and apples, and play games. In England, the poor often went from parish to parish "a-souling," singing and begging for soul cakes. In *Two Gentlemen of Verona*, a page refers to this tradition when he says, ""To watch, like one that fears robbing; to speak puling [singing small], like a beggar at Hallowmas."

Accession Day

November 17th was a secular holiday commemorating Queen Elizabeth's accession to the throne in 1558. It was also called Queen's Day and Coronation Day.

Christmas

December 25th was a day for feasting on pickled pork, nuts, and pies; drinking Wassail; singing carols; and exchanging gifts. Throughout the twelve days of celebration, people decorated their homes with rosemary, bay, holly, ivy and mistletoe. A man chosen as Christmas Lord presided over the festivities and Yule logs burned in the fireplaces.

TWELFTH NIGHT
OR, WHAT YOU WILL

APPEALING PAGE SHAKES UP HIGH SOCIETY SET; REVELERS SEND PRIGGISH PRUDE TO PADDED CELL

Period

16th century

Setting

Illyria, a mythical, madcap kingdom by the sea (also the name of a region on the Adriatic coast)

This gender-bending romantic comedy is like a present given on the twelfth and final night of Renaissance Christmas merrymaking. There is music (a lot of it) and witty conversation, and quite too much drinking going on. The gift of this play is presented neatly wrapped in brightly colored paper—but look again! There are blue ribbons of midwinter melancholy and heartbreak tied around it.

Viola, our gutsy heroine, has come ashore from the shock of a shipwreck in which her twin brother Sebastian may have drowned. Not one to wallow at the water's edge, she firmly takes her destiny in hand and disguises herself as a high-voiced eunuch named Cesario. Her disguise is effective, and she is promptly hired as a page to run messages for dashing Duke Orsino, who is in love with a beautiful countess named Olivia. His are the famous opening words of the play:

If music be the food of love, play on,
Give me excess of it, that, surfeiting,
The appetite may sicken and so die.

O is for obsession. Duke Orsino is obsessed with the idea of himself as a lover of the perfect woman, but, not willing to risk much on reality, he sends his page to do his wooing for him. Countess Olivia is obsessed too—with mourning her dead brother. For a year, she has hidden behind a dark veil, refusing suitors, though her house has slowly filled with an odd assortment of characters. There are the servants, Fabian and Maria, and the clown, Feste. Sir Toby Belch, Olivia's fat, drunken uncle, and Sir Andrew Aguecheek, a would-be suitor, are houseguests whose names proclaim their true natures. And then there is Malvolio, Olivia's pompous, sour steward, a killjoy destined for comeuppance before the play's end.

Viola, dressed as a boy, shows up at Olivia's door and refuses to leave without a hearing. The countess, hiding behind her veil, eventually relents and the two women, whose names are almost mirror images, meet. Both are mourning lost brothers, both are in disguise, both are ready for love, whether they know it or not. When Viola, as the page, conveys the duke's message of love, her sincerity reaches through Olivia's stubborn grief. As if shocked back to life, Olivia falls in love—not with the duke, but with the duke's messenger boy who, we know, is really a girl. Viola is in love too, with the duke. For his part, the duke becomes entirely too fond of his messenger than is generally thought proper. Gender identity and class bias, which usually function to narrow the field of suitable suitors, are cast aside as so much meaningless flotsam and jetsam on the landscape of love in Illyria.

Meanwhile, Malvolio has antagonized everyone with his self-righteousness and interfered with the festivities one time too many. "Dost thou think, because thou art virtuous, there shall be no more cakes and ale?" Sir Toby, like a drunken Lord of Misrule, famously asks. As a prank, Maria, an educated gentlewoman with the ability to copy her mistress's handwriting, pens a love letter to Malvolio, signing Olivia's name. In the letter, she proclaims her secret love and begs Malvolio to wear yellow stockings and crossed garters as a sign of affection (a color and style Olivia actually loathes). The letter sounds authen-

tic with its nod to class concerns: "In my stars I am above thee; but be not afraid of greatness. Some are born great, some achieve greatness, and some have greatness thrust upon 'em." Malvolio is ready to have greatness thrust upon him and dreams of marrying the countess. He seems most excited about the prospect of being able to boss around the hired help.

The aim of the prank is revenge, and it is almost too successful. When Malvolio appears before Olivia, grinning in his garish stockings and flirting with the bewildered countess, he is taken for mad and locked up as a lunatic.

Sebastian, Viola's almost-drowned twin brother, eventually reaches Illyria. Like a magnet, he attracts confusion. Lovesick Sir Andrew, insulted that the countess has ignored him in favor of a mere messenger boy, mistakes Sebastian for the disguised Viola and challenges him to a duel. Olivia, also mistaking Sebastian for the duke's page, drags him to a chapel to get married. Sebastian is a stranger in a strange land, where half the people seem to be in love with him and half want to fight him. In the end, the disguises are dropped and reality quickly realigns the personalities with their socially appropriate roles. The countess, surprised that she had fallen in love with a girl, is happy enough to marry the girl's twin brother. The duke, who has been strangely attracted to his page, is delighted to learn that this boy is really a girl who is in love with him. In mere seconds, he readjusts his thinking. Viola and Sebastian are reunited as sister and brother, each with the extra bonus of having lovers by their sides.

Only the puritanical Malvolio, the maltreated, is bitter in the end, vowing revenge for the trick played on him. Feste the world-weary clown, gets the last word in this comedy which is darker than we expected it to be. He sings a song of resignation with the repeated phrase, "For the rain it raineth every day."

Likely Source of the Plot

Shakespeare named his own characters but the primary source of the main plot was the story of "Apolonius and Silla" from *Farewell to Militarie Profession* (1581) by Barnabe Rich. The Malvolio sub-plot is thought to be Shakespeare's own invention.

Notable Features

This is the only play to which Shakespeare attached a subtitle, the exact meaning of which has puzzled scholars. Some think *What You Will* was the Renaissance equivalent of the modern "whatever," which is in keeping with the spirit of abandon that informs the play. Others claim that the play is a sustained meditation on the meaning of "will." This theory is backed by the observation that Viola and Olivia are near anagrams of "volli," the Italian word for "will," and Malvolio, with the preface "mal," hints at ill-will or bad will. The primary title, *Twelfth Night*, refers to the last night of Christmas festivities celebrated each year in Elizabethan England—memorialized in the song "The Twelve Days of Christmas." January 6th was the Twelfth Day, also known as Epiphany (see Elizabethan Holidays, page 105), a day honoring the three kings. Outside of the church walls, the day was given to madcap revelry, disguises, and pranks.

Notable Productions and Performances

Some believe that the play was first performed on January 6, 1601, at Whitehall for an Italian nobleman, Duke Orsino of Bracciano. Others believe its first performance was on February 2, 1602. Viola, a coveted role for Shakespearian actresses, has been notably played by Charlotte Cushman (1846), Ellen Terry (1884), Peggy Ashcroft (1950), and Judi Dench (1969). In a 1937 production featuring Laurence Olivier as Sir Toby, Jessica Tandy played both Sebastian and Viola, an experiment that was more successful in a 1969 televised performance by Joan Plowright.

The music of the play has inspired a range of composers, including Smetana, who composed the opera *Viola* (1881), as well as Brahms, Schubert and Sibelius.

Other Use of Basic Plot

Directed by Trevor Nunn, 1996 film starring Helena Bonham Carter as Olivia, and Imogen Stubbs as Viola. It is more morose than comic.

Shakespeare In Love, 1998, directed by John Madden, starring Gwyneth Paltrow and Joseph Fiennes, with Judi Dench as Queen Elizabeth. Winner of seven Academy Awards, including Best Picture, this blockbuster success opens with Will struggling to write a new play, the working title of which is *Romeo and Ethel, the Pirate's Daughter*. Writer's block stops his creative flow until he meets Viola. She will inspire from within long after she is lost to an arranged marriage. As the movie ends, we watch Viola bravely walk out of the sea from a shipwreck and listen to the voiceover as Will, begins to construct the plot of a new play, *Twelfth Night*.

THE WINTER'S TALE

UNFOUNDED JEALOUSY ANNIHILATES BLISSFUL REALM, KING SUFFERS SELF-IMPOSED SEASONAL AFFECTIVE DISORDER (SAD)

Period

Once upon a time

Settings

Sicilia and Bohemia

This story is the stuff of fairy tale, a tragedy played in reverse. Leontes, the King of Sicilia, has been entertaining his childhood friend, Polixenes, the King of Bohemia. When the guest insists he must leave in the morning, both the king and his winsome wife, Hermione, beg him to stay a little longer. It is the captivating queen who succeeds in convincing her husband's friend to postpone his departure. Instead of being delighted, however, King Leontes surprises himself and the entire court by suddenly suspecting his wife and his best friend of long-term infidelity, to the point of doubting his son's paternity.

King Leontes instructs Camillo, one of his most trusted lords, to murder his old friend from Bohemia, but Camillo warns the bewildered guest and they escape together. Succumbing to suspicion, and crazed by unfounded jealousy, Leontes has now driven away his best friend and his most trusted lord. He is about to do even worse.

Unaware of the impending turmoil, a very pregnant Queen Hermione asks her lively, talkative son to entertain her with a story. The little prince wisely quips that, "a sad tale is best for winter." He begins to whisper a scary story in his mother's ear, his eyes wide with mock fear. Suddenly, his make-believe story is interrupted by his father, the king—and it is no longer the prince's little story, but the larger story of their lives which is abruptly transformed into a nightmarish winter's tale, full of woe.

Like a man in a fairy tale, King Leontes voices his suspicion and sends his queen to prison, where she gives birth to a baby girl. When Paulina, the queen's wise and devoted defender, brings the infant princess to his majesty, the king denies he is the father and commands that the baby be taken to a remote island and left to die. With the verdict already in, he puts the queen on trial. The Delphic oracle—that legendary Greek source of prophecies—is consulted, then ignored by the king when it too confirms Hermione's faithfulness. Perceiving that her case is hopeless, the queen speaks in her own defense, without tears or melodrama, concluding matter-of-factly, "I never wished to see thee sorry. Now I expect I will." She is right, of course.

Just then, word is sent that the little prince, overcome with worry, has died. Hearing this news, Hermione collapses and is carried out. It is a turning point for King Leontes, who suddenly regains his sanity, as if awakening from a fairy tale curse. The damage has been done, however, and it seems irreversible. The king's brief sojourn into irrational jealousy has transformed his once happy kingdom into a barren landscape of loss. There is one more nail in the coffin: word comes that Queen Hermione has died too.

Meanwhile, the baby princess, in accordance with the king's order, has been taken to a far Bohemian shore by Antigonus, Paulina's husband. Prompted by a ghostly vision of the queen, he names the baby Perdita and laments, "Thou'rt like to have A lullaby too rough," as he leaves her on the desolate shore. It is Antigonus, however, and not the baby, whose time is up. He is pursued by a bear and dies a gruesome death (offstage), while the baby is discovered by a kind old shepherd and his son, the Clown. They also find the bundle of gold tucked in the folds of the baby's blanket.

Suddenly, Time steps forward to announce that sixteen years have passed. King Leontes has been in mourning, tormented by regret and shame. The years he has lost can never be regained, not even in this fairy tale, but forgiveness is in the cards. Polixenes, the Bohemian king, has a son, Prince Florizel, who has fallen in love with Perdita, the shepherd's found daughter. She is the very picture of springtime, blossoming youth, birdsong, and blessing. King Polixenes is most unhappy that his fine son has fallen for a commoner. He plots to go to a sheep-shearing festival in disguise with his faithful attendant Camillo to somehow stop the mismatched romance. Amidst the festivities, the king angrily reveals himself, threatens to disinherit his son and have Perdita put to death.

Everyone, one way or another, makes their way to Sicilia. There, Prince Florizel professes his love for Perdita to King Leontes and begs his help. The king is strangely taken with the sweet shepherdess, Perdita, and is moved by the strength of the young couple's beleaguered love. He gives his royal blessing.

The two old kings are reconciled, and rejoice together when they hear the old shepherd tell that Perdita was discovered as an infant, abandoned on the seacoast. King Leontes is overjoyed to be reunited with his long-lost daughter, and the King of Bohemia is relieved to learn that the shepherdess is a really a princess, a good match for his lovesick son after all.

Paulina invites everyone over to her house to see a statue of the long-lost Hermione. The statue is remarkably lifelike and this prompts a new speech of remorse from King Leontes for all the wrongs he committed long ago. To everyone's amazement, the statue suddenly comes to life and descends her pedestal, taking the king by the hand. It is Hermione, not dead, but very much alive. She has let the king stew in misinformed misery all these years. When she first speaks, it is to her beloved daughter. Questions rush from her lips, "Tell me, mine own, Where hast thou been preserv'd? Where liv'd? How found Thy father's court?" In this scene of restoration, if not resurrection, the king, reunited with his wife and daughter, proclaims that the faithful widow Paulina should marry the faithful wise man Camillo. Then all three couples depart, arm in arm, to prepare for the marriage of Perdita and Florizel.

Likely Source of the Plot

The primary source for the play was *Pandosto*, a romantic novel written in 1588 by Robert Greene, the same fellow who may have been referring to Shakespeare when he wrote, in 1592, of "an upstart Crow."

Notable Features

"Exit, pursued by a Bear" (act 3, scene 3) is widely regarded as Shakespeare's most famous and problematic stage direction. The other oddity in this play is the placement of a rugged seacoast in Bohemia. If Shakespeare meant to describe the central European region which is currently a part of the Czech Republic, he—to put it politely—erred. There is no seacoast there. In his defense, however, it can be noted that medieval Bohemia, as it was then defined, briefly controlled a small stretch of the coast bordering the Adriatic Sea. Further, Shakespeare used the same exotic locations as were used in his original source, Greene's *Pandosto*. Finally, since this is the stuff of fairy tale, he was more concerned with establishing an accurate psychological landscape, than a literal geographic one.

Notable Productions and Performances

Since its first performance in May 1611, the play was popular in the courts of Kings James I and Charles I, and was performed at the wedding festivities of Princess Elizabeth. Then, it abruptly disappeared from the stage after 1640 and was not performed for one hundred years, until its revival at Covent Garden in 1741.

In the 18th century, a number of adaptations removed Leontes and Hermione from the story and simply told the tale of Florizel and Perdita. In the 19th century, Charles Kean put on an elaborate show with extensive program notes in a performance that was both popular and ridiculed. Ellen Terry, aged eight, spoke her first Shakespearean lines in this production playing the little doomed Prince of Sicilia. Fifty years later, the actress played Hermione in Beerbohm Tree's production.

In most productions, Time steps forward with an hourglass to tell the audience that 16 years have passed. In a 1992 Royal Shakespeare production, however, Time's words were on a scroll attached to a balloon that drifted down on the stage to Camillo. He opened the scroll and read aloud Time's words, then popped the balloon with a pin.

In a number of productions, the roles of Hermione and Perdita have been played by the same actress, notably by Mary Anderson in 1887, Judi Dench in 1969, and Penny Downie in 1986. Ian McKellen, Patrick Stewart and Jeremy Irons all played Leontes in 20th century productions.

Other Use of Basic Plot

Three silent films of *The Winter's Tale* were made before 1915, two movies in the second half of the century and two television productions.

Wintermärchen, 2000, an opera in German and English, by Belgian composer Philippe Boesmans, produced in Brussels and at the Lyon Opera. In this version, Perdita is a silent role played by a dancer and, at the end of the opera, Hermione steps from a wall of ice.

"Sad Stories of the Deaths of Kings"

Let us sit upon the ground, and tell sad stories
of the deaths of kings. —Richard II

hakespeare was a dramatist, not a historian. He chose the subjects of his dramas for their potential conflict and also—particularly with his royal histories—for their familiarity to his audience. He also had, consciously or not, a set of assumptions about the lessons taught by the lives and deaths of England's monarchs, about the importance of stability to the military and civil future of the kingdom and the lives of the common people. But he never hesitated to sacrifice all of them in order to engage the audience with a rip-roaring yarn.

Experts have studied the history plays from a variety of viewpoints. One school looks at them in the order in which he apparently wrote them—an order almost the reverse of their chronology. But particularly for readers who do not share the knowledge and assumptions of English history that Shakespeare's audience took for granted, here is the order of their historical story.

Shakespeare's Kings

King John—an early and unpopular English monarch, who was forced by his nobles to sign the Magna Carta (although Shakespeare never mentions it).

Richard II—weak and ineffective king deposed by his cousin, with negative consequences down the generations.

Henry IV (in two parts)—Richard's deposer, never secure in his reign.

Henry V—Henry IV's wastrel son who converts himself into the greatest English monarch and military hero of the period.

Henry VI (in three parts)—Henry V's son and heir, well-intentioned but inept enough to lose all of his father's gains; his poor leadership fosters the civil wars known as the Wars of the Roses.

Richard III—the Yorkist faction, winners of the Wars of the Roses, deposes Henry VI and the Lancasters; as one of the Yorkists, Richard—after a succession of murders—claims the title until he too is defeated and Henry VII is crowned.

Henry VIII—king by normal succession from his father, Henry VII, and like his father a personalization of the union of the Lancastrian and York factions, and father of Shakespeare's Queen Elizabeth I.

Foreign Quarrels and Domestic Turmoil
—Shakespeare's History Plays

hakespeare's history plays take as their subject the foreign entanglements and civil conflicts that occupied England from about 1200 (the setting of *King John*) to roughly 1533 (the baptism of Elizabeth during the reign of her father, Henry VIII). But *King John* and *King Henry VIII* mark the bookends of the cycle. Most of the plays cover the period from about 1398 during the reign of Richard II, to 1485 and the death of Richard III at the battle of Bosworth.

These nine decades include some of the most turbulent in English history, the reign of six kings (only two of whom died in bed, the others victims of war or murder), several coups d'etat, a long intermittent war on French soil, repeated battles against the Irish, Scots, and Welsh who resisted English hegemony, popular rebellion, and decades of internal strife among the ruling classes, often leading to pitched battles between sizable armies.

While people caught up in these fractious times no doubt saw these as intermingled, popular history has categorized the external conflict as the Hundred Years' War and the internal one as the Wars of the Roses.

Hundred Years' War (1337–1453)

The seeds of the long conflict with France were sown centuries before the war began. England was invaded and then abandoned by the Romans, colonized by northern European tribes (Angles, et al.) and then invaded repeatedly in the ninth and tenth centuries by Viking raiders. So great a hold did the Norsemen acquire in England that much of the north and east became a predominantly Scandinavian settlement, a reality recognized in the ninth century with the creation of the Danelaw, a substantial area where Danish rather than English law prevailed.

In 1066, the English King Harold Godwin repelled yet another Viking invasion in the battle of Stamford

Bridge. History has tended to overlook this victory, since Harold almost immediately wheeled from the east of England to repel a simultaneous invasion from France in the south. He lost this battle at Hastings near the Channel coast to William of Normandy (William the Conqueror to his chroniclers). England's native ruling class was largely replaced by French-speaking knights and lords (who were actually misplaced Vikings themselves, the descendants of Scandinavian invaders of France who had adopted—more or less—French language and customs).

English men and women in later generations—the climate and cuisine of France to that of England.

To many nominally English monarchs, like Richard I (the Lionhearted), England was just a northern extension of their Continental holdings. The mother of Richard I (and of King John of the earliest play in Shakespeare's cycle), was the heir of the Duchy of Aquitaine, encompassing much of the Mediterranean coast of France. Richard himself is thought to have spent no more than a year of his decade-long reign in England, and it is doubtful that

One effect of Hastings was to move England squarely into the orbit of continental Europe rather than Scandinavia. The Norman lords, through conquest and marriage, had holdings all over France, and for centuries England's rulers had much more in common with their French-speaking cousins on the Continent than with the native English over whom they ruled. William's immediate descendants often spent much more time in their European possessions, preferring—as did thousands of

he, along with kings for generations, could actually converse in the English language. The action in King John is primarily concerned with the king's holdings in France.

Edward III Opens Hostilities

That subject was still a matter of serious concern more than a hundred years later, during the reign of King Edward III. In medieval times property was thought to reside first of all in the king, and for hundreds of years after the Conquest the lives and heritage of nominally English and French nobles were so tangled that the English King was a vassal or subject of the King of France to the extent he owned French estates. When in the 14th century the French King Charles VI died without a male heir, the English King Edward III, not only a major landowner in France but Charles's nephew, claimed—with considerable justification—that *he* was the rightful heir to the French throne. Other branches of the French royal family disagreed, and in 1337 Edward III mounted an expeditionary force to back up his claim, kicking off, from the historian's viewpoint, the Hundred Years' War.

In the early years the English amassed considerable success, particularly at Crecy and Poitiers, battles where English and Welsh longbowmen helped turn the tide against armored French knights. There were periods of truce, followed by renewed conflict, then truce again. A principal and successful war leader was the king's son, Edward (known to history as the Black Prince, from the color of his armor). But the son died in 1376, his father in 1377, and the monarchy passed to Richard II, the Prince's then ten-year-old son.

Richard, occupied by internal problems, eventually married the daughter of the French King and concluded a long-term treaty with the French. His successor, Henry IV, spent most of his reign consolidating his position against internal opposition and then struggled long against debilitating illness, though he did send expeditions to France to back local allies in French disputes. The war

with France assumed a new importance with the accession of Henry IV's son, Henry V.

"No King of England Unless King of France"

So proclaimed Henry V in Shakespeare's play as he embarked for France with his army in 1415 to reassert his great-grandfather's (Edward III's) claims. Henry V's actual successes enshrined in the play—the capture of Harfleur and the decisive victory at Agincourt—had little long-term significance. However, later campaigns did leave Henry with a marriage to the French king's daughter and a treaty that said that on the French king's death Henry would inherit that throne. Henry died too soon to take advantage of that inheritance.

Contributing to early English success under both Edward III and Henry V was the fact that France was going through a series of its own internal conflicts. The country was divided into areas where local rulers held much more sway than did the king, and important nobles rivaled the king in wealth and resources. England had ancestral and commercial links with Burgundy, for example, and for important periods in the Hundred Years' War the Duke of Burgundy was either neutral or fought on the English side.

On the death of Henry V in 1422 his realm in France was overseen by his brother, the Duke of Bedford, on behalf of the infant Henry VI. But Joan of Arc successfully began, in 1429, to rally the French, starting with the raising of the English siege of Orleans. Joan was eventually captured by a group of French combatants and sold to the English, who had her tried for witchcraft and burned. However, the military successes she helped bring about on behalf of the Dauphin (the son of the French king who had made the deal with Henry V) continued to gather momentum. By 1435 Burgundy had switched to the French side, Paris fell to the French, then Normandy and Gascony in 1453, and English claims on French soil were all but eliminated.

One effect of this extended conflict was to help both England and France forge individual identities. While nobles on both sides continued to marry into each other's families, France became more unified as the king's party increased its reach, while the English began more and more to see themselves as their own unique society. The English language, rather than being supplanted by the conqueror's tongue, took on thousands of new words from French and Latin and emerged eventually as the language of all classes.

At the death of Henry V, the English influence in France was at its height. The decline in English fortunes there happened during the long, interrupted, and generally unhappy reign of Henry VI (1422–61/1470–71). There were many reasons for England's losses on the Continent, but they were inextricably tied up with the English preoccupation with their internal conflict—the Wars of the Roses.

The Wars of the Roses

The internal stresses that were features of all kingdoms of the period often led to civil conflict. And there was no issue around which conflict was more likely to break out than that of a disputed succession.

Laws of succession were not universally agreed upon, though English kings had generally been succeeded by their eldest surviving son. Even when the unpopular and unsuccessful Edward II had been forced to abdicate in 1327, his successor was his son, Edward III. But the succession issue came to a dramatic head in 1399, when Richard II, Edward III's grandson and successor, managed to nearly bankrupt his kingdom and offend almost every important group in English society with a combination of arrogance and mismanagement. He was deposed by his cousin Henry Bolingbroke.

Bolingbroke's coup had wide support among the ruling class. Richard's general high-handedness in dealing with the nobles eventually included his seizing the vast estates of Bolingbroke's father, John of Gaunt, at John's death. Such a seizure threw into potential question the inheritances that established the rank and wealth of an entire class. Bolingbroke had returned from exile in France allegedly only to claim his father's estates, but emboldened by the general distaste for Richard (and his absence on campaign in Ireland) he successfully declared himself king.

Like Richard himself, Bolingbroke was a grandson of Edward III, and thus had an arguable claim to the throne if it had been empty (although there were other grandchildren with more or less equivalent claims). Particularly after Richard's murder, the deposition created a cause that dissident elements could use to question the king's authority—including that of Bolingbroke's descendants.

Bolingbroke Maintains the Throne

Bolingbroke, as Henry IV, managed to head off counter-coups by Richard's adherents and others who felt that the change in power had not brought them sufficient gain. In 1403, he won an important victory against a combination of rebellious Welsh and northern English lords at Shrewsbury. His success there, and previous victories against the Welsh in their homeland, owed a good deal to the help of his son, who succeeded him on his death in 1413 as Henry V.

Two years later, on the eve of his expedition to France, Henry V uncovered and headed off a conspiracy to replace him with another descendant of Edward III. In general, however, his internal diplomacy and military successes in France insulated him from dynastic uncertainty. This was emphatically not true of *his* son and successor, Henry VI.

The Long Decline

Since Henry VI was an infant when he succeeded to the throne, the realm was overseen by his father's relatives. It

became clear to many during the king's adolescence that despite his admirable qualities, including real piety, he was unlikely to be much of a monarch. He was married in 1445 to Margaret of Anjou, who assumed considerable power. When in 1453 he underwent a period of insanity, his internal rival Richard, the Duke of York, who was descended on both his mother and father's sides from Edward III, was designated Protector. York may well have imagined himself the next line for the throne, but Queen Margaret gave birth in 1453 to Henry VI's son, frustrating York's hopes.

Henry VI's inability to govern, and York's continuing conflicts with the queen and her sympathizers, led eventually to a series of battles won by York and his allies. York proclaimed himself king, and when he died shortly thereafter his son Edward took the throne as Edward IV.

But the Wars of the Roses had barely begun. (The red rose eventually became identified with King Henry's party, known as the Lancastrians from Henry's descent from John of Gaunt and Blanche of Lancaster. The white rose became the Yorkist emblem.)

Edward had the crown, but Henry VI was still alive in the Tower and his queen and their son were in France. Edward had also alienated the powerful Duke of Warwick, along with his own brother Clarence. Warwick, Queen Margaret, and their forces deposed Edward in 1470, but he survived to flee to France, from which he returned in 1471 and defeated them at the battle at Tewkesbury, with the help of his now-reconciled brother Clarence. The son of

Margaret and Henry VI was killed at Tewkesbury, King Henry was murdered in the Tower, and Edward finally held the throne with relatively clear title.

Edward died in 1483 and power was seized by the sole surviving brother, Richard, taking the title Richard III (their brother George, Duke of Clarence, having earlier been executed on Edward's order). Edward's young sons died in the Tower under suspicious circumstances, generally believed to have been at Richard III's hands. Their deaths and a rebellion by the Duke of Buckingham helped destabilize Richard's reign. He was defeated by still another claimant to the throne, Henry Tudor, in the battle of Bosworth in 1485. Richard's son had died previously; many of the children of his brothers were in their graves; the people of England, particularly the nobles, were weary of the civil war. Tudor, who was spoken of as a Lancaster (though in fact he was descended from John of Gaunt's mistress rather than Gaunt's first wife, the duchess of Lancaster), married Elizabeth, daughter of Edward IV and the niece of the man he killed at Bosworth. Tudor by his marriage thus "united the red rose and the white" and his reign as Henry VII brought to an end a turbulent period of English history.

What the Plays *Don't* Cover

Shakespeare concentrates on certain external and internal conflicts in this volatile period. But there were other issues that figure largely in the history of the period. They include the Black Death, popular political and religious movements, and the long English effort to pacify the "Celtic fringe" around their kingdom. Shakespeare may have chosen to ignore or slight these issues because they were difficult to dramatize, unlikely to interest his audience, or even because of a fear of incurring the kind of official displeasure that could easily have ended his career and that of his theater company. But any balanced historical picture of the period must include some mention of them.

The Plague

The Black Death, which had begun in southern Europe, hit England in 1348. Its horrors are hard to overstate. Hundreds of thousands died, emptying entire villages, turning town fields into mass burial grounds. As much as one-third of the population of England may have fallen victim to "the great mortality," and repeated attacks in ensuing years caused further havoc.

While the plague comes well after the reign of King John and its worst depredations precede the action that begins in the 1390s with Richard II, its effects were felt for generations, and indeed England's population may not have recovered for more than a century. Shakespeare makes occasional reference to plague or sickness, but "the great mortality" is not a subject that is dealt with in the history plays.

One effect of the plague, however, was a significant change in social roles and economic realities. Before the plague in England, productive land was relatively scarce, labor abundant. Rural *villeins* and laborers had little power over the noble or ecclesiastical owners (and their managers) of the estates on which they

A plague scene

labored, or from whom they held their few acres. In the wake of the plague labor became scarce, wages rose, and workers broke many of the bonds that held them to the land and their employers.

A newly empowered peasantry, resentful both of new taxes and attempts by Parliament and local magnates to retain the old system, led in 1381 to a Peasants' Revolt spearheaded by Wat Tyler and John Ball. The rebels swept into London and executed some of the king's ministers (they met with a young Richard II, but were persuaded that he was their ally). The rebellion failed to spark a nationwide rising, and the rebels dispersed. In 1450, one Jack Cade led a similar movement, although this one was apparently more representative of the opinions of local gentry and smallholders than of the peasants and artisans who had supported the 1381

revolt. Shakespeare does make use of Cade's rebellion in *Henry VI, Part Two,* but its peasant nature and general anti-authoritarian tone ("let's kill all the lawyers,") owes its reality more to Wat Tyler's uprising during Richard II's reign than to Cade's.

Matters of the Spirit

Although major and minor characters make routine mention of God or the saints, and bishops and other religious men are portrayed in their secular roles, there is little or no discussion of religion per se in the history plays. Even the break with Rome implied in *Henry VIII* is matter of politics, not religion, and the accusation in that play of heresy against Archbishop Cranmer is never developed, much less proven.

But there was religious unrest in

A deathbed

England during this period. John Wycliffe, a priest, scholar, and reformer, had his views on a variety of doctrinal issues condemned in 1380, but he attracted many followers, known as Lollards. They and other reformist preachers may well have had a role in stirring up popular sentiment that resulted in the 1381 revolt ("When Adam delved and Eve span, who then was the gentleman?") It was the Lollards who sponsored the first complete translation of the Bible into English and their movement set the scene for the religious revolution of Henry VIII's reign.

Some students of the plays and the period believe that Shakespeare maintained a secret loyalty to the Roman Catholic church despite the Protestantism of his sovereign, Queen Elizabeth. Whether or not this was true, religion was an explosive political issue during this period, and a subject difficult for a popular playwright to navigate without personal and political risk.

The Celtic Fringe

For hundreds of years after the Norman invasion, the English sought to extend their dominion in Wales, Scotland, and Ireland, and to resist incursions by the Welsh and Scots onto English territory. Such military adventures absorbed considerable energy during both the Hundred Years' War and the Wars of the Roses, when the Scots in particular allied themselves with the French and Scotland provided a haven for rebel refugees.

Only in *Henry IV* does Shakespeare make substantial mention of these rebellions, and then in the character of Owen Glendower, the Welsh rebel who allies himself with Hotspur and the rest of the Percy family from the north of England. In *Henry V* Shakespeare makes repeated mention, through the voice of the Welsh captain Fluellen in Henry's army, of the king's Welsh connections, since Henry was born at Monmouth in Wales. Henry had actually distinguished himself militarily first in Wales; but it was in fighting his father's enemies—and Fluellen's fellow Welsh—there.

Sources and Methods

Shakespeare's principal sources for his plays included Edward Hall's *The Union of the Two Noble and Illustrious Families of Lancaster and York*, and Raphael Holinshed's *Chronicles of England, Scotland and Ireland*, two of the most current historical works then available. He may also have relied on an English translation of the works of the French writer Jean Froissart, and other plays and stories in circulation at the time, including the historical writings of Sir Thomas More.

Shakespeare rarely strayed far from his sources (sometimes repeating what later historians found to be their mistakes). But he had no hesitation in telescoping events (a series of messages in *Henry VI* combines decades of English losses in France into one scene), or eliminating or combining characters to make a point or keep the drama moving.

The plays fit together relatively seamlessly, but they were not written in historical order. Dating Shakespeare's plays on the basis of external and internal evidence is always a controversial

practice, but one potential sequence is that *Henry VI, Parts Two* and *Three*, were written first, followed by *Henry VI, Part One*; *Richard III*; *Richard II*; *King John*; *Henry IV, Parts One* and *Two*; and *Henry V*, all between 1590 and 1599, with *Henry VIII* coming more than a decade later. Such a system, while it may seem complicated to us, would not have seemed so to Shakespeare and his contemporaries. Although the comparison is a rough one, we might think of a modern American dramatist (in more than a decade of writing), beginning a historical series with plays about the Vietnam War and the counterculture of the 1960s, followed by a drama about the Cuban missile crisis, jumping ahead to Watergate and Nixon's resignation, back again perhaps to World War II, then forward yet again to the Reagan years.

The Art of Storytelling

Despite hundreds of years of analysis and debate over Shakespeare's political attitudes and goals, a thorough reading of the history plays establishes few controversial political views. English warriors on foreign soil are generally noble and their cause portrayed as just; men ambitious beyond their station can cause great harm to themselves and others; honest men may disagree on who should be the king, but a strong king is better than a weak one; civil war is a tragedy for the entire nation.

Again and again, Shakespeare portrays individuals with complex motives who incorporate both good and evil—Richard III, his most closely drawn villain, is a brave and effective warrior; Richard II, who so mismanages his kingdom that he loses his crown, speaks some of the most affecting poetry in the history of the language; Henry VI's Queen Margaret, brutal and manipulative, sends her supposed lover off to banishment with lines of startling beauty.

Shakespeare's goal was not to teach history, but to *dramatize* it. His plays bring alive stories much of his audience already knew, with a goal of creating characters with whom *all* his audience, however unlettered or unsophisticated, could identify. On this basis it is hard not to agree with the statement of the Duke of Marlborough, who took the view that Shakespeare's plays contained "all I know, and all I need to know, of English history."

KING JOHN

BAD KING OPPRESSES SUBJECTS, GETS COMEUPPANCE

Period

ca. 1200

Settings

England and France

King John, last surviving son of Henry II, ascended to the throne after his brother Richard I, nicknamed Couer-de-Lion (the Lionhearted), died on a campaign in France. It is less than 200 years since the Norman knights crossed the Channel and won the battle of Hastings, and because his mother is the only heir to major French estates, the English king retains extensive claims to lands in France (and members of much of the French nobility have similar claims in England).

Now a courier comes from Phillip, the King of France, telling John to resign his throne in favor of a claimant the French are championing, his nephew Arthur, the son of another of his late brothers. John's response is to mount a campaign against the French king. But while both are in the field outside the French city of Angier, they conclude a peace when John agrees to marry his niece to the French king's son (the Dauphin) and throw in as her dowry all the French lands that are in dispute.

The deal falls apart when an emissary from the pope arrives and condemns John in an unrelated matter (his refusal to permit the pope's candidate to become Archbishop of Canterbury). The papal condemnation of John swings the French against him despite their recent treaty, but John manages to beat them in battle.

One of the trophies of the battle is the aforesaid nephew Arthur, whom John captures and brings back to England. The king orders one of his associates, Hubert De Burgh, to kill the boy, but Hubert is moved by the boy's pleadings and refuses. Arthur, however, dies accidentally while trying to escape. The discovery of his death by some English noblemen is the excuse they need to break their allegiance to the king. They join the French, who—emboldened by the papal condemnation and the fact that the French king's son now has a claim on the English throne through his new wife, John's niece—are invading England.

Seeing his danger, John makes a deal with the pope and tries to get the pontiff's emissary to call off the French and their English allies. The French are having none of it, however, and fight a battle against John's forces. The result is not decisive but John dies—apparently of food poisoning in a nearby monastery—and the Pope's ambassador manages to work out a peace agreement while John's son Henry succeeds him.

One of the most important subplots involves an illegitimate member of the Plantagenets, England's royal family. In an early scene John is asked to judge between two claimants to the estate and name of Faulconbridge; one bears a strong resemblance not to his putative father, Robert Faulconbridge, but to King John's brother, Richard Couer-de-Lion, and the man claims that Couer-de-Lion was in fact his father. On the basis of his appearance and attestation, King John adopts him into the Plantagenets, and (under the title The Bastard) he functions as both commentator and principal in much of the action.

Notable Features

Arthur's mother, Lady Constance, learning of her son's capture and presuming his eventual death at John's hands, says:

Grief fills the room up of my absent child,
Lies in his bed, walks up and down
  with me.

Many authorities believe that these lines were written after the death of Shakespeare's only son, Hamnet, in 1596.

The warrior queen appears in a number of Shakespeare's histories. Here it is Elinor of Aquitaine, King John's mother, who goes to war with him ("I am a soldier now and bound to France.")

Several scenes echo incidents in the other history plays. When in *King John* the French king sends a message to England's monarch calling for his resignation:

Desiring thee to lay aside the sword
Which sways usurpingly these several
  titles.

The scene has much in common with the Dauphin's message to Henry V in the play of that name. The lines King John uses to send a trusted man to murder an inconvenient contender for the throne:

...throw thine eye
On yon young boy. I'll tell thee what,
  my friend,
He is a very serpent in my way...dost
  thou understand me?
...Death.

fit nearly as well in the mouth of Richard III, dispatching Tyrell to murder the royal nephews.

Likely Source of the Plot

The play is based on the general record of John's reign, from Holinshed's *Chronicles of England*, but the events are rearranged for dramatic effect. Some authorities believe it was John himself who killed his nephew (though it was in France, not England).

Notable Features

There are a number of references to artillery in the play ("The thunder of my cannon shall be heard," John tells the French ambassador) but they are not historical. Cannon were not part of European warfare until the 1300s.

Not mentioned in the play is the fact that it was the tyrannical rule of John—serving as regent while his brother Richard was off on Crusade—against which Robin Hood and his followers rebelled. John's exactions of his barons led to their rebellion and the creation of the Magna Carta in 1215 (though the Magna Carta was not generally identified as a milestone in English history until centuries later, when it was used as a precedent for other attempts at limiting monarchical power).

Notable Productions

Not one of Shakespeare's more popular efforts, *King John* was apparently not staged between his death and 1737, when the play was revived with an actress playing the role of Arthur, an innovation that became something of a tradition. The 19th-century actor William Charles Macready led a number of productions in mid-century, and the first recorded film of a Shakespeare play was made of part of *King John* in 1899. In the 20th century, a number of notable actors (Paul Scofield, Richard Burton) have preferred the role of the Bastard to that of King John himself.

The 1984 *Time-Life*/BBC production stars Leonard Rossiter as King John, with Mary Morris as Elinor. Claire Bloom delivers a memorable performance as Lady Constance. There was also a 1951 BBC-television production starring Donald Wolfit.

Although King John himself has excited little interest on the part of dramatists, the same is not true of his parents, Henry II and Elinor of Aquitaine. The 1964 film *Becket*, based on a Jean Anouilh play and elements of T. S. Eliot's *Murder in the Cathedral*, and starring Peter O'Toole and Richard Burton, concerns the relationship between Henry II and the friend he created archbishop and later caused to be murdered, Thomas à Becket. *The Lion in Winter*, a 1968 film (from the play of the same title by James Goldman) starring O'Toole and Katharine Hepburn, treats the tumultuous relationship of Henry II and Elinor, a fascinating historical figure who is the only person who has served as queen both of France and England (though not at the same time).

KING RICHARD II

RASH KING ALIENATES HIS NOBLES, LOSES JOB TO COUSIN

Period

1400

Setting

England

Richard II was the eldest son of Edward (the Black Prince), himself the eldest son of King Edward III, who ruled from 1327 to 1377. Since the Black Prince died before his father, the grandson Richard, then little more than a child, succeeded to the throne. As an adult, Richard is surrounded by members of his extended family, including two of his father's surviving brothers, their sons, and the sons of several other deceased brothers. Key to the story are Richard's uncles, the Duke of York and John of Gaunt, along with Gaunt's son Henry Bolingbroke.

The play opens with Bolingbroke accusing another noble, Thomas Mowbray, of treason. Unable to settle their dispute, Richard orders a trial by battle. However, just before the contest is to begin, he changes his mind and banishes both men, Bolingbroke for six years, Mowbray forever. News of rebellion in Ireland prompts Richard to lead his troops there in person. To raise money for the expedition, he permits some of his royal hangers-on to "farm" the revenues of his realm, in effect to collect oppressive taxes. Before he leaves for Ireland he visits the dying John of Gaunt, who catalogs his shortcomings as a monarch. In anger, Richard seizes all of Gaunt's fortune at his death, thus disinheriting the banished Bolingbroke (Gaunt was, after the king himself, the richest man in England).

While Richard is campaigning in Ireland, Bolingbroke raises an army and lands in England, ostensibly only to reclaim his father's title and inheritance. Nobles flock to his cause, including at last the Duke of York, whom Richard left in charge of the realm. When Richard arrives to discover his Welsh forces have dispersed and all his friends are dead or joining the rebellion, he surrenders to

Bolingbroke, in the knowledge that Bolingbroke in fact seeks more than John of Gaunt's title and properties.

Back in London, Bolingbroke seizes the throne as Henry IV, despite the dire predictions of the Bishop of Carlisle, "What subject can give sentence to the King...the blood of English shall manure the ground, and future ages groan for this foul act."

A humbled Richard, in the long and moving deposition scene, tells Bolingbroke,

You may my glories and my state depose,
But not my griefs. Still am I king of those.

Richard is imprisoned in the north of England. Bolingbroke, now Henry IV, utters the fateful words about his rival, "Have I no friend will rid me of this living fear?" and his followers, led by Lord Exton, get the message. Richard gives a good account of himself in the final fray, seizing a weapon and dispatching four of his attackers before he himself is slain. As the play ends, Henry hears about Richard's death, and vows to go on Crusade to atone for his misdeeds and Richard's murder.

One of the key subplots revolves around the question of who killed Richard's uncle, the Duke of Gloucester, the brother of John of Gaunt, and the Duke of York? Gloucester's offstage death is the issue at the play's opening, in the confrontation between Bolingbroke and Thomas Mowbray. Gloucester's widow asks John of Gaunt to take up the issue, but Gaunt tells her sadly that he believes King Richard was responsible and thus is beyond justice.

Further attempts to discover the truth lead to a series of challenges to duels among fiery nobles after Bolingbroke has seized power, but the challenges are not resolved in the play. One of the men accused of complicity in Gloucester's death was Lord Aumerle, the son of the Duke of York. Aumerle later ends up begging for Bolingbroke's (now Henry IV) mercy for plotting an attempt on *his* life in a planned countercoup. Aumerle's mother joins in the pleas while his father, the redoubtable duke, says his son should pay the price of his treason. Moved by the mother's request, Bolingbroke pardons Aumerle, though he orders the deaths of his co-conspirators.

Likely Source of the Plot

Holinshed's *Chronicles of England* was Shakespeare's source for the story.

Background

Implied but not included in the play are long years of conflict with his nobles in Richard's troubled reign that preceded his loss of the throne. Although there was a deposition scene in Westminster Hall, Richard was not present— Bolingbroke was far too strategic to let even an unpopular Richard plead the case for his kingship before the leading figures of the nation. Richard's moving farewell to his adult wife is also Shakespeare's creation. Isabelle of France was married by proxy to Richard after the death of Richard's first wife. She was only seven at the time of her marriage and eleven when her husband lost his crown. (She went back to France and married the Duke of

Orleans.) The actual circumstances of Richard's death are also a mystery.

John of Gaunt and his son Bolingbroke represent the house of Lancaster. Richard II was the last direct lineal descendant of William the Conqueror, and despite his shortcomings as a king, Bolingbroke's usurpation of the throne threw into jeopardy the tradition that had long determined the leadership of English society. The Wars of the Roses—the civil wars between the followers of Lancaster and York— were the eventual result of Bolingbroke's action.

Notable Features

The dying John of Gaunt's description of England,

This royal throne of kings, this
*   sceptred isle*
This earth of majesty...
This blessed plot, this earth, this realm,
This England....

is usually employed as a jingoistic paean to Great Britain. In the play, however, John of Gaunt uses this praise as an ironic comparison between the England that could be and the England that did exist under Richard's rule, "Bound in with shame...a shameful comport of itself" thanks to Richard's ineptitude and mismanagement.

Unmentioned in the play is the fact that Richard II had a scholarly side and was probably the first English king since the Conquest who was fluent in English (in addition to the French that had been spoken at Court since the time of William the Conqueror). He thus could read the works of one of his Crown officials, Geoffrey Chaucer, author of *The Canterbury Tales*.

Notable Productions and Performances

The play is thought to have been written about 1595, before both parts of *Henry IV* and *Henry V*, but after the Wars of the Roses plays—the three parts of *Henry VI* and *Richard III*. Early editions of *Richard II*—perhaps given royal sensitivities—were printed *without* the crucial deposition scene. The American actor Edwin Booth (brother of Abraham Lincoln's assassin John Wilkes Booth) was a famous interpreter of the title role in the 19th century; John Gielgud is accorded similar honors for the 20th.

A 1970 film version stars Ian McKellen, while a 1979 production features Derek Jacobi and Jon Finch, with John Gielgud as John of Gaunt. David Birney has the title role in a 1982 production from the Shakespeare Collection, which includes an excellent Paul Shenar as Bolingbroke. A 1997 television version of the play featured the actress Fiona Shaw as Richard II.

So Near and Yet So Far
—Shakespeare's Language

he language of the Shakespeare plays is remarkably close to our own, in spite of the passage of 400 years (and is much more comprehensible than that of Chaucer, writing only 200 years before Shakespeare's time). But as transparent as "to be or not to be" or "my kingdom for a horse" may seem, in truth much of Shakespeare is in fact a good deal harder for modern audiences to follow.

Shakespearean syntax is often different from the "subject-verb-object" we take for granted; many words have fallen out of use, and in others the meaning has migrated, often a considerable distance; the plays are full of references to what is now obscure—classical myth, falconry, astrology, or the theory of "humours" that were thought to determine personality. In addition, changes in the language over four centuries have meant the loss of subtleties and colors that contemporary audiences for the plays could appreciate and enjoy, and that add considerably to the dramatic impact of the words.

The Origins of English

Elizabethan English traces its roots to Old English, basically a Germanic tongue. It changed dramatically—if slowly—after the invasion by William the Conqueror, who overthrew the native reigning house and became King of England after 1066. For decades, William's followers and descendants ruled England while continuing to speak Norman French. But by about 1400, when *The Canterbury Tales* were written, English had absorbed thousands of French and Latin words and had become what we now know as Middle English, spoken by all classes.

Chaucer's English is sufficiently different from ours to require careful study. The opening line of *The Canterbury Tales* "Whan that Aprille with its shoures soote" ("When April with its sweet showers") can be all but incomprehensible to the modern reader. But only 200 years later, in Shakespeare's time, the language had evolved to the point of Early Modern English, and its evolution since has been much more gradual.

Poets & Writers, Inc. 20th anniversary celebration chapbook
A Garden of Earthly Delights. *M.G. Lord*

Syntax and Structure

In Latin, the base for all modern European Romance tongues, and in many other languages, word order is unimportant, because words are inflected—they have slightly different endings or forms depending on what role they play in the sentence structure. They also may have gender, as nouns in Romance languages still do, but English gave up long ago. Modern English is generally uninflected, so the role of a word in a sentence is almost always indicated by word order, and the order that has evolved as the standard is "subject, verb, object" (*The woman drove home*).

Shakespeare's plays rely less on this structure, so some lines require more careful reading. "Thus with imagined wing our swift scene flies," says Chorus in *Henry V*; and "there's naught in France that can be with a nimble galliard won," says the French ambassador to the king in the same play. In some circumstances the subject, verb, and object may not only be inverted, but separated by several lines.

Standard syntax was still evolving, but in addition, one of the reasons for Shakespeare's syntactical choices was the need for the lines to scan—to have the rhythm of poetry rather than prose.

Blank Verse

The plays were mostly written in blank—that is, unrhymed—verse (except for rhymed couplets, often used to close out scenes or sequences). The rhythm is iambic pentameter, a way of saying that the typical line has five two-syllable "feet" or units, and the typical unit is stressed on the second syllable. Blank verse was a common dramatic vehicle at the time and for centuries later. As many experts have pointed out, it is relatively close to the natural form spoken English takes. (*he WENT to SEE a MAN aBOUT a CAR*.)

Of course, of the thousands of lines in the plays, not all are blank verse. *Richard II*, for instance, is almost entirely in verse, while *The Merry Wives of Windsor* is predominantly prose. In general, serious characters discussing important issues speak in verse, while comic characters are less likely to do so, particularly the lowborn.

Thus, while King Henry IV says lines like

> *unEAS-y LIES the HEAD that*
> *WEARS the CROWN,*

the same play has Falstaff saying "Hang ye, ye gorbellied knaves, are ye undone? No, ye fat chuffs."

Changes in Vocabulary

Many words used by Shakespeare have effectively disappeared. Others, including simple ones, have changed their meanings. Who now uses *roynish* (base or coarse), *orgulous* (haughty), *micher* (a petty thief), *kibe* (a chilblain or sore), or *slubber* (to be clumsy or messy)? *Fond* now conveys affection; in Shakespeare's plays it means foolish. *Nice* now means agreeable (a nice day) or even effective (a nice job); to Chaucer it meant ignorant or even wanton; in Shakespeare's time it could mean finely drawn, as in a *nice* distinction, or even diffident. *Bootless* to Shakespeare did not mean lacking footwear, but useless or meaningless. *'A* could mean he. *Meat* now means flesh; in Shakespeare's time it meant any solid food (and it rhymed with our modern *mate*).

In Shakespeare current and outmoded forms exist side by side, sometimes in the mouths of the same character. Shakespeare uses both *has* and *hath*, *do* and *doeth*, *go* and *goeth*.

Thou and *you* are both widely used in the plays, but they are not interchangeable. In Shakespeare's time, *thou* was the equivalent of the modern French *tu*—an informal mode of address used between family members or friends, or to indicate status. Thus, the king could use *thou* with almost anyone and in most situations. Theoretically only his family members could use it with him, and then in private, and the usage continued down through the Elizabethan social hierarchy. In *Richard III*, the king discusses with Tyrell the murder of the royal nephews, addressing Tyrell as "thou," while Tyrell uses "you" or "my lord." But King Lear's Fool, as a measure of his standing outside the social hierarchy, refers to Lear as "thou."

Shakespeare's plays, as popular entertainments, also used popular language that we would term bawdy, from *whoreson jackanapes* to Princess Katherine's mistaking of the English word *gown* for the French *conne* (pudenda). They also made reference to many things familiar to Shakespeare's audiences that are now obscure. *Pitch* in the plays often means height, taken from the sport of falconry (it referred to the high point of the flight of a bird of prey, a sense that we retain in musical pitch).

Uncommon Pursuits

The revival of classical learning in the Renaissance had led to a rediscovery of Greek and Latin authors, and their myths. The plays contain references to Hercules, Jupiter, Diana and other gods

The sport of falconry

and goddesses, to myths like that of Icarus, the phoenix, the River Stxy and Charon, ferryman to the classical underworld.

That same Renaissance learning had helped reawaken interest in astrology and the influence of the stars on human life. "Happier the man whom favourable stars allot thee" says Katherina in *The Taming of the Shrew*; Gloucester, referring with unconscious irony to the heir apparent to the throne, speaks of "the right and fortune of his happy stars" in *Richard III*.

Elizabethans believed that the physical and mental characteristics of people were derived from the balance of the four fluids or humors that made up their constitution—blood, phlegm, choler, and bile. It was in terms of these "elements" that Antony praises the dead Brutus at the end of *Julius Caesar*, "the elements so mixed in him that Nature might stand up and say to all the world 'this was a Man.'"

Wordplay

In Elizabethan times, thousands of new words were coming into the language from Latin and Greek texts, Italian and French. It is estimated that of the roughly 25,000 different words in the plays, about 2,000 are new, either coined by Shakespeare or first recorded by him.

Elizabethans also loved puns, and Shakespeare provided them. The rotund Sir John Falstaff, faced with the criticism of the Lord Chief Justice that "Your means are very slender, and your waste (spending) is great," replies "I would my means were greater, and my waist slenderer." Lord Northumberland on the news of the death of his son, nicknamed Hotspur, asks "said he that young Harry Percy's spur was cold? Of Hotspur Coldspur?"

What It Sounded Like

When a contemporary English actor says Macbeth's lines about sleep being "sore labour's bath," the sound we are likely to hear is not at all what Shakespeare had in mind. Today no one knows for sure what Shakespeare's actors sounded like, aside from some clear dialect humor written phonetically, like the voice of the Welsh Captain Fluellen in *Henry V* ("For look you, th'athversary...is digt himself four yards under the countermines.... By Cheshu, I think 'a will plow up all...."). But it is possible to get some sense of how different Shakespeare's language sounded from ours.

Great Vowel Shift

One of the ways English began to differentiate itself from its Germanic and French roots was a change in vowel sounds known as the Great Vowel Shift, which began sometime before Shakespeare and continued (though it was not completed) through his time.

Anyone familiar with grand opera knows that its usual vowel sounds have what is known as "Continental" values *ah/eh/ee/oh/oo* (largely retained in Romance languages even today). But thanks to this shift, vowel forms are closer to *eh/ee/aye/owe/yew* in both the English upper/middle-class accent known as Received Pronunciation and current American Standard, also known as Inland Northern. (It is the *eh/ee/ah/oh/yew* that makes the language of the American South distinct).

Spelling and Pronunciation

Although Romance languages are spelled generally as they sound, English is full of idiosyncrasies. Why don't *roof* and *blood*, with the same vowel combination, share the same vowel sound? Why do *ruff* (the Elizabethan garment) and *rough* (with different vowels and final consonants) sound the same, while *tough, dough,* and *cough,* with virtually identical spellings, sound very little like each other?

The answer is that they once sounded as they are still spelled, due to something of an accident of history. Printed books had been produced in England for much of the 16th century, but books in English rather than Latin or French found their market as literacy spread only later in the century. Printers—most of whom were based in London—used the pronunciations they heard in the capital as their standard, and for a variety of reasons their spellings became the standard even as pronunciation evolved.

In modern English *cloud* and *bowed* rhyme, although they are spelled differently. In Shakespeare's time *cloud* was probably pronounced *cloe-ud. House* was pronounced *how-oose.* (It had been *hoose* for Chaucer).

Letters that are now silent in our language were probably pronounced, such as the *t* in *often,* the *w* in *sword,* and, at least in passing the *k* in *knee* and *knife.* The latter probably sounded closer to *k-naif,* since *wife* and *knife* are rhymed in a number of the sonnets and Shakespeare's pronunciation of wife was close to *waif,* a descendant of the *wif* that would have been pronounced in Chaucer's tale of the Wife of Bath. All the letters in *ion* endings were probably sounded.

Whereas for Chaucer every syllable and every vowel was pronounced (*smalle foules* of the Prologue to *The Canterbury Tales* was *small-e fool-es*), by Shakespeare's time many final *e*'s had been dropped in writing, and probably more in actual speech. Meanwhile *-ed* words like *dropped,* once pronounced *drop-ed,* had become closer to our modern *dropt.* Nevertheless, it appears that either pronunciation was acceptable, and a number of his lines scan and/or rhyme properly only if the *-ed* is pronounced, whether marked or not.

One of the many differences between upper-class English and American Standard is the use of the broad "a" in words like *bath,* making most English actors utter a sound like *bawth.* But this did not come into wide use even in upper-class English until the late 18th century, and never really found its way to America. Even *labour,* pronounced *lay-ber* now by both British and American actors, was probably much closer to *lah-boor,* a sound closer to the way the British still spell it.

> *"If it falls your lot to be a street sweeper, sweep streets like Michelangelo painted pictures, Shakespeare wrote poetry, Beethoven composed music."*
> —**Martin Luther King**

We use a broad "a" sound in *want*; to Shakespeare it probably rhymed with our pronunciation of *can't. Father*, *(fah-thur* in American Standard), is thought to have been closer to a rhyme with our *lather* (as in soap), with a trilled final *r* *(fatherrr)*. Hamlet's famous lines, written phonetically today, would be—*Too bee or not too bee, that is the kwes-chun*—but to Shakespeare's audience they may have sounded much more like *Ta bay, or not ta bay, that iss the kwess-tee-on.*

Rhymes

Although rhymes are only an approximate guide to sounds, it is interesting to note that in one long passage of couplets in *Henry VI, Part One*, Shakespeare rhymes *slain/again, swear/fear, son/afternoon, word/sword, blood/maidenhood, encountered/shed, fly/chivalry, wot/boat, boot/foot, alone/none* and *have/grave. Love* and *prove* are rhymed in a number of references.

Most modern versions of how we believe Shakespeare's actors spoke sound like a kind of backwoods/archaic American with something of a Scotch burr or Irish brogue (though in Shakespeare's day the Irish and many Scots spoke Gaelic, not English.) It is an oversimplification to assert that Irish or American speech—or elements of Australian—come closer to Shakespearean English than modern Received

Pronunciation. But it is not entirely untrue.

The Missing Music

Listening to Shakespeare in a version that tries to capture the original sound can be a remarkable experience. Although such renditions can be difficult to follow if one doesn't know the text well, these reproductions reveal a compelling musicality to the lines that is too often missing from modern readings.

The use of contemporary pronunciation can illuminate the lines in a new way. When Cassius says

Upon what meat doth this our
    Caesar feed,
That he hath grown so great.

the music of the line is much more evident when one hears

Upon what mate doth this our
    Caesar feed

and a whole different rhyme scheme.

A few lines later Cassius plays with the words *room* (in the sense of area for Caesar's reign) and *Rome*. The wordplay becomes much more evident when we realize that in Shakespeare's time *room* and *Rome* had the same vowel sound— they were homonyms.

KING HENRY IV, PART ONE

PRODIGAL PRINCE MATURES, KING FIGHTS TO KEEP HIS CROWN

Period

Early 15th century

Setting

England

Henry IV, Part One, begins the story of the maturing of Prince Hal from a tavern wastrel to a king—a story that reaches its climax in *Henry V*. This evolution is played against one of Shakespeare's most popular characters, Sir John Falstaff: gourmand, thief, belligerent coward, and all-around endearing rogue. The dramatic background is the uneasy confidence in which Henry IV, the former Henry Bolingbroke, holds the throne he plans to bequeath to Hal. Bolingbroke, in the story told in the previous play, deposed Richard II and assumed the crown, then was implicated in Richard's murder.

While Richard had few friends when alive—their absence contributed to Bolingbroke's ability to mount a nearly bloodless coup—his reign has sweetened in the reminiscence for many English nobles. Even the most fervent opponents of Richard's policies retain some belief in the divine right of kings, and recall with discomfort the details of his being stripped of power by one of his subjects. Meanwhile, as king, Henry IV has offended many of his own supporters. By the time of this play King Henry's opponents include the northern lords Henry Percy and his son Harry, nicknamed Hotspur. This young noble's martial spirit and accomplishments mark such a striking contrast with the feckless Hal that Henry IV wishes aloud that Hotspur rather than Hal was his son.

The play opens with news of rebellion in Wales and Scotland and a recap of Henry IV's perilous circumstances. The scene then shifts to a tavern and the beginning of the other major plot line—the relationship between Prince Hal and Falstaff. Falstaff and his cohorts plan to rob a group of merchants and pilgrims and Hal agrees to participate (though with a secret plan to rob the robbers). Back at court, the breach between Henry IV and the Percys becomes more open as Henry IV refuses to ransom from the Welsh a Percy relative whom he considers a traitor, and Hotspur withholds from the King the prisoners he has captured in Scotland.

Outside London, Falstaff and his gang set upon and rob the travelers, but themselves are routed easily by Prince Hal and his friend Poins, both in disguise. Falstaff returns to the inn bellowing about being overcome by his assailants, their number growing in the retelling under the prod of wine and Hal's questioning. Hal confronts Falstaff with the truth and without missing a beat Falstaff claims he knew it was Hal all the time and thus refused to fight back—"The lion will not touch the true prince."

In a mock court scene in the tavern Falstaff speaks of Hal's life when he becomes king, and urges him to turn his back on most of the low company of his youth. "Banish Peto, banish Bardolph, banish Poins; but for sweet Jack Falstaff, kind Jack Falstaff, true Jack Falstaff...banish not him thy Harry's company—banish plump Jack, and banish all the world." As Falstaff falls into a drunken slumber, Hal protects him from the sheriff looking for the robbers, and makes plans to return the money to the travelers.

In Wales, meanwhile, the uncertainty of the rebels' alliance becomes clear as Hotspur and Owen Glendower quarrel over ego (*Glendower: I can call spirits from the vasty deep. Hotspur: Why so can I, or so can any man. But will they come when you do call for them?*) and then over the division of the spoils of their expected victory. At court the King confronts Hal with his dissolute life and compares him unfavorably with Hotspur. Hal pledges to redeem himself.

Matters come to a head at Shrewsbury. Hotspur learns that a number of his allies, including his father, will not be joining him in time for the battle now drawing near. In a statement that presages Henry V's address to his troops before Agincourt, Hotspur is undeterred. The lack of allies lends "a larger dare to our great enterprise."

In comic contrast Falstaff, given charge of a company of foot soldiers by Hal, has kept the money for their pay and provisioning, extracted more from sturdy young men he has allowed to buy their way out of service, and proceeds slowly toward the battle with "a hundred and fifty tattered prodigals...most of them out of prison."

Before the battle, Henry IV offers a truce "...will they take the offer of my grace...every man shall be my friend again, and I'll be his." Hotspur's uncle, convinced that the King's offer is not in good faith, keeps the truce offer from Hotspur. In the fighting Hal, though wounded, refuses to leave the field, saves his father's life, and eventually finds and kills Hotspur. Falstaff is a silent witness to their confrontation, pretending to be dead on the field nearby.

> "What is honor? A word. What is that word, honor? Air."
> —*Henry IV, Part One*

Orson Welles as Falstaff in Chimes at Midnight.
Courtesy Museum of Modern Art/Film Stills Archive

Before the battle Falstaff comments on bravery. "What is honor? A word...What is that 'honor'? Air." Then after the fighting, rising from the field where he feigned death, he announces, "The better part of valor is discretion, in the which better part I have saved my life." Falstaff then claims to have been the cause of Hotspur's actual demise, saying that Hotspur had recovered from his wound at Hal's hand and had to be dispatched by none other than Sir John himself after Hal had left the battlefield.

Likely Source of the Plot

The play is drawn largely from Holinshed's *Chronicles of England.* Falstaff, originally named Oldcastle, is entirely Shakespeare's own creation.

Background

In what amounts to a hagiography of Hal leading to his triumphs as Henry V, Shakespeare draws a dramatic contrast between his misspent youth and that of his contemporary, Hotspur. However, there is some question about the depth of the young Hal's dissoluteness. While Shakespeare has him in taverns, in real life he was on the Welsh border fighting his father's wars. The contrast Shakespeare draws between Hal and Hotspur as young men is also solely for dramatic purposes. In reality Hotspur was not only older than Hal, he was older than Hal's father.

Notable Productions and Performances

The best lines in the play are almost always Falstaff's, who is by far the most memorable character and the focus of most productions. Great actors of the 19th-century stage made careers of Falstaff (who also appears in *Henry IV, Part Two*, and *The Merry Wives of Windsor*.) Modern interpreters of note include Sir Ralph Richardson, Anthony Quayle, and in the 1968 New York Shakespeare Festival, Stacy Keach.

The *Time-Life*/BBC production includes Anthony Quayle as Falstaff. Orson Welles directed and starred in his own Falstaff story, entitled *Chimes at Midnight*. As much Welles as it is Shakespeare, the film pulls together Falstaff scenes from both parts of *Henry IV*, *The Merry Wives of Windsor*, and ends with Mistress Quickly's account of Falstaff's death from *Henry V*.

KING HENRY IV, PART TWO

FALSTAFF CAPERS, BAD BOY PRINCE FINDS HIMSELF

Period

Early 15th century

Setting

England

In the opening scene, the Earl of Northumberland learns of the failure of the rebel alliance at the battle of Shrewsbury and the death of his son, Hotspur. But he urges his friends to join with the remaining rebels, led by the Archbishop of York, who "turns insurrection to religion," and bolsters his followers with relics of the dead King Richard II.

Meanwhile Falstaff, in a tavern, complains that merchants refuse him credit despite his exalted station. On the street he encounters the Lord Chief Justice, who tells him that only his part in the battle at Shrewsbury has prevented him from being charged

> He hath eaten me out of house and home.
> —Henry IV, Part Two

(and presumably hanged) for the robbery at Gad's Hill (in the previous play, *Henry IV, Part One*).

The remaining rebels debate the wisdom of taking on King Henry's forces before all of theirs are assembled, essentially the mistake that Hotspur made in the previous play. Tipping the balance in favor of action are the fact that the king's forces are fighting other battles with the French and the Welsh, and the Archbishop of York's statement that "the commonwealth is sick of their own choice" of Henry IV as king, and "they that when Richard lived would have him die are now become enamored on his grave."

The Lord Chief Justice and Falstaff meet again, this time as the jurist is called upon to mediate between Falstaff and the mistress of a tavern to whom he owes money. Prince Hal, who disguised himself and robbed Falstaff of his ill-gotten gains in the previous play, in this one disguises himself as a waiter and is witness to an alehouse brawl as Falstaff defends the somewhat tattered honor of Doll Tearsheet from his drunken aide, Pistol.

"Uneasy lies the head that wears the crown," mutters Henry IV, speaking of his own state. He is ailing, beset by doubts, and unable to sleep as the rebels gather, though his nobles assure him that loyal troops will put down the rebellion. However, the reliability of at least some of those troops is called into question as Falstaff, with the help of an old acquaintance named Simon Shallow, interviews potential draftees in a country village. Persuaded by bribes, he lets the likeliest candidates for service go, filling out the ranks with the eponymous Wart and Feeble.

The decisive encounter happens at the Forest of Gaultree when the archbishop and Thomas Mowbray (not the denouncer of Bolingbroke at the beginning of *Richard II*, but his son) and other rebels face Prince John of Lancaster (Hal's brother) and the Earl of Westmoreland. The rebels offer a list of grievances which Prince John accepts and agrees to remedy. The rebels then disperse their army, after which Prince John has the leaders arrested and taken away for execution.

Despite the good news from Gaultree and a similar victory in Yorkshire, Henry IV is troubled in body and spirit. Hal returns to find his father apparently dead, and takes the crown from his pillow. But Henry IV, rallying briefly, awakens to find it gone, and rebukes his son. Hal tearfully says he believed his father dead, and they reconcile.

Henry IV tells him that while his own reign was constantly troubled by the fact that he got the crown by usurping Richard, Hal should be more secure, since he will become king by normal succession. Yet, before he dies and knowing the temper of his nobles, he urges Hal to "busy giddy minds with foreign quarrels."

When the news of Hal's accession is brought to Falstaff he rushes to London, certain that he will become one of the great figures of the kingdom. But as he shouts at the royal procession leaving the coronation, the new king publicly turns his back on his past. Hal stops and says to Falstaff, "I know thee not, old man. Fall to thy prayers." Falstaff and his followers are banished from the court, though Hal, now Henry V, adds, "as we hear you do reform yourselves, we will...give you advancement."

Likely Source of the Plot

In addition to Holinshed's *Chronicles of England*, a source play for these dramas may have been an anonymous play called *The Famous Victories of Henry V*.

Notable Features

"A man can die but once. We owe God a death," says one of the characters. The words, with irony that came so easily to Shakespeare, are spoken not by the noble Hotspur or a valiant defender of the king, but from the mouth of a woman's tailor and Falstaffian draftee named Francis Feeble.

The play offers an unusually clear contrast in language. The drama switches continually between the high life of England—court and castle—to the tavern and the street. In the former the characters, such as the Archbishop of York, speak in blank verse and with words that need no translation:

Thus have you heard our cause and
known our means;
And, my most noble friends, I pray
you all,
Speak plainly your opinions of our hopes.
And first, Lord Marshal, what say
you to it?

But Doll Tearsheet addresses Falstaff's aide, Pistol, in the alehouse in the following way:

Away, you cut-purse rascal. You filthy bung, away. By this wine I'll thrust my knife in your mouldy chaps and you play the saucy cuttle with me. Away you bottle-ale rascal. You basket-hilt stale juggler, you.

Henry IV, Part Two, has had mixed success on the stage, but it is full of memorable lines: "*Never so few, never yet more need,*" says the Earl of Northumberland about the rebel forces; "*An habitation giddy and unsure, hath he that buildeth on the vulgar heart,*" says the Archbishop of York about Henry IV's popularity; "*He hath eaten me out of house and home,*" says Mistress Quickly of Falstaff.

> "**Away, you scullion!**
> **You rampallian!**
> **You fustilarian! I'll**
> **tickle your catastrophe.**"
> **—Henry IV, Part Two**

Notable Productions and Performances

Although *Henry IV, Part One,* is in many ways a complete play able to stand on its own, *Part Two* in many eyes falls short. It revisits, in the maturation of Prince Hal, an issue that arguably was settled in *Part One,* when Hal joined his father's army, saved the king's life, and killed Hotspur. *Henry IV, Part Two,* has structural shortcomings that have led to its often being staged in some altered form, with the interpolation of scenes from *Henry IV, Part One,* or even *Henry V.*

Rather than advance the historic story, *Part Two* provides many opportunities for the crowd-pleasing jokes and low humor of Falstaff's tavern scenes, and thus productions often focus on Falstaff's role. Anthony Quayle plays Falstaff in the 1979 *Time-Life*/BBC production, with Jon Finch and David Gwillim reprising their roles as Henry IV and Prince Hal.

Other Notable Uses of Plot

My Own Private Idaho, a 1991 film by Gus Van Sant, consciously uses the model of Falstaff and Hal in a modern story about West Coast hustlers.

Which Is the Way to London Town?
One Foot up, the Other Foot Down

n Shakespeare's day, London was bursting at its seams and spilling over with new immigrants. Just one square mile, "The City" was enclosed by a wall twenty feet high which had been built centuries before by the Romans to protect the settlement they called *Londinium*.

**Pussycat, Pussycat, where
  have you been?**
**I've been to London to visit
  the Queen!**

In Elizabeth's prosperous England, London had become a magnet, drawing to its busy streets the desperate—including thousands fleeing the reli-

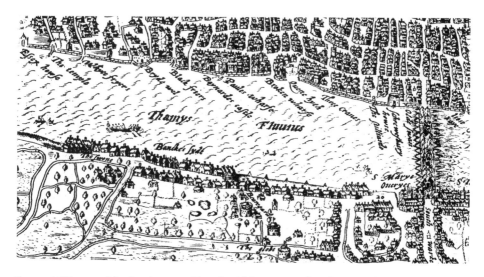

From a 1600 map of the London area. Note the Globe, very small, at bottom. Above it is a playhouse believed to be the Rose, with a bear-baiting arena slightly to the northwest. Royal Academy Stockholm

The severed heads of traitors looked down from the entrance to London Bridge. Detail from J. C. Visscher, Londinium Florentissima Britanniae Urbs *(Amsterdam 1616)*

gious wars on the Continent; the creative—artists, poets, musicians, playwrights; and the industrious—peddlers, merchants, and entrepreneurs looking for business opportunities.

Though small, London was big enough. It was, in fact, the largest city in England, the third largest in all of Europe, after Naples and Paris. In 1500, the population of London had been only 40,000. By 1550 London was a thriving 120,000; by 1600 it had swelled to well over 200,000.

All roads, no matter how muddy or dangerous, led to London. The best were paved highways still intact from the days of the Romans. There were also well-worn horse paths, saltways (for the distribution of salt) and drove roads (for the cattle).

London, England's center for trade and commerce, stretched its boundaries to accommodate the migrating masses in areas outside of its wall. To the west was Westminster, where William the Conqueror had been crowned King of England on Christmas Day, 1066, in the newly completed abbey. This area was where power resided, the place of the royal palace and court.

To the South, across the Thames, was seedy and resourceful Southwark. It had everything—from the hottest "red light district" to hospitals and monasteries.

In Shakespeare's play, *King Henry VI, Part Two*, act 4, scene 8 takes place in Southwark and opens with Jack Cade's cry to the rebel mob,

*Up Fish Street! Down Saint Magnus'
    Corner!
Kill and knock down! Throw them into
    the Thames!*

Most of the city's theaters were in Southwark, including Shakespeare's Globe, because the Puritans opposed theaters inside the city walls. The area had a reputation for pickpockets and peddlers and for brothels (called "stews"). There were so many prostitutes in Southwark that they even had their own burying-ground, discretely named the Single Woman's Churchyard.

A popular "bear garden" was also located here with an arena to seat 1,000 spectators. Bear-baiting was a cruel form of entertainment: a bear, chained to a stake, would be set upon by five or six big dogs, usually mastiffs, while the crowds roared. When the surviving dogs were exhausted or too seriously mauled, fresh dogs would be brought out to begin a new attack. The game would end when the mutilated bear, too tired to continue, would be led away and nursed back to health in time for the next fight. The queen enjoyed this spectator sport, as had other monarchs before her, and, in 1591, decreed that theaters would be closed on Thursdays so as not to compete with the bear-baiting audiences.

**Hark, hark, the dogs do bark,
The beggars are coming
    to town;
Some in rags, and some in tags,
And one in a velvet gown.**

Entering walled London from the south meant crossing the Thames—London's main delivery route and thoroughfare (it was easier to travel by river than through the narrow streets). There were two thousand licensed "watermen" ready to ferry passengers across the river, but many travelers entering the city crossed London Bridge. Built of stone in 1209, the bridge supported rows of shops and houses, some seven stories high. One section was a drawbridge, to let ships through.

In Shakespeare's day London didn't exactly put out the welcome mat. A traveler entering the city across London Bridge first had to pass under the gateway to the bridge where the severed heads of traitors were displayed. The grisly heads, stuck on top of poles, lasted a long time (one was up for eleven years); they'd been parboiled and dipped in tar.

Once over the bridge, the traveler would not be far from the disreputable neighborhood known as Eastcheap, the location of the Boar's Head Tavern where Falstaff and Prince Hall go drinking and "wenching" in the plays *Henry IV*, *Parts One* and *Two*.

A little farther on was the Tower of London with its walls fifteen feet thick in some places. It was used as a command post, an armory, and a meeting place for the royals, where celebrations were held and treaties were signed. Monarchs spent the night before their coronation in the Tower, and it was the only mint in England. The Tower had a treasury for jewels and a zoo where exotic animals were exhibited—lions, tigers, crocodiles, wolves, camels, and porcupines. For a time a woman was put on

display there—a Pygmy, "only six thumbs high."

But the Tower was primarily famous as a prison for aristocrats deemed traitors. Elizabeth I was imprisoned there before she became queen, and her mother, Anne Boleyn, was executed there at the Tower Green. In Shakespeare's play *Henry VI, Part Three*, Richard kills King Henry in his Tower cell. In *Richard III*, the Duke of Clarence, brother of the king, has a nightmare there and then is murdered, as are Richard's young nephews.

At the other end of the city was St. Paul's Cathedral, which had lost its spire

in a thunderstorm in 1561. Less a cathedral than a center for news and gossip during the week, its middle aisle was actually a thoroughfare called "Paul's Walk" where business was transacted. Delivery boys carrying their wares used it as a shortcut to Fleet Street.

St. Paul's Churchyard was the center of London's book trade for publishers and booksellers. It was crammed with stalls where readers and scholars could buy joke books and chapbooks, folios on law, theology, and the occult, ballads and songbooks, wordy editorial pamphlets about the nature of the sexes, broadsides with bits of news, and dramatic quartos by Shakespeare and other playwrights of the day.

St. Paul's was not the only church in town. There were over one hundred others, transformed during the reign of Henry VIII from Catholic to Protestant—stripped of their incense and statues of saints. Many had bells which rang every evening to mark the time for "retreat from work" and again at nine, the hour of curfew—thus the later nursery rhyme:

Gay go up and gay go down, to ring
   the bells of London Town.
Bull's eyes and targets, say the bells
   of St. Margaret's.
Brickbats and tiles, say the bells of
   St. Giles'.
Halfpence and farthings, say the
   bells of St. Martin's.
Oranges and lemons, say the bells
   of St. Clement's.
Pancakes and fritters, say the bells
   of St. Peter's.
Two sticks and an apple, say the bells
   at Whitechapel....

**To market, to market to buy
   a plum bun:
Home again, home again,
   market is done.**

There were a hundred and one ways to spend money in the lively city where strolling vendors selling everything from hot cakes to new brooms competed with the shopkeepers. Apprentices called out, "What d'ye lack!" to catch the ear of potential buyers. Cheapside was lined with goldsmith shops, four stories high, whereas Thames Street was famous for cook-shops and dried fish. For "wet" (fresh) fish, one would have to go to Bridge Street.

In 1571, Queen Elizabeth opened the Royal Exchange, between Cornhill and Threadneedle Street. It was something like a modern shopping mall, four stories high, housing over 100 shops—apothecaries, haberdashers, goldsmiths, stores full of armor and glassware. On Sunday evenings and holidays, musicians gave concerts there.

The lucky had some silver coins in their purses—pennies (the most common coin), halfpennies (very tiny coins, only half an inch across), groats, and shillings. Even luckier were the ones with gold coins jingling on them—crowns, angels, half-sovereigns, and pounds.

A penny (1d) bought a loaf of bread or a broadside ballad or admission to the theater. Threepence could get you across the Thames. Sixpence could pay for a meal at an inn or a quickie with a prostitute, while a pair of shoes might cost one shilling (12d). You could buy a horse for one pound (20s) and a Bible for two.

To put this purchasing power in perspective, a laborer generally made a penny a day plus meat and drink in winter, two pennies in summer. A craftsman could make £4–10 a year, a successful merchant £100, a knight £1000–2000.

Stealing goods worth at least 12 pence was considered grand larceny and, like murder, rape, sodomy, arson, and treason, was a capital offense. The law was harsher than the people enforcing it, consequently up to 80 percent of the suspects escaped trial, and up to 50 percent of those who went to trial were acquitted. On an average year, about

150 felons were executed in London, many of them at the permanent gallows called Tyburn, erected in 1571.

A man who could read could claim "benefit of clergy" and be branded on the thumb instead of hanged, but this was good for one time only. The reading test was often Psalm 51, verse 1, "Have mercy upon me, O God, according to thy loving kindness: according unto the multitude of thy tender mercies blot out my transgressions." A useful line of Scripture, it was dubbed the "neck verse" because it could literally save one's neck from the noose.

A woman, whether she could read or not, could not claim benefit of clergy unless she had been a nun before the Reformation, but if she was pregnant she could postpone her execution until after childbirth.

Those who stole goods valued at less than a shilling were guilty of petty larceny and were likely to be sentenced to a public flogging.

There was an old woman, and what do you think? She lived upon nothing But victuals and drink!

Home was a dark place, lit by candles made of beeswax, which was expensive but burned brightly, or tallow, which was smelly and smoky, and dripped gobs of animal fat. The very poor used only "rush dips," reeds soaked in grease and held in place with an iron clip.

People with money had windows of glass or oiled paper to let in sunlight, but the poor kept such openings to a

A moated Elizabethan brothel (or "stew")

minimum to conserve heat. The houses were drafty, heated by burning wood in a fireplace. Hot coals were sometimes put in earthenware jars and used to heat rooms without hearths or in metal "warming pans" to heat the beds at night.

Instead of carpets, floors were covered with rushes, reeds and straw mixed with herbs. In *The Taming of the Shrew*, Grumio, the comical servant, asks, "Is supper ready, the house trimmed, rushes strewed, cobwebs swept?" In *Two Noble Kinsmen*, the jailer's daughter brings "strewings" or rushes to place on a cell floor. At the coronation of Henry V, described in *Henry IV, Part Two*, the procession is accompanied by the cry, "More rushes, more rushes." Carpets were for the wealthy who didn't walk on them, but used them to cover furnishings.

The Elizabethans used very little fur-

niture, most of it made of oak and other hardwoods. People sat on backless stools and benches. Chairs were rare and were usually reserved for the head of the house. Only the wealthy had anything upholstered.

For most people, the main meal of the day was eaten around noon. Breakfast was usually a bowl of porridge on the run, but the noon meal was substantial. Bread was central to the Elizabethan diet. Wheat was most popular, but the poor often ate rye, barley, or mixed-grain breads. When it went stale, bread was used to make bread puddings or to thicken stews.

More important than bread, however, was meat. The Elizabethans were big meat eaters. They ate beef, mutton, veal, lamb, kid, pork, deer, and rabbit. In addition to chickens, ducks, and geese, they ate pheasants, partridges, quail, even sparrows. They also ate fish—cod and herring, oysters and mussels. Those who could not afford meat, poultry or fish ate cheese and eggs.

Without refrigeration, foods had to be salted, smoked, dried or pickled. Salted meats were soaked before cooking and most dishes were prepared the easiest way—boiling. Roasting was more time consuming, as the meat had to be constantly turned on a spit with a dripping pan below, and baking required an oven.

For most people, fruits were the main source of sugar, along with honey. Aristocrats satisfied their sweet tooth with gingerbread, cake, marmalade and marzipan. They made flavorful dishes with spices like cinnamon and nutmeg. Most people seasoned their foods with easy-to-grow herbs—fennel, mint, parsley, sage, rosemary, and thyme.

The least exciting part of the meal was usually the vegetable—carrots, spinach, cabbage, leeks, peas, turnips. Few could afford potatoes, which were considered an expensive delicacy.

The meal was washed down with ale or beer. Water was too polluted to drink and wine was expensive, twelve times the cost of ale. Cider was sometimes available, as was mead (an alcoholic drink of water and honey) and fruit drinks—perry (made from pears), raspie (from raspberries), blackberry or cherry juice.

People drank from ceramic mugs or pewter tankards. A "black jack" was a mug made of leather, sealed with pitch. The poor sometimes drank from wooden bowls, while the rich drank from glass goblets. There were no forks at the tables in England until the 1700s, only spoons and knives, so people often ate with their fingers. Plates were most

often square blocks of wood with a circular depression cut in the middle.

Prayers began and ended the meals, and everyone was expected to wash their hands first in a basin of water pro-

A lidded close-stool

vided near the table. After eating, some people cleaned their teeth with toothpicks, or with linen tooth-cloths.

There were no bathrooms, no sinks, no showers, only small basins filled with fennel-scented water and wooden tubs for the occasional bath in front of the fireplace. There were no toilets, either, only clay chamber pots, which people of the upper classes might hide inside lidded "close-stools." Sometimes this contraption, with its donut-shaped seat, was placed in a separate room called a privy (from the French word for private). Sir John Harington, godson to Queen Elizabeth, invented a hydraulic water closet, the predecessor to our flush toilets, but no one was interested, not even the queen.

Bedsteads were often hung with curtains to keep in warmth, after the fires had been extinguished and to keep out the night air, which was considered unhealthy by Elizabethans. The well-off had mattresses stuffed with feathers or wool and down pillows. The poor stuffed their pallets with straw or wheat chaff and sometimes rested their weary heads on logs.

Golden lads and girls all must, Like chimney-sweepers, come to dust.
(from *Cymbeline*)

Perhaps because of poor sanitation, outbreaks of plague, as noted, were common in London. Some years were worse than others. In 1563, the year before Shakespeare's birth, 20,000 died of it in the city. 1593 was another particularly bad year, with upward of 18,000 deaths, but not as bad as 1603 with 34,000 deaths or 1625 when 50,000 people died of the plague in London.

No one was sure what caused the plague. Some thought it was God's punishment for sin. Preachers quoted pas-

Rat-catcher

sages from the Bible, such as Numbers 16:46, "There is wrath gone out from the Lord: the plague is begun."

Others thought the problem was the air. In *Timon of Athens*, Shakespeare writes of a "planetary plague, when Jove Will o'er some high-vic'd City, hang his poison In the sick air."

Astrologers could usually explain it by the position of the stars and planets. Others blamed bad blood. Dogs had a rough life in London though the streets swarmed with them. Now and then, they were ordered banished from the city or killed, and they were always prime suspects in time of infection. The chief culprit, the rat, was rarely suspected, though rat catchers did a good business.

Theories of protection and remedy were varied and plentiful. Some people carried orange peels stuffed with vinegar-soaked sponges and cloves. Others wore amulets filled with arsenic. Some tried cleansing the air in their rooms by burning old shoes. Others dipped red-

A sermon at St. Paul's Cross during an outbreak of plague

hot bricks into basins of vinegar or burned dried rosemary, juniper or bay leaves. There was a common belief that three or four peeled onions left in a corner of the house for ten days would draw any infection out of the air. Some people trusted garlic, others, tobacco, but the best remedy of all was a mixture made of unicorn's horn; many quacks grew rich selling the make-believe potion.

Beginning in 1518, the government of London drew up plague-orders that were printed and fixed on posts. Wandering beggars were to be arrested and theaters closed when the plague was rampant. Graves had to be dug six feet deep.

Homes with infected persons were to be quarantined. Their houses had to be marked with the words, LORD HAVE MERCY UPON US and a red cross. All members of the household were to remain indoors for a specified time, although servants were often cast out of the house to die in the street. Any member of an infected house who had to go outdoors was required to carry a white rod. The rich were allowed to go to their country estates, but were denied re-entry to the city for a month.

Elderly women were hired to shop for and assist afflicted families of marked houses, and "warders" were hired to watch the houses, lest family members try to leave. In 1594, the first "pest-house" was opened in London for people with infectious disease, but still the death carts rolled down the streets as the corpse-bearers called, "Bring out your dead."

KING HENRY V

YOUNG KING'S LEADERSHIP LEADS TO TRIUMPH IN FRENCH WARS

Period

ca. 1415

Settings

England and France

The action of the play opens with an elaborate set-up scene, a conversation between two leading churchmen whose discussion recapitulates Henry V's misspent youth, when he was known as Hal, ("his hours filled up with riots, banquets, sports"), his newfound gravity, and the current geopolitical situation. Henry has demanded of the French that they give up certain dukedoms he claims as his own from his great-grandfather, Edward III. It falls to the churchmen to research and establish the rightness of his claim (the church's near-monopoly on literacy meant it had a similar hold on the profession of law).

Permitting the king to make this claim will divert his attention from backing a previous measure that would strip the Church of much of its land and temporal power. Unsurprisingly, in an audience before the king and his nobles, the bishops not only endorse the rightness of his plans, they pledge "such a mighty sum as never did the clergy at one time bring in to any of your ancestors," for his campaign.

The issue now clear, Henry admits the French ambassador, who brings greetings not from the King of France but from his son, the Dauphin. His gift recalls Henry's youth—tennis balls. "You cannot revel into dukedoms" in France, runs the Dauphin's message. Henry is not amused. "When we have matched our rackets to these balls we...shall strike his father's crown into the hazard."

Comic balance—and a further link with the preceding *Henry IV* plays—is represented in a scene that reintroduces the disreputable and comic characters Bardolph, Nym, and Pistol, along with Mistress Quickly. The quarreling Nym and Pistol are barely kept from a murderous duel by the offstage death of Sir

John Falstaff, the comic hero of the earlier plays.

"No King of England, if not King of France," cries Henry on his departure for the Continent. In France the king and his nobles debate the seriousness of the threat Henry poses, given his youthful reputation. Cooler heads, remembering "with what great state" he heard the ambassador's demands, urge caution, while the king recalls French losses to Henry's forbears at the Battle of Crecy in 1346, a famous English victory.

When Henry's uncle and messenger, the Duke of Exeter, appears, he calls upon the king to give up not only the dukedoms in question, but to "resign your crown and kingdom" to Henry, "the native and true challenger" by right of inheritance.

Before the French town of Harfleur, Henry urges his troops forward with what has become a classic speech, "Once more unto the breach, dear friends, once more" while it takes the threats of the Welsh captain Fluellen to get Bardolph, Nym, and Pistol, though they have joined the expedition, to actually join the battle.

Henry's bloodcurdling threats to the town fathers "...the blind and bloody soldier with foul hand defile the locks of your shrill-shrieking daughters...your naked infants spitted upon pikes..." are balanced by his orders to his uncle once the town has surrendered to "use mercy to them all."

A comic scene between Princess Katharine of France, the king's daughter, and her maid amounts to little more than a vulgar joke on French pronunciation of English words. Her father, meanwhile, sends the flower of the French nobility to meet Henry's forces. Before the final battle is joined Henry demonstrates the finality of his conversion from wastrel to sovereign. Bardolph, the tavern companion of Henry and Falstaff, has been caught stealing from a church and is to be hanged for the offense. Although Henry could pardon him he says, "We would have all such offenders so cut off," and the French protected from thievery and abuse by his troops.

Shakespeare draws two very different scenes the night before the battle. As the French nobles await the dawn—their troops fresh and their numbers overwhelmingly larger than Henry's now tattered forces—their only anxiety is that there will not be enough fight left in the English to justify a great victory. Meanwhile, "the poor condemned English, like sacrifices, by their watchful fires sit patiently and inly ruminate the morning's danger." Henry goes unnoticed through the English camp, his disguise fooling first Pistol, then a group of common soldiers who debate the rights and wrongs of soldiers' lives (and deaths) in the service of their sovereign.

As the battle is about to begin, Henry rallies his outnumbered and disheartened troops with one of the great such speeches in English literature. "We few, we happy few, we band of brothers." His "warriors for the working day...our gayness and our gilt are all besmirched with rainy marching...and time hath worn us into slovenry" compare poorly with the French in their finery only 1,500 paces away, "But, by the Mass, our hearts are in the trim."

So confused is the battle itself that Henry and the English do not know who has won until the French herald asks for a truce to retrieve the dead. "I know not if the day be ours or no," says Henry. "The day is yours," the Frenchman tells him and Henry, not for the first time, cites divine intervention. "Praised be God, and not our strength for it.... God fought for us."

In the last act Henry, as part of a truce agreement brokered by the Duke of Burgundy (who will fight on the English side in the first of the *Henry VI* dramas), woos Katharine. "Is it possible dat I sould love de ennemi of France?" she asks. "In loving me you should love the friend of France, for I love France so well that I will not part with a village of it," Henry replies. The play ends on the announcement of their marriage, but the narrator Chorus, in an epilogue, cites their son Henry VI "whose state so many had the managing that they lost France, and made his England bleed...which oft our stage has shown" (the *Henry VI* plays were written and performed before this one).

Principal Source of the Plot

The outlines of the play are based largely on Holinshed's *Chronicles of England*.

Background

Henry V invaded France in an attempt to exert a claim to territory conquered by his great-grandfather. He did capture the town of Harfleur, and on his way to Calais was brought to battle by a vastly larger French force. The English won an overwhelming victory. Henry actually returned to France in a second successful campaign a few years later, resulting in the peace treaty and his marriage to Katharine.

The Battle of Agincourt may have involved as many as 60,000 French and 12,000 English. According to the play, more than 10,000 French, the overwhelming number lords, knights and squires, were killed and another 1,500 taken prisoner. English losses amounted to fewer than thirty. Holinshed cites these numbers, but adds that other authorities put English losses at 500–600. While exact numbers will probably never be known, there is no question that this was a major English victory.

The enormous discrepancy in casualties is ascribed by most authorities to two principal factors—the superiority of the English longbow over the French crossbow; and tactical blunders by the French dismounted knights, who continued to charge into a mudpit in the center of the English line and exposed their flanks to withering fire and hand-to-hand attacks by the lightly armed but far more nimble English archers.

Notable Features

The questionable circumstances by which his father achieved the crown are never far from this story. Henry, before embarking for France, pauses at Southampton to expose and execute three noble traitors to his cause. He accuses them of selling out their sovereign for French gold, but the Earl of Cambridge, one of their number, protests that for him "the gold of France did not seduce." In fact, although Shakespeare neglects to mention it, the

Reproduction of the Globe Theatre in the 1944 Henry V *starring Laurence Olivier. Note the audience in the background at right. Courtesy Museum of Modern Art/Film Stills Archive*

Earl of Cambridge had a significant and arguably more legitimate claim on the kingship that Henry himself.

Before the battle of Agincourt Henry sees that "the sword, the mace, the crown imperial, the intertissued robe of gold and pearl" that represents his kingship, "not all these, laid in bed majestical, can sleep so soundly as the wretched slave.... " He prays to God to "think not upon the fault my father made" by usurping Richard's crown. His speech on sleep could well have been given by his father, who in *Henry IV, Part Two*, asks "Why, rather, sleep, thou liest in smoky cribs, upon uneasy pallets...than in the perfumed chambers of the great?"

A standard feature of American movies about World War II is the pla-toon that includes an Italian from New York City (usually Brooklyn), a southern boy, a young man from one of the western states, and other indications of the country's unity in the face of adversity. Similarly, a major subplot of *Henry V* involves Captain Fluellen, the Welsh student of ancient wars and head of the sappers (miners) who tunnel under castle and town walls to bring them down. A brave but comic figure who speaks with a strong accent, he is linked with equivalent Scot and Irish officers, and his simple virtues are contrasted with the dissembling and cowardly Pistol. (Fluellen represents a marked contrast with the Welsh rebel, Owen Glendower, who worked in the previous play to overthrow Henry V's father).

Laurence Olivier as Henry V, left, and Kenneth Branagh, right, in the same role.
Courtesy Museum of Modern Art/Film Stills Archive

Notable Productions and Performances

Laurence Olivier's 1944 *Henry V*, with Olivier as producer, director, and star, is in many ways a straightforward treatment. The French are supercilious and often ineffectual, the English largely noble and brave. As a morale booster for the British during World War II (although the French were English *allies* in that conflict), it may well have been effective. Cinematically it is fascinating, beginning on the stage of the Globe, complete with backstage preparations and a bow from the prompter, Shakespeare himself. Moving to France, the filmed play expands into a movie, eventually returning to a play again at the close.

Kenneth Branagh's 1989 film, which be both directed and starred in, is eminently watchable as grand drama and compelling moviemaking. Backed by an A-list of talent including Paul Scofield, Derek Jacobi, Ian Holm, Emma Thompson, and Judi Dench, Branagh embodies the English king Shakespeare tried to create—brave, resolute, considerate of his men, merciful, capable of believably wooing the daughter of his adversary. His speech before the battle and the battle sequences themselves—a muddy, confused, and brutal undertaking—are particularly memorable.

There is also a *Time-Life*/BBC-TV version starring David Gwillim.

The Elizabethan World

ational life in late 16th century England was dominated by two great public issues and one memorable monarch. The issues, often intertwined, were the international religious battle between orthodox Catholicism and Protestant reform, and the transfer of the center of European political and economic power from the Mediterranean states to those on the Atlantic coast. The religious dispute led to persecution and brutal massacres in Europe, helped spark a series of Continental wars, and prompted an ambitious plan by Spain to redraw the power map of Europe by mounting an invasion of the British Isles. The geopolitical contest, while not concluded during this period, laid the groundwork for England's emergence as a great maritime force and the holder of the balance of power in Europe.

As the monarch who faced these challenges, Queen Elizabeth I walked a successful tightrope between religious extremists inside and outside her boundaries. She led the country through the defeat of Spain's invasion attempt, and managed for more than forty years to preserve and increase England's international power. And whatever the internal tensions during her reign, Elizabethan society experienced a growing prosperity and a new sense of possibility in many fields, including drama.

The Question of Religion

Christianity had dealt with reform movements through much of the middle ages, ignoring them when possible, condemning them or absorbing them when necessary. But Martin Luther's posting of his 95 theses on a church door in Wittenberg in 1517 set off a conflagration that was to affect all of Europe and eventually the New World.

Luther, an Augustinian monk and professor of philosophy, in some respects echoed earlier reformers who attacked shortcomings in the administration of the Church, which by the 14th century had become a major landowner and political player all over the Continent. But in addition to criticizing things such as the sale of indulgences or the abuse of clerical power, Luther eventually attacked basic doctrine and the organization of the Church as it had evolved over the centuries. He found his first religious adherents among the faithful who were looking for a more compelling and involving religious practice than Latin rituals dominated by a priestly hierarchy. He found his political support among nobles and monarchs who resented church influence and papal meddling in their political and dynastic affairs.

The Movement Accelerates

His success emboldened other reformers, many more radical than he, including Huldrych Zwingli, John Calvin, and John Knox. These reformers quarreled with Luther and with each other, while a whole series of political, economic and social movements either grew out of their doctrines or fastened themselves upon them.

Germany was the site of the first disorders associated with this religious reform, including the Peasant Rebellion of 1524–25 (which Luther opposed and urged be put down with great severity.) Protestantism also gained a foothold in the Netherlands and northern France, where in 1572 the massacre of thousands of Protestants in Paris occurred on the feast of St. Bartholomew. Much of northern Europe eventually ended up in the Protestant camp, while Italy and Spain remained bastions of orthodoxy and founts of the Counter-Reformation.

16th Century Realpolitik

Spain, conquered by the Moors in the eighth century, had spent centuries reasserting its European roots, uniting under the reign of Ferdinand and Isabella, whose support for Columbus's voyages paid a remarkable return. Thanks in large part to those voyages and Spain's conquests in the New World, the central economic fact of the 16th century was the rise of Spain from a minor player on the European continent to a major force, based in part on the gold and silver that flooded into Spain from the mines of Mexico and Peru.

By the late 16th century, the ruler of Spain was Philip II, who because of his Hapsburg family ties, had also inherited control of the Netherlands. While Spain was the leading maritime power of its

Martin Luther

Philip II

supplant Elizabeth as Queen, he vowed to return England to the Catholic fold by sponsoring the largest invasion yet attempted.

The Armada

Spain had helped lead the Christian forces in one of the largest and most successful naval encounter of the period, the Battle of Lepanto in 1571, when Europe broke the naval power in the Mediterranean of the Ottoman sultan. Spanish successes there, along with the experience of its ocean sailors and the size and armament of its fleet, made the Armada a real threat to the future of England as an independent and Protestant country. But despite its overwhelming numerical superiority, the invasion suffered from a number of tactical weaknesses. The plan was for the Armada to sail from the Atlantic ports and come together at anchor in the English Channel while the 30,000 troops of the Duke of Parma in the Netherlands were ferried to the ships in small boats.

But the plan foundered on a combination of bad weather, the superior sailing skill of the English, who managed to get upwind of the Armada (a decisive tactical advantage in the age of sail) and the longer and more accurate gunnery of the English.

The English fleet proved its superiority at the battle of Gravelines in the English Channel in 1588. The English sent in fireships, which broke the Spanish formation, and hammered the Spanish with superior long-range cannon fire. Eventually the surviving Spanish ships fled to the north, forcing

day, its treasure fleets often fell prey to English sailors (the line between piracy and war was ill-defined). Philip was also a stalwart of Catholic orthodoxy, alarmed at England's drift into Protestantism.

When Protestant rebels in the Netherlands received English aid, his displeasure with the English turned to anger. After Mary, Queen of Scots, was executed for her role in Catholic plots to

them to go all the way around the British Isles in the North Sea before trying to make their way back to Spain.

Fewer than half the Armada returned to Spain, and many of the ships were damaged beyond repair. Thousands of Spanish sailors were lost to the battle or to the hazards of the return journey.

The Source of English Protestantism

England's conversion to Protestantism had begun not as a doctrinal dispute but as a jurisdictional problem. King Henry VIII, whose marriage to Katherine of Aragon had produced no surviving sons, was anxious to produce a male heir, in part to avoid the kind of dynastic struggle that had led to the Wars of the Roses (see pages 118 and 122–24).

He had originally married Katherine, the widow of his older brother, on the basis of a papal dispensation. He sought to reverse that dispensation, effectively annulling the marriage. While such an accommodation to a ruling house was not uncommon at the time, other political issues intervened. The pope had no desire to offend Katherine's uncle, the Holy Roman Emperor, and failed to rule on Henry's request. Henry took matters into his own hands and declared himself in 1534 head of the Church of England.

His reforms were relatively modest, including introducing more English into services and suppressing the monasteries, confiscating their extensive properties. He prosecuted not only Catholics who refused to countenance his takeover of the English church, but also Lutherans who sought more extensive reforms. His break with Rome enabled him to marry Anne Boleyn, a union which produced the future Queen Elizabeth, though Anne herself was executed a few years later.

Henry's marital saga is too extensive to go into here, but his liaisons produced one son, Edward, who succeeded in 1547 to the throne, encouraged the growth of Protestantism, and died in 1553; Elizabeth's half-sister, Mary, daughter of Katherine of Aragon, who ruled for five years and is known as Bloody Mary for her attempts to suppress Protestantism by executing many of its leading adherents; and Elizabeth herself.

Her Royal Highness

Elizabeth came to the throne in 1558. She was well educated by the standards of the time, particularly for a woman. She had been reared a Protestant, although she had concealed that fact under a veil of orthodoxy during Mary's reign. Although her Protestantism was by all accounts genuine, she was more concerned with a stable and prosperous nation than with "opening a window into men's consciences." She made sure that leading figures of the state and church were religiously reliable, but probably the great

Queen Elizabeth borne in her palanquin

mass of commoners, along with many gentry, remained Catholic in their hearts if not in their practice.

As Queen, Elizabeth fined Catholics who refused to attend services of the official church (recusants), but there was no widespread persecution of those who clung to the old faith, and Elizabeth tried to ensure that services and prayers were conducted in a way that both Catholics and Protestants could in good conscience attend. Particularly in the north of England, many important families remained Catholic, and at the same time there was a very vocal and determined minority across the country who felt that the religious reforms instituted by both her father and Elizabeth herself did not go far enough.

To the extent these were private views, Elizabeth remained unconcerned. Only when such views threatened her reign did she act, including her execution of some Jesuits smuggled into England from France, presumably in an effort to destabilize her monarchy and install her cousin Mary on the throne.

England's Religious Factions

Meanwhile, as on the Continent, the English reform movement was splitting into various camps along doctrinal and jurisdictional lines. A significant splinter group was the Puritans, who sought to minimize or eliminate many of the ritual and doctrinal elements remaining in the English Protestant church. (Puritans played a significant role in the founding of the English colony at Jamestown in Virginia in 1607, and it was a Puritan congregation—one that had left England for the more reliably Protestant Holland in 1607—that took ship on the *Mayflower* in 1620 for Massachusetts Bay.)

Many devoted adherents of both the old and new faiths no doubt felt ill-served by Elizabeth's moderate course. But the fact is that while on the Continent thousands died in massacres and wars fomented by religious discord, or eventually the depredations of the Inquisition, England was generally spared these fatal turmoils, at least on the scale experienced elsewhere.

Shakespeare's Attitude

There is much debate over Shakespeare's own religious views (or lack of them). His father was fined for recusancy, although there is evidence he refused to attend church not out of sectarian loyalty but because he was trying to avoid debt collectors. His extended family also included prominent adherents of the old religion. But Shakespeare's actual practice of religion appears to have elicited no undue attention from the authorities. Nor do his plays deal in any serious ways with this great issue that absorbed so much of the nation's attention. In some plays, priests perform their sacramental function—such as the priest who marries Romeo and Juliet. Churchmen also appear in the history plays, but their roles reflect the power and influence of their official positions and the issues they deal with are political, not religious.

In *Henry V* leading churchmen scheme to give the king the legal justification to invade France, and promise him large sums from the Church treasury. Their motive is to forestall other official levies on Church property. The Bishop of Winchester is one of the many power-mad schemers in *Henry VI, Part Two*, while Cardinal Wolsey is a leading character in the drama of *Henry VIII*, and a representative from the pope is a supporting player, as is Cardinal Pandulph in *King John*. One of the few who acts honorably in the exercise of his office is the Bishop of Carlisle in *Richard II*, who predicts dire results from the deposition of the anointed king.

But religion itself, or the disputes around it, are not a major feature of the plays. Shakespeare's company, purveyors of popular entertainment, no doubt saw little to gain from taking sides in these matters, and had little desire to incur the kind of official displeasure that could close down their operations—although they would have had little to lose by publicly disparaging the Puritans, who found the theater too ungodly to attend under any circumstances, and were active voices seeking its suppression.

The Virgin Queen

Like a modern politician, Elizabeth was highly conscious of her image as the leader of her country and her court as an expression of her ascendancy. Though known for her thrift, she owned a vast wardrobe, and her court entertainments included both music and drama at a time when England's were regarded as among the best in Europe. Whatever her religion, she was a potential marital prize for any of Europe's leading families

and royal households, and she was pursued relentlessly by players on both sides of the the religious divide (not to mention by domestic candidates). It is a measure of her diplomatic skills that in decades of on-again, off-again deliberations, she encouraged, then discouraged one party after another, including Spain's Philip II, who had been married to her predecessor on the throne. Most authorities now believe she never seriously intended to dilute her power by marrying.

The defeat of the Armada marked a high point not just for Elizabeth's reign, but for the Tudor dynasty. Demonstrating her fitness to rule in dangerous times, Elizabeth appointed her leading officers to plan the defense, then abandoned the safety of her palace. She rode to the South of England, exhorted her troops in person, and behaved like a strong and capable monarch.

The Armada, along with continuing Spanish threats, helped fuel a wave of xenophobia in England, reflected in part in Shakespeare's early plays (although the foreign power in those historical dramas was France, England's Cont-inental adversary in the 14th and 15th centuries). Philip II died in 1598, and was succeeded by his son, Philip III. Elizabeth, though clearly in decline, lasted until 1603, at seventy having outlived most of her early critics and presided over a nation whose naval power had become a principal geopolitical factor in Europe. It was under her leadership that the nation's domestic economy was bolstered by extensive exploration and new trading links forged under the protection of that navy. Among these were the East India Company and the Virginia Company, joint-stock entities that were keystones in the foundation of Britain's eventual overseas empire, which would far surpass that of 16th century Spain.

KING HENRY VI, PART ONE

JOAN OF ARC RALLIES THE FRENCH, BOY KING CANNOT DO SAME FOR THE ENGLISH

Period

15th century

Settings

England and France

The previous play ended with the Dukes of Bedford, Gloucester, and Exeter (the brothers of Henry V) with him in France, where Henry V's marriage to Katharine of France is proclaimed. This play opens with the same characters, this time following Henry V's coffin into Westminster Abbey.

While the King's brothers bemoan his death (of disease while on campaign, although the play does not specify), a parade of bad news stuns the English. Messengers bring news of the loss of Guienne, Champagne and other English holdings in France, and the wounding and capture of Lord Talbot, the senior English commander there. The Duke of Bedford, regent of France, vows to restore English power.

But the scene shifts to France, and in flashback we see the French campaign to dislodge the English from Orleans. It is unsuccessful until Joan La Pucelle (Joan of Arc) is introduced to Charles, the heir to the French throne (the Dauphin), and bests him in single combat. Assigned by God "to be the English scourge," she effectively takes command of the French forces. She duels with the renowned Lord Talbot, fights him to a draw, and leads her troops into the city ("A witch, by fear, not force...drives back our troops," Talbot complains).

In England, the civil strife that forms a major subtext of the play becomes clear as the Duke of Gloucester is denied entrance to the Tower of London by the Bishop of Winchester. Their retainers come to blows, and the riot is broken up only by the intervention of the lord mayor of London.

The scene switches to France again, this time Talbot and company reclaiming Orleans from Joan and the French, while Talbot, invited to dine with a

French lady, sees through her stratagem to have him captured.

Well into the play, Shakespeare offers two scenes that frame the issues for much of the material for his historical series set around the Wars of the Roses. In a scene set in the garden outside the law courts he has Richard Plantagenet (of the House of York) disputing with the Earl of Somerset (of the House of Lancaster) on a point of law. While the question they are debating is never mentioned, it is clear that the real matter is their competitiveness as rival claimants to the throne. They and their sympathizers—for York the Earl of Warwick and Sir Richard Vernon, for Lancaster the Earl of Suffolk—each pluck a rose, the Yorkists choosing white and the Lancastrians red.

Richard Plantagenet then meets in the Tower of London with his dying uncle, Edmund Mortimer, who has been imprisoned for years because of an attempt by his partisans to put him on the throne. In the last play, as Henry V was about to embark for France, he uncovered a plot and executed three ringleaders.

One of those ringleaders was the Earl of Cambridge, the brother-in-law of this imprisoned Mortimer. "Thus the Mortimers, in whom the title rested, were suppressed," sighs Mortimer to Plantagenet. The rebellious motives of the Earl of Cambridge included not just the promotion of his brother-in-law, but the restoration of the legitimate line from the deposed Richard II. The next in line for the throne after the childless

Joan of Arc

173

Mortimer would be the Earl of Cambridge's son—the Richard Plantagenet who stands before his dying uncle.

In a clear attempt to heal the scars of civil conflict, Henry VI restores Richard Plantagenet to his estates, and even names him Duke of York. But the action comes after a scene of different civil discord at Court, where the retainers of the Bishop of Winchester and the Duke of Gloucester come once again to blows and subside only at the king's plea. Exeter sees the falsity of their reconciliation: "This late dissension grown betwixt the peers burns under feigned ashes of forged love."

Back in France, Joan and the French take Rouen only to lose it almost immediately to Talbot and the English. But as Talbot leaves the city for Paris for the coronation there of Henry VI, Joan manages to separate the Duke of Burgundy from his English allies and persuades him to come over to the side of the Dauphin. Burgundy's decision proves decisive. Talbot attempts to take Bordeaux (his threats to the city fathers of "lean famine, quartering steel and climbing fire" if the city does not surrender echo Chorus's "famine, sword and fire" in the Prologue to *Henry V*). But he is surrounded by French forces. Joined by his son, who refuses to leave his side, Talbot is overcome because confusion and mismanagement among the English—including the new Duke of York and his rival, the Earl of Somerset—prevent him from being reinforced. Military fortunes switch again, this time before the French town of Angers, where the French are defeated and Joan is captured and eventually burned to death by the English.

Meanwhile, as the French and English conclude a truce in which neither side has much confidence, final plot lines anticipate problems in later plays. The Bishop of Winchester, Gloucester's foe, appears before the king in the habit of a cardinal, as the pope has appointed him. In an aside he pledges not "to be inferior to the proudest peer." In France, the Earl of Suffolk has captured Margaret, daughter of one of the French lords he has been fighting, the Duke of Anjou. Besotted by her beauty but ever with an eye to the main chance, Suffolk woos her not for himself but for the king, and eventually persuades King Henry VI to choose her as his queen.

Likely Source of the Plot

Holinshed's *Chronicles of England* was Shakespeare's general source, although he telescoped the action and made other changes to dramatize the story. However compelling the play, the demands of the dramatic form thus make *Henry VI* an unreliable guide to the actual history of the period. Henry VI was a child when his father died, though the play soon has him in an adult role. In the play, English losses on the Continent follow closely on one another. In reality, it took decades of campaigning to drive the English out of most of their French possessions. While some areas like Poitiers were lost shortly after Henry V's death in 1422, it was not until mid-century that the French reclaimed Guienne and Rouen. And whereas the overall pattern of English fortunes is accurate, the details are often at variance with the facts. For example, the play has Burgundy changing sides thanks to Joan of Arc's persuasion; in reality he switched well after her death. Never was Margaret of Anjou the prisoner of Suffolk or any other English noble before she became queen. And there is no historical basis for the Temple Garden scene, where adherents of York and Lancaster choose white and red roses to mark their loyalties.

Notable Features

Joan La Pucelle, or Joan of Arc as we know her, enjoys a generally favorable reputation today as a fighter for her people. But to the English of Shakespeare's time she was an enemy, a liar, a harlot, and a witch. In Shakespeare's play she displays a good deal of martial spirit ("Fight to the last gasp," is her line), but she confirms the English charge of witchcraft by meeting with fiends from hell, who refuse to offer her aid. When facing her death she denies the truth of her peasant upbringing (in the face of her shepherd father), claims first to be a virgin, then to be pregnant by a variety of men. The Duke of York's disdain for her ("Thou foul accursed minister of hell") goes far beyond his attitude toward his male French enemies. And Joan's calling out of the spirits, complete with peals of thunder and her reminder of "where I was wont to feed you with my blood," anticipates many of the scenes of demons and ghosts in later Shakespeare plays.

Some of Shakespeare's plays, particularly his later works, have a contemplative quality. *Henry VI, Part One*, however, provides constant opportunities for the "alarums and excursions"—groups of armed and armored men sweeping back and forth across the stage—that entertained Elizabethan audiences.

There is a battle scene before Orleans, where the English push back the French; Joan fights the Dauphin to demonstrate her soldierly qualities; the retainers of Gloucester and the Bishop of Winchester brawl before the Tower of London; a French cannon shot kills the Earl of Salisbury; Joan and Talbot fight to a draw as part of another skirmish, once again before Orleans, this time with the French winning the town; Talbot and the English turn them out again in the next scene;

Gloucester's and the bishop's men riot again, this time before Parliament; the French capture Rouen, then lose it to Talbot in the next scene; Talbot attempts to take Bordeaux, but in a long battle scene is surrounded and slain, along with his son and many other English soldiers.

"She is beautiful and therefore to be wooed; she is a woman, therefore to be won" is Suffolk's aside about Margaret, daughter of the French Duke of Anjou. Shakespeare liked the line so much he relied on a variant in *Richard III* ("Was ever woman in such humour wooed...") and in *Titus Andronicus*.

Notable Productions and Performances

Henry VI, Part One, is sometimes combined with parts two and three in a cycle of production, telescoping the three plays into two. The BBC-TV version produced by Jonathan Miller has a very memorable Talbot in Trevor Peacock.

KING HENRY VI, PART TWO

QUARRELING NOBLES
SPARK CIVIL WAR

Period

15th century

Setting

England

As *Henry VI, Part Two,* begins, the English have all but lost France. And into their midst comes a new queen, Margaret, the daughter of one of the French nobles whom they have been fighting. Adding insult to injury, she comes not with the usual dowry but at the price of Anjou and Maine, two of the contested regions of France that Henry VI ceded to her father in return for her.

First among the unhappy nobles is Henry's uncle, the Duke of Gloucester, Protector of the Realm. ("Shameful is this league...fatal this marriage..."). And while all but the Duke of Suffolk, who arranged the marriage, agree with Gloucester, their unease serves not to bind them together but helps split them

into warring camps. In one is Gloucester, first peer of the realm; in another the queen and Suffolk, the man who brought her to England; still another is Gloucester's adversary, Cardinal Beaufort, the Bishop of Winchester; another group is headed by York, not the least grateful that the king has forgiven his father's treason and elevated him to the status of duke. There is also the Duke of Somerset, who has hated York since their quarrel in the Temple Garden in the previous play and their reciprocal blame for military disasters in France; the Duke of Buckingham, a man whose most sincere emotion is ambition; and the Earls of Salisbury and Warwick.

The only thing all the conspirators can agree on is the necessity of getting rid of Gloucester. Their opportunity presents itself in the ambition of Gloucester's wife, Eleanor. ("She sweeps it through the court with troops of ladies, more like an empress than Duke Humphrey's wife. Strangers in court do take her for the Queen," the unhappy real queen observes.) Eleanor has asked a priest to set up a kind of seance with a witch to foretell the future. The priest, however, is an agent of Suffolk and the cardinal.

The witch calls forth a spirit, which gives ambiguous answers to questions about the fate of the king and other characters. But the seance is interrupted by York and Buckingham and their guards, who take the party into custody, including Gloucester's wife. Gloucester is all but undone by the news of his wife's arrest.

York persuades Salisbury and Warwick of the justice of his claim to the

tenced to death, while Gloucester's wife is banished to the Isle of Man, but not before predicting to Gloucester that the conspirators are preparing his death. He, of course, refuses to believe it. "All these could not procure me any scathe, so long as I am loyal, true and crimeless."

At Parliament, the queen gives the king a lecture about Gloucester's alleged ambition. "With what majesty he bears himself...he is near you in descent, and, should you fall, he is the next will mount...by flattery he hath won the commons' hearts...." The rest of the conspirators join in, Suffolk raising the issue of his wife's consorting with witch-

Elizabethan lawyers arguing a case

throne, and accepts their allegiance. But he cautions them to show no sign, but rather to "Wink at the Duke of Suffolk's insolence, at Beaufort's pride, at Somerset's ambition, at Buckingham and all the crew of them," until Gloucester's downfall is complete.

The witch and the priests are sen-

es, the cardinal questioning his legal judgment, York accusing him of diverting to his own use tax money meant for English soldiers in France.

Gloucester denies it all, and while the king believes him, he refuses to overrule his arrest and trial. After the king leaves in grief, the conspirators decide to make sure that Gloucester dies before he can be tried. Their unity is already breaking up under the antagonism between York and Somerset when news comes of a rebellion in Ireland. It falls to York to deal with the rebellion, and he muses to himself that by choosing him to put down the rebellion his co-conspirators have undone themselves (" 'Twas men I lacked, and you will give them me...whiles I in Ireland nourish a mighty band, I will stir up in England some black storm"). The assassins hired by Suffolk report to him their successful murder of Gloucester. When the king arrives Suffolk tells him Gloucester has died in his bed. The king is inconsolable, while the queen is offended by the depth of the king's grief. Warwick arrives with members of the Commons and determines from the evidence ("his face is black and full of blood, his eyeballs further out than when he lived.") that Gloucester was strangled.

Warwick and the Commons accuse Suffolk, and the Commons threaten to break into the palace and execute him unless the king orders him either to death or banishment. The king agrees to his banishment, despite the queen's protestations. Cardinal Beaufort dies raving. "So bad a death argues a monstrous life," Warwick observes.

Suffolk, kidnapped by pirates as he goes into exile, is murdered by them, though he disputes their right to kill him ("It is impossible that I should die by such a lowly vassal as thyself").

York returns in arms from Ireland, but agrees to dismiss his army when Buckingham assures him that his foe, Somerset, has been confined to the Tower by the king. When he discovers that in fact Somerset is at liberty, York declares to Henry "thou art not King, not fit to govern and rule multitudes... that head of thine doth not become a crown...thou shalt rule no more o'er him whom Heaven created for thy ruler."

Warwick and Salisbury having declared for York, they join him in the first engagement of the Wars of the Roses, the battle of St. Alban's. York kills Clifford (the elder), while York's son Richard kills Somerset. But the king and queen escape and head for London.

Likely Source of the Plot

Holinshed's *Chronicles of England* was the principal source of the story. While there may be some question of just how blameless the character of the Duke of Gloucester was in real life, his virtues in the play provide a dramatic counterbalance to the schemes of the other players in the drama. There were rumors after his death that he had been smothered, but the official cause of death was a stroke, a finding not contradicted by the evidence.

Gloucester's wife was banished for consorting with witches, but it was well before Queen Margaret arrived in England. And there is no real evidence of a romantic relationship between Suffolk and Queen Margaret, who were far apart in age.

Notable Features

One feature in this play is the rebellion of Jack Cade, who leads an army of artisans and peasants to London demanding free food and drink for all and property held in common. Their riots and rebellions provide plenty of opportunity for stage mayhem that Elizabethan audiences enjoyed. "The first thing we do, let's kill all the lawyers," Cade's followers cry, including in that fatal category anyone who can read and write. Cade's forces triumph in a battle against forces led by Sir Humphrey Stafford and threaten London. Buckingham and Clifford confront Cade and his army, offering the king's pardon to any and all who abandon Cade and return to their homes. The mob sways first one way, then the other, and finally—after Clifford has invoked the victories of Henry V—turns on Cade, who flees and is eventually slain by a householder whose garden he invades.

There are also several painful scenes of leave-taking. Gloucester tries to intercede with his wife's jailers ("use her well; the world may laugh again; and I may live to do you kindness if you do it her") but does not say good-bye to her ("Witness my tears, I cannot stay to speak.") The Duke of Suffolk, banished by the king, takes his farewell of the queen. "Give me thy hand, that I may dew it with my mournful tears;" says she. He replies, "For where thou art, there is the world itself . . . and where art not, desolation . . . live thou to joy thy life; myself no joy in nought but that thou livest."

What makes their emotion so remarkable (and so ironic) is that they have just colluded in the slander and murder of the Duke of Gloucester, the play's most selfless and admirable character.

Notable Productions and Performances

Thought to have been written in the early 1590s, some experts believe *Henry VI, Part Two*, to be the first of Shakespeare's histories. Titles of early printed editions refer to "the Contentions" between the houses or York and Lancaster, and the plays are sometimes thus known as the "contention" plays. Given their relatively continuous story, they are often produced as part of a series. Jonathan Miller's *Time-Life*/BBC production includes David Burke as Gloucester and Trevor Peacock (who was the noble English warrior Talbot in *Part One*) as the rebel Jack Cade.

Although *Henry VI, Part One*, has battle scenes to keep the audience interested, the BBC production of *Part Two* effectively captures the alternate tack that Shakespeare takes in this play—the contrast of normal, everyday characters and their conflicts against that of court intrigues. In one scene Peter, an apprentice armorer, accuses Horner, his master, of having said that the Duke of York is the rightful King of England. They are ordered to fight to establish who is telling the truth. Peter, drunk and terrified but supported by a crowd of cheering apprentices, manages to overcome Horner, who confesses to treason before he dies. In another, a man named Saunder Simpcox claims to have been cured of congenital blindness at St. Alban's shrine, a claim disproved by Gloucester, who sends the miscreant scampering away, pursued by village officials.

KING HENRY VI, PART THREE

HOUSE OF YORK IS APPARENT VICTOR IN WARS OF THE ROSES

Period

15th century

Settings

England and France

As the previous play closed, the forces of the Duke of York had won the Battle of St. Alban's and the king and queen had fled to London. This play opens in the palace of Westminster, where the Duke of York and his partisans come together to celebrate their victory.

King Henry enters to find York in the chair of state. "Thou factious Duke of York, descend my throne...I am thy sovereign," says Henry. "I am thine," York replies, and their dialogue reprises Henry IV's usurpation, Henry V's military virtues, and the fact that it is the Yorkists who at the moment have the upper hand militarily. The compromise they reach is that Henry will continue to reign, but at his death York will succeed

him. The compromise is celebrated by all, except Queen Margaret when she arrives, accompanied by their son. Unimpressed by King Henry's excuse that York and his forces made him do it, ("thou preferest thy life before thine honour," she remarks), she takes the boy and departs to raise an army among the northern lords in order to restore the rights of Henry and their son. The duke agrees and gives orders for the raising of forces, but the news of the queen's arrival with an army disturbs their discussion. In the field Clifford, still enraged by his father's death at the hands of the Yorkists, comes upon the Earl of Rutland, youngest of York's children and no more than a child. Despite the unarmed Rutland's pleas, Clifford ("Thy father slew my father; therefore die") kills him.

Later York, alone, encounters Queen Margaret and the leadership of her forces. He offers to fight, but they capture him, and taunt him with a paper crown upon his head and with the news that his youngest son has been murdered by Clifford. "That face of his the hungry cannibals would not have touched," York says, and describes Margaret as a "tiger's heart wrapped in a woman's hide." Even Northumberland is moved to pity by York's suffering at the news of his son's death. "Think but upon the wrong he did us all," Queen Margaret says, before stabbing York and ordering his head stuck on the gates of the neighboring city, "So York may overlook the town of York."

York's sons, Edward and Richard, are brought the news of their father's death, and then of the loss of another battle at St. Alban's, this time a force led by Warwick routed by the queen and her allies. Despite these losses, York's son Edward, now claiming the title of duke and the crown as well, meets the forces of Margaret and King Henry outside of York.

This time the Yorkists win the day. As the battle ends Edward, Richard, and Warwick come upon Clifford. In a dramatic counterpoint to the Queen and Clifford's tormenting of York they try to humiliate Clifford. Unfortunately for them he is already dead, and they have to settle for replacing York's head on the city gates with Clifford's. The victorious Edward and his Yorkist forces proceed to London; Margaret flees for France, and Henry for Scotland, though he later steals back into England "to greet my own land with my wishful sight." He is recognized and captured by two gamekeepers.

In London, Edward, now King Edward IV, is much taken with the widow Lady Elizabeth Grey, whose husband died fighting on the Lancastrian side at St. Alban's, and who seeks the return of her seized estates. Edward proposes to make her his mistress, an offer she chastely refuses, but she succumbs to his offer to make her the queen.

Warwick, meanwhile, has gone to France to seek the sister of the French king as Edward's wife. At the court he encounters Queen Margaret lobbying the French to take the part of King Henry. Given the obvious political advantages of forging a link with the sitting King of England (rather than the one in exile), the French are disposed toward Warwick's suit. But their discussions are interrupted by word that Edward has married Lady Grey. Outraged by this insult, the French embrace the cause of King Henry; equally outraged, so does Warwick, and even pledges his daughter in marriage to Prince Edward, the son of King Henry and Queen Margaret. Remarks Warwick of his former ally, King Edward, "I was the chief that raised him to the crown, and I'll be the chief to bring him down again."

Back in England the new king's brothers are also offended that he has turned his back on a critical alliance with France to marry Lady Grey. George, who is to marry Warwick's other daughter, abandons his brother the king and joins Warwick's forces. Richard remains at Edward's side, though he remarks to the audience "not for the love of Edward, but the crown."

It is once again the Lancastrians' turn to win. In the first battle of the new alliance, Warwick and George capture Edward, then proceed to London to recrown King Henry. Henry, saying "although my head still wears the crown," resigns the government to Warwick and proposes "I myself will lead a private life, and in devotion spend my latter days." Edward, however, aided by Richard, escapes. In the bishop's palace in London, the newly recrowned King Henry urges the Lancastrians to raise an army to resist Edward and Richard. But they arrive before Henry's allies can organize and capture him once more.

The Lancastrians now face reverse after reverse. Warwick holds the city of Coventry as his allies gather and the Yorkists draw near. Oxford and Montague join their forces to his, but George, when he arrives, switches sides back to the Yorkists and his "brother and the lawful King." In battle Warwick is wounded, and dies talking of "my parks, my walks, my manors that I had, even now forsake me...live how we can, yet die we must," (he was one of the richest men in England).

At Tewkesbury Queen Margaret tries to hearten her troops despite the Lancastrians' losses and Warwick's death. "Great men ne'er sit and wail their loss, but cheerly seek to redress their harms." But despite Margaret's spirit, the Yorkists triumph. Margaret and her son, Prince Edward, are cap-

tured. The young prince, undaunted by his loss and peril, talks to his captors as if *he* has captured *them*, accusing them of usurping "my father's right and mine." Edward and Richard kill him before Queen Margaret's eyes, then Richard hastens to London. He comes to King Henry in the Tower. King Henry, if not warlike certainly brave and fully aware of why Richard has come, predicts that "many a thousand...shall rue the hour that ever thou wast born," before Richard stabs him. "Clarence, thy turn is next, and then the rest," Richard says for the ears only of the audience.

Yet again installed in power, "Once more we sit in England's royal throne," says King Edward, "having my country's peace, and my brother's loves...here, I hope, begins our lasting joy." The audience, of course, knows otherwise.

Likely Source of the Plot

Holinshed's *Chronicles of England* was the source of much of the story. The action is greatly telescoped, and thus the play is not a good guide to the actual history of the conflict. Richard was a child during most of the early years and took no part in the first battles of the Wars of the Roses. Rutland, cast as a boy, was actually seventeen when he was killed. Although the Duke of York was killed and his head impaled on the walls of York, it was not by Queen Margaret, who was in Scotland at the time.

The second battle of St. Alban's was not a clear-cut Yorkist victory; their greatest triumph was at the battle of Towton some weeks later. King Henry's wandering—actually in England not Scotland—came after yet another battle. The young Prince Edward, son of Henry VI and Margaret, was killed during or after the battle of Tewkesbury, but not before his mother's eyes.

Notable Features

In the previous play, Richard of York (later to be Richard III) was portrayed primarily as a soldier. Two scenes in this play establish his character. In one Richard, his brother the Duke of York, and the Marquess of Montague debate the legitimacy of the oath that the duke has taken to set aside his claim to the throne until King Henry's death. Richard's view is that since the oath was not taken before a magistrate it is not binding, and, in any case, "I would break a thousand oaths to reign one year."

In a later soliloquy, Richard ponders his physical deformity. "Am I man then to be lov'd?... Since this earth affords no joy to me but to command...I'll make my heaven to dream upon the crown." To free himself from the torment of desiring the kingship, "I can smile, and murder whiles I smile...frame my face to all occasions...and set the murderous Machiavel to school."

In *King John* the pleadings of young Arthur, the competing claimant to the throne, soften the heart of his potential killer. In *Henry VI, Part Three*, Rutland's similar pleas for his life fall on deaf ears.

King Henry is prevailed upon to leave the fighting to others ("The Queen hath best success when you are absent," Clifford tells him). Alone away from the battle, Henry remarks that the homely life of a shepherd, including his sleep "under a fresh tree's shade," is much the superior to that of a monarch "his body

couched in a curious bed, when Care, Mistrust and Treason waits on him." These musings are echoed in *Henry IV* and *Henry V*.

In this play and elsewhere, Shakespeare is unsparing in his criticism of civil conflict. He itemizes two reasons for the conflict. Edward accuses Margaret of fomenting the unrest. "For what hath broached this tumult but thy pride? Hads't thou been meek, our title still had slept; and we, in pity of the gentle King, had slipped our claims until another age."

The dying Clifford, however, is inclined more to blame the king for whom he has fought. "And Henry, hadst thou swayed as kings should do, as thy father and his father did, giving no ground unto the House of York...thou this day hath kept thy chair in peace, for...what makes robbers bold but too much lenity?"

As King Henry awaits the outcome of a battle, the stage is taken over by a son that has killed his father, not realizing he was in the opposing forces; he is succeeded by a father who in similar circumstances has killed his son. "Erroneous, mutinous and unnatural," is how the father describes this civil war.

Notable Productions and Performances

As mentioned previously, *Part Three* is often produced in conjunction with *Part Two*, and also *Part One*. The *Time-Life*/BBC production stars Julia Foster as Queen Margaret, Peter Benson as Henry VI, Bernard Hill as the Duke of York, and Brian Proetheroe as York's son Edward, later Edward IV.

Shakespeare in the Garden

ubbed "the Poet of Nature," some scholars believe that Shakespeare may have been a student of botany or had close association with gardeners in his life.

Beware the Untended

To stray from the ordered path in life is to risk meeting the prickly and unexpected. In a light-hearted exchange from *As You Like It*, Rosalind frets about briars, while Celia shrugs at the burs.

*Rosalind: O, how full of briars is this
    working-day world!*
*Celia: They are but burs, cousin, thrown
    upon thee in holiday foolery; if we
    walk not in the trodden paths our
    very petticoats will catch them.*

Straying from the beaten path is more dangerous in *Henry VI, Part Three*. Richard muses about the murders he'll have to commit or arrange before he can become the king:

*And I—like one lost in a thorny wood
That rents the thorns and is rent
    with the thorns,
Seeking a way and straying from the way;
Not knowing how to find the open air,
But toiling desperately to find it out
Torment myself to catch the
    English crown;
And from that torment I will free myself
Or hew my way out with a bloody axe.*

Weeds most often represent what is unruly and unwanted. In *Hamlet*, Denmark, a country under the thumb of a drunk and murdering monarch, is compared to "an unweeded garden, / That grows to seed; things rank and gross in nature, / Possess it merely!" The prince, begging his mother to repent and change her wanton ways, warns her not to "lay the compost on the weeds to make them ranker."

There are lessons to be learned in Shakespeare's gardens. Neglect kills. Vigilance is vital. What is unhealthy or hurtful must be gotten rid of when it first appears in our lives. In *Henry VI*,

Elizabethan gardeners. The British Library

Part *Two*, the queen tries to convince the popular king that the Duke of Gloucester is planning a coup. They should act before Gloucester attracts more followers. She says:

Now 'tis the spring, and weeds are
    shallow-rooted;
Suffer them now, and they'll o'ergrow
    the garden
And choke the herbs for want of husbandry.

Cultivating Our Lives with Care

In *Othello,* Iago, villainous and manipulative, scoffs at a lovesick friend and proclaims the power of reason over raging emotions, comparing human will to a gardener, shaping a life, wisely or unwisely, capable of making choices:

'Tis in ourselves that we are thus or thus. Our bodies are our gardens to the which our wills are gardeners; so that if we will plant nettles or sow lettuce, set hyssop and weed up thyme, supply it with one gender of herbs or distract it with many, either to have it sterile with idleness or manured with industry—why, the power and corrigible authority of this lies in our wills.

Tended gardens reflect control and choice. On the other hand, a human life, no matter how intentionally shaped, is subject to predictable stages and to inevitable wear and tear of the seasons and the weather. In *Henry VIII,* when Cardinal Wolsey, the scheming and power-hungry adviser to the king, is finally brought low, stripped of status and possessions, he muses:

Farewell, a long farewell, to all my
*   greatness!*
This is the state of man: to-day he puts
*   forth*
The tender leaves of hopes; to-morrow
*   blossoms*
And bears his blushing honors thick
*   upon him;*
The third day comes a frost, a killing frost,
And when he thinks, good easy man, full
*   surely*
His greatness is a-ripening, nips his root,
And then he falls, as I do.

In *Cymbeline*, Belarius remembers being in King Cymbeline's court, and considers how he was framed, falsely accused, and sent into exile:

Then was I as a tree
Whose boughs did bend with fruit;
*   but in one night*
A storm, or robbery, call it what you will,
Shook down my mellow hangings, nay,
*   my leaves,*
And left me bare to weather.

In *Richard II*, the gardener, using as metaphor the beneficial pruning of fruit trees, laments that the king has not tended his dominion with as much care as his workers have tended the royal gardens:

We, at time of year
Do wound the bark, the skin of our
*   fruit trees,*
Lest, being over-proud in sap and blood,
With too much riches it confound itself:
Had he done so to great and growing
*   men,*
They might have liv'd to bear, and he to
*   taste*

Their fruits of duty. Superfluous
*   branches*
We lop away, that bearing boughs may
*   live;*
Had he done so, himself had borne the
*   crown,*
Which waste of idle hours hath quite
*   thrown down.*

A Plant for All Seasons— The Function of Foliage on Shakespeare's Stage

Shakespeare knew his greenery, the look of the plants, the lore and superstitions imposed on them.

In *Hamlet*, before she commits suicide, Ophelia distributes flowers.

There's rosemary; that's for remembrance; pray you, love, remember. And there is pansies, that's for thoughts.... There's fennel for you, and columbines. There's rue for you; and here's some for me. We may call it herb of grace a Sundays. O, you must wear your rue with a difference. There's a daisy. I would give you some violets, but they withered all when my father died.

Ophelia prepares herself for drowning by making a garland of wild flowers to wear in her hair. As the queen describes it, "Therewith fantastic garlands did she make / Of crowflowers, nettles, daisies, and long purples, / That liberal shepherds give a grosser name, / But our cold maids do dead men's fingers call them."

In *King Lear*, the monarch, "As mad as the vex'd sea, singing aloud," wanders the wilderness wearing a crown of wild flowers and weeds, "Crown'd with rank fumiter and furrow weeds, / With hardocks, hemlock, nettles, cuckoo-flowers, / Darnel, and all the idle weeds that grow / In our sustaining corn."

In Shakespeare's day, there were strong superstitions about the **mandrake** plant. It had a forked root that crudely resembled the lower half of the human body, and many believed it screamed or groaned when it was pulled from the ground. Anyone who actually heard a screaming mandrake would go mad or die. In *Romeo and Juliet*, the young lover is filled with foreboding as she prepares to drink the Friar's potion. Alone in her bedroom, Juliet worries first that it may actually kill her, then that she might awaken and find herself buried alive in the family crypt where she imagines she might hear "Shrieks like mandrakes torn out of the earth, / That living mortals, hearing them, run mad." In *Henry VI, Part Two*, Suffolk says,

Would curses kill, as doth the mandrake's groan,
I would invent as bitter searching terms,
As curst, as harsh, and horrible to hear.

There were superstitions, too, about **ferns.** It was believed that fern-seed held the power to render people invisible, and it was gathered on Midsummer Eve. A snatch of dialogue in *Henry IV, Part One*, reflects the old belief:

Gadshill: We have the receipt of fern-seed, we walk invisible.
Chamberlain: Nay, by my faith, I think you are more beholding to the night than to fern-seed for your walking invisible.

When Shakespeare wanted a symbol of virtue, elegance, dignity, or honorable ancestry, he sometimes used the image of a **cedar tree.** In *Henry VIII*, Archbishop Cranmer, in his long blessing on the royal infant Elizabeth, predicts she will bring "a thousand thousand blessings" and that her successor also will be a great ruler: "He shall flourish, / And, like a mountain cedar, reach his branches / To all the plains about him; our children's children / Shall see this, and bless heaven." Likewise, at the end of *Cymbeline*, a soothsayer predicts good fortune:

The lofty cedar, royal Cymbeline,
Personates thee; and thy lopp'd branches point
Thy two sons forth, who, by Belarius stol'n,
For many years thought dead, are now reviv'd,
To the majestic cedar join'd, whose issue
Promises Britain peace and plenty.

In *Titus Andronicus*, Titus says to his brother, "Marcus, we are but shrubs, no cedars we."

Another tree, the **cypress**, did not grow in Britain, but its hard black wood was used for coffins. In *Twelfth Night*, Feste the Clown sings a sad song, "Come away, come away, death, / And in sad cypress let me be laid." In *Henry VI, Part Two*, Suffolk curses his enemies and, though it sounds lovely, he's thinking about their deaths when he wishes, "Their sweetest shade, a grove of cypress trees!"

Aspens, too, provide a provocative image. According to one medieval legend, Jesus died on a cross made of aspen wood and it is because of this that the tree trembles, even when there is no breeze. According to another legend, Judas, the disciple who betrayed Jesus, hanged himself from an aspen tree, and ever since, the tree has trembled in shame. Perhaps Shakespeare knew these legends. In *Titus Andronicus*, Marcus finds his niece, Lavina, after she's been raped and mutilated. Her tongue has been ripped out and her hands cut off. His first image is that of a tree: "What stern ungentle hands / Hath lopp'd, and hew'd, and made thy body bare / Of her two branches...?" Then, he remembers that her hands had been beautiful. "O, had the monster seen those lily hands / Tremble like aspen leaves upon a lute / And make the silken strings delight to kiss them, / He would not then have touch'd them for his life!" At the other end of the emotional spectrum, in *Henry IV, Part Two*, Hostess Quickly, of the Boar's Head Tavern, has joined in some rowdy banter and gotten herself worked up. She loudly proclaims that she dislikes swaggering and swaggerers, to the extent that she doesn't even like the word "swagger." Then she says, "Feel, masters, how I shake: look you, I warrant you...Yea, in very truth, do I, an 'twere an aspen leaf. I cannot abide swagg'rers."

As far back as the psalmist's song in the Bible, "We hanged our harps upon the willows and there we wept..." **willow trees** have been symbols of sadness. Cultural tradition has made them especially meaningful for those disappointed in love. In *Othello*, shortly before Desdemona is murdered by her husband, she remembers that her mother's maid had been left by her lover.

She had a song of willow,
An old thing 'twas, but it express'd her
fortune,
And she died singing it: that song tonight
Will not go from my mind.

In *Hamlet*, Ophelia hangs some of her flowers on a willow tree before she wades into the brook to drown herself.

The **yew tree** was frequently found in churchyards and used at funerals. In *Romeo and Juliet*, Paris says,

Under yon yew trees lay thee all along,
Holding thine ear close to the hollow
ground;
So shall no foot upon the churchyard
tread,
Being loose, unfirm, with digging up of
graves,
But thou shalt hear it.

And in *Twelfth Night*, the lyrics of a song make reference to the custom of putting yew in a shroud:

My shroud of white, stuck all with yew,
O, prepare it!
My part of death, no one so true
Did share it.

The witches in *Macbeth* use "slips of yew" in the brew they mix in their cauldron.

The **rose** is a symbol of innocence and beauty. In *Richard III*, Tyrell, reporting that he has killed the two little princes as ordered, describes the scene: "Their lips were four red roses on a stalk, / And in their summer beauty kiss'd each other. / A book of prayers on their pillow lay." In *Othello*, just before he murders Desdemona, the Moor thinks of roses: "When I have plucked the rose, I cannot give it vital growth again, / It needs must wither."

Violets are the flowers of early death. In *Hamlet,* Laertes mourns the dead Ophelia saying, "Lay her in the earth: / And from her fair and unpolluted flesh / May violets spring."

Flowers bloom heralding spring after the long, cold season of woe in *The Winter's Tale*. Perdita, not yet aware she's of royal blood, greets those gathered at a sheep-shearing festival with a wild array of colorful blossoms. First she greets the older men with **rosemary**, a flower used to strengthen memory and traditionally used in weddings and funerals and at Christmas commemorating old friends.

Give me those flowers there, Dorcas.
Reverend sirs,
For you there's rosemary and rue; these keep
Seeming and savor all the winter long.
Grace and remembrance be to you both!
And welcome to our shearing.

There are more flowers to be given out, but Perdita is not impressed with the horticultural art of grafting:

The fairest flow'rs o' th' season
Are our carnations and streak'd gillyvors,
Which some call nature's bastards.
Of that kind
Our rustic garden's barren; and I care not
To get slips of them.

A virtual summer goddess, Perdita has more flowers:

Here's flowers for you:
Hot lavender, mints, savory, marjoram:

The marigold, that goes to bed with the sun,
And with him rises weeping...
   Daffodils, that come before the swallow dares, and take
The winds of March with beauty; violets, dim
But sweeter than the lids of Juno's eyes
Or Cytherea's breath; pale primroses,
That die unmarried ere they can behold
Bright Phoebus in his strength...bold oxlips, and
The crown-imperial; lilies of all kinds,
The flow'r-de-luce being one.

Greenery abounds too in *A Midsummer Night's Dream,* where young lovers romp in a wood ruled by fairies. One of the most beautiful passages is spoken by Oberon, the Fairy King:

I know a bank where the wild thyme blows,
Where oxlips and the nodding violet grows,
Quite over-canopied with luscious woodbine,
With sweet musk-roses, and with eglantine;
There sleeps Titania sometime of the night,
Lull'd in these flowers with dances and delight.

The Bard in Our Backyards

Around the world, modern botanic gardens feature Shakespeare gardens. Often, the boast is made that such a specialty garden contains all the flora mentioned in the plays of William Shakespeare.

A Shakespeare garden in Johannesburg, South Africa, includes a stage surrounded by sloping lawns on which spectators sit to watch dramatic performances.

In Paris, there is a garden of Shakespearean landscapes made with plants—the witches' moors from *Macbeth*, the woods from *A Midsummer Night's Dream*, the rocky inlets from *The Tempest*.

There are Shakespeare gardens in England, Canada, and in Japan, and throughout the United States. There are two in New York City. One is located in Central Park on the western slope leading up to Belvedere Castle. The other, a cozy English "cottage style" garden, is part of the Brooklyn Botanic Garden.

The Shakespeare garden at Golden Gate Park in San Francisco is a favorite spot for weddings. There are other gardens in Wichita, Kansas; Plainfield, New Jersey; Camden, Maine; Manteo, North Carolina; Tulsa, Oklahoma; and one in Portland, Oregon, which was founded in 1917. The Shakespeare garden in Montgomery, Alabama's Wynton M. Bount Cultural Park, features an amphitheater with rock-ledge seats for concerts and theatrical productions, and boasts an astonishing number of plants, including 8,000 narcissus bulbs, 570 rosemary and lavender plants, and 55 shade trees.

Sometimes the gardens are found on middle school, high school, or college grounds, usually as part a student project. Many are dedicated on April 23rd, Shakespeare's observed birth date. There are Shakespeare gardens at Kilgore College Campus in Texas and at the University of Tennessee at Chattanooga. A sculpture of the Bard overlooks the Shakespeare garden at the University of South Dakota. There are Shakespeare gardens at Northwestern University's Evanston campus and at Vassar and Purdue.

The Mountain Heritage High School in Burnsville, North Carolina, has a garden maintained by students. The school's Shakespeare Society cultivates the garden which was dedicated on April 23, 1998. Students from English, biology, art, carpentry, and agriculture classes participate in planning and planting, and provide ongoing care of the garden.

KING RICHARD III

MURDEROUS DESPOT CLAWS
HIS WAY TO POWER

Period

15th century

Setting

England

The play opens on the Yorkist triumph. Richard reflects in his opening soliloquy, that "all the clouds that lowered upon our house" are "in the deep bosom of the ocean buried." But while others (notably his brother, King Edward IV) have turned their martial skills to the arts of love, Richard is "rudely stamped...deformed, unfinished" and since he "cannot prove a lover...I am determined to prove a villain."

His career as such is well underway, and he itemizes for the audience how he has persuaded King Edward that their brother George, Duke of Clarence, has conspired against him. Then, as George passes by in custody on his way to the Tower, Richard blames the queen for

setting the king's mind against both of them, and promises to redeem him. As his brother is taken away, however, Richard muses for the audience's benefit, "Simple plain Clarence, I do love thee so that I will shortly send thy soul to heaven."

In the preceding play, Richard helped clear the Yorkist path to the throne by murdering an unarmed Henry VI in the Tower. Henry's daughter-in-law Lady Anne, widow of Henry's son (whom Richard also helped kill in the previous play) enters with bearers who bring Henry's body to be re-interred.

Since marrying Anne would strengthen Richard's own eventual claim to the throne, he has set his sights upon her, and in a memorable scene begs her forgiveness for his crimes, pledging his love and seeking her hand. "I'll have her, but I will not keep her long," he muses after she leaves, having at first described him as "villain" and "lump of foul deformity" but eventually saying that "much it joys me too to see you are become so penitent."

As King Edward's health deteriorates, Richard pretends to the queen that he has not been the source behind rumors and plots against herself and her family. At this point the old queen, Margaret, widow of Henry VI, enters with a bad word for just about everyone. To Elizabeth, who has replaced her as Queen, she says, "die neither mother, wife or England's Queen." For Richard, the principal target of her ire, she wishes that "the worm of conscience still begnaw they soul, thy friends suspect for traitors...and take deep traitors for they friends."

In the Tower, Clarence awakes from a terrifying dream of a watery death. "What a pain it was to drown, what sights of ugly death within my eyes." Asleep again, he wakes to find two murderers, whom he assumes have been sent by King Edward. He urges them to go to Richard, who he says will reward them for sparing him. " 'Tis he that sends us to destroy you here," they tell him, before stabbing him and then drowning him in a wine barrel.

King Edward in his final days tries to cure the dissension in his court. He brings together all the rival figures, including Richard, who allows that "I do not know that Englishman alive with whom my soul is any jot at odds." He relays the news of Clarence's death, which the king apparently had ordered and then reversed. "Some tardy cripple" carried the message that would have saved Clarence, Richard says.

The news of King Edward's eventual death, however expected, sends Queen Elizabeth into a state of "black despair." The Duchess of York, mother to Edward, George, and Richard, now has only Richard left, and she has no illusions about her only surviving son ("one false glass that grieves me when I see my shame in him.") But Elizabeth has two surviving sons from Edward, and the oldest is sent for to become king in his father's place. Richard, however, has other plans.

While the young man is on his way to London, Richard and his ally the Duke of Buckingham have the Queen's brothers taken into custody at Pomfret Castle. "I see the ruin of my house," says the prescient queen, while the Duchess of York, whose "husband lost his life to get the crown," now sees her family "make war upon themselves, brother to brother." Both flee to sanctuary, theoretically out of reach of civil law.

The young prince Edward arrives and Richard, as Protector, sends him and his brother to the Tower, ostensibly for their own protection. Meanwhile he sends an emissary to Lord Hastings, the Lord Chamberlain, to determine whether Hastings can be recruited to join the conspiracy to put Richard on the throne. As for Buckingham, Richard pledges, "when I am king, claim thou of me the earldom of Hereford and all the moveables whereof the King my brother was possessed." Hastings, despite being informed that Richard has seen that his internal enemies have been put to death at Pomfret Castle, refuses to join the conspiracy. The result is Richard's turning on him at a council meeting in the Tower—"Thou art a traitor. Off with his head."

Richard and Buckingham persuade the Lord Mayor of London that Hastings was plotting Richard's death. Buckingham is then sent to persuade

"The bloody dog is dead." The death of Richard III

the London officials that King Edward was in fact not the son of the Duke of York ("Yet touch this sparingly...you know my mother lives.") Despite their initial coolness to Richard's ambitions, eventually the Lord Mayor appears at Bayward Castle, where Richard has two prominent churchmen join him in a charade of piety. With Buckingham stage-mastering the performance, Richard at first refuses and then accepts the suit of the Mayor and Aldermen that he proclaim himself king.

Richard ascends the throne, and from it immediately confides his next concern to Buckingham. "Young Edward lives. Think now what I would speak." But Buckingham has had enough and balks at dispatching the dead king's sons. An angry Richard turns to Tyrell, "whose humble means match not his haughty spirit." As Richard outlines his concerns about the boys, "foes to my rest and my sweet sleep's disturbers," Tyrell promises, "soon I'll rid you from the fear of them." When Buckingham returns to claim the earldom that Richard has promised him, Richard dismisses him. "I am not in the giving vein today." Knowing trouble when he sees it, and recalling the death of Hastings, Buckingham flees.

"Oh God," Queen Elizabeth says on learning of the deaths of the princes in the Tower, "when didst thou sleep when such a deed was done?" Richard then reveals that his wife, Anne, has died, and determines that his next wife shall be the daughter of Queen Elizabeth by his dead brother Edward. Marriage to this princess, he reasons, would further confirm his claim on the throne.

Richard's unpopularity is growing, and his enemies have taken arms, with the Duke of Richmond coming by sea to claim the crown and Buckingham raising an army. But Buckingham's army is dispersed and he is shortly taken and executed, musing on how Queen Margaret's prophecies have come to pass. The forces of Henry Tudor, Duke of Richmond and claimant to the throne, meet those of King Richard at Bosworth Field. The night before the battle, the ghosts of Richard's victims—among them Henry VI, his son Prince Edward, Clarence, Hastings, the young Princess Anne, and finally Buckingham torment his sleep with maledictions, and offer encouragement to Richmond. "If I die, no soul will pity me," Richard reflects, in an uncharacteristic display of humanity. But the pressure of the nearing battle heartens him. "Let not our babbling dreams affright our souls...our strong arms be our conscience, swords our law."

Whatever his faults, Richard at least is brave. In the battle he is unhorsed, yet refuses to withdraw, calling "a horse, a horse, my kingdom for a horse" so that he can remount and find his enemy, the Duke of Richmond. Richmond finds Richard, however, and kills him. "The day is ours. The bloody dog is dead," he tells his followers, promising to fulfill his pledge to marry the Princess Elizabeth, and "unite the White Rose and the Red," ending the civil war. Richmond thus becomes Henry VII.

Likely Source of the Plot

The story is principally based on Holinshed's *Chronicles of England*, but Shakespeare also drew on the work of Sir Thomas More, written while many

Laurence Olivier as Richard III. Courtesy Museum of Modern Art/Film Stills Archive

fountain of murder and deceit. Some historians and other writers, notably the mystery author Josephine Tey in her book, *The Daughter of Time*, paint Richard as something less than noble but not as villainous as the play would have us believe.

Central to the dramatic picture of Richard is his misshapen figure, which serves as an outward manifestation of his twisted soul. Many historians believe he was a good deal less physically deformed than the play indicates, and contemporary portraits show him with little or no deformity (although it would not be unheard of for a portraitist to downplay such a physical problem, particularly for a royal patron.)

Notable Features

Given the bitterness of Lady Anne's reaction to the sight of Richard "dreadful minister of hell...foul devil...thy deeds inhuman and unnatural..." her submission to marriage with him is a problem in the dramatic structure of the play. But Elizabethan audiences were well aware of the changing alliances of the Wars of the Roses. In the previous plays Lord Warwick (Anne's father) had fought for both sides at various points, and the king's brother, George, had done so also; the current queen had first become a widow when her then husband was killed fighting her current husband's allies. Anne and the audience were also aware that while the Yorkists had killed innocent people, the Lancastrians had done so too, including Richard's unarmed teenage brother, Rutland, murdered by the Lancaster ally Lord Clifford.

participants in Richard's government were still alive. Shakespeare takes enormous liberties with the historic events in this play. There is no evidence for the kind of presence Queen Margaret has in this drama. In fact, she was in France after 1475 and died in 1482. Lady Anne had been betrothed to Henry VI's son, but they were not actually married when he died. Clarence was executed on order of his brother, Edward IV, in 1478 after a history of fomenting disorder, and any involvement of Richard in his death is purely speculative. Edward, in this play on his own deathbed at the time of Clarence's death, actually died five years later.

Shakespeare's sources were very anti–Yorkist, and there are serious questions about the truth of their (and Shakespeare's) portrayal of Richard as a

The importance of dreams is a recurrent theme in this play. Queen Margaret curses Richard that "no sleep close up that deadly eye of thine, unless it be while some tormenting dream affrights thee," as indeed occurs before the final battle. The Duke of Clarence dreams of drowning before Richard's murderers choke out his life in a wine barrel. Lord Stanley dreams of being pursued by a boar (the boar was Richard's standard) and warns Hastings to flee before he (Hastings) is executed by Richard on a trumped-up charge.

Ian McKellen as Richard III. Courtesy Museum of Modern Art/Film Stills Archive

In addition to the prophetic power of dreams, prophecy—both direct and in the form of curses hurled at characters—prepares the audience for steps in the drama that is unfolding. Richard's plots against his brother George take the form of prophecy to King Edward that "G" will murder Edward's heirs. Of course it is the "G" of the Duke of Gloucester, Richard's official name,

rather than that of George (Duke of Clarence). Anne curses Richard that any wife of his should be made more miserable by his life than she is by her husband's death. The object of that curse eventually is herself after she marries Richard. Queen Margaret's curses on Elizabeth and Richard, and her prophecy of Richard's treachery toward Buckingham, all come to pass.

The play employs two sets of murderers. The first two have no names but a number of lines as they debate the justice of their plans for the Duke of Clarence, recall the pay that they are to receive, and talk to their victim. The second two—Dighton and Forrest, employed by Sir James Tyrell to accomplish the offstage death of the princes in the Tower—have names but no lines.

Notable Productions and Performances

Richard III has always been one of Shakespeare's most popular plays. An 18th-century English impresario and Shakespeare editor, Colley Cibber, crafted a revised version incorporating Henry VI's death from the earlier play, and omitting much or all of Queen Margaret and other characters. This version was far more popular than the original for decades, and influenced Olivier's 1955 film *Richard III*, still quite watchable. Ian McKellen's *Richard III*, set in a postwar fascist Britain, is visually remarkable and memorable for McKellen's performance. The most illuminating cinema treatment of all may be *Looking for Richard*, Al Pacino's 1996 documentary film about his attempt to mount a modern production of the play.

KING HENRY VIII

AMBITION BRINGS DOWN
A CARDINAL,
A KING FINDS A NEW QUEEN

Period

16th century

Setting

England

The play opens with the Dukes of Norfolk and Buckingham, along with Lord Abergavenny, discussing a recent meeting of Henry VIII and Francis I, King of France, a meeting set up by Cardinal Wolsey, Lord Chancellor and the most important person in the kingdom after the king himself. Buckingham criticizes a recent treaty negotiated by the cardinal, and is warned by Norfolk that his opposition to Wolsey is dangerous. Indeed, at the scene's end Buckingham and Abergavenny are arrested and taken to the Tower.

In an appearance before the king, Queen Katherine pleads that recent taxes levied by Wolsey are too heavy, and have led to both unemployment and potential rebellion. Wolsey defends the taxes while noting that his is only one of the votes on the king's council that created them. But when the king orders them remitted, Wolsey whispers to his clerk to ensure that he, rather than the king, gets public credit.

Henry then calls upon the former surveyor (overseer) of the estates of the Duke of Buckingham, who relates a series of treasonous statements by his former employer. Katherine notes that the surveyor was discharged by Buckingham on his tenants' complaints, but the king has no trouble believing the charges. At a banquet and ball thrown by Wolsey at his estate, the king strikes up a friendship with one of the queen's ladies-in-waiting, Anne Bullen (Boleyn in modern spelling).

Buckingham, convicted offstage by the testimony of his employee and other alleged conspirators, is led to execution. Pausing on a London street, he proclaims his innocence to passersby, forgives his enemies, and compares his fall to that of his father (in the previous play), who befriended Richard III, then opposed him, and was captured and executed after being betrayed by a servant.

The king has become troubled by the fact that his marriage of more than twenty years to Queen Katherine has produced no male heir, and nobles speculate that the cause of this attack of conscience is Cardinal Wolsey. The dukes of Norfolk and Suffolk attempt to break into the king's meditations. They are rebuffed, but the king welcomes the arrival of Wolsey and Cardinal Campeius, sent from Rome to sit in judgment at arguments over whether Henry's marriage to Katherine (his brother's widow) was incestuous and thus illegal.

Anne Bullen and an elderly lady companion discuss the travails of Queen Katherine, and given the depths a bad turn of fortune can offer the mighty, Anne vows that she would never be a queen. "'Tis better to be lowly born...than to be perked up in a glist'ring grief and wear a golden sorrow," she says. The old lady, in a series of bawdy double entendres, disputes her before the Lord Chamberlain arrives to tell her that she has been made Marchioness of Pembroke (an area in Wales) with an income of 1,000 pounds a year—a very substantial sum at the time.

At a hearing in the hall of Blackfriars Abbey, Queen Katherine pleads her case before the king himself. "Heaven witness, I have been to you a true and humble wife..." and summarizes the complaints of so many about Wolsey, "you sign your place and calling...with meekness and humility, but your heart is crammed with arrogancy, spleen and pride." She leaves, insisting that her case be judged only by the pope himself.

At Wolsey's behest, the king clears him in front of the assembled court of the queen's charge that he had fomented the potential break between Henry and Katherine. Henry claims that it was his own conscience, stimulated by questions raised about the legitimacy of their daughter, Mary, for a potential marriage into the French royal family, and the fact that all their sons had died at birth or in infancy, a sign of God's displeasure.

A group of lords who are Wolsey's enemies discuss with pleasure the fact that documents from Wolsey have fallen into the king's hands. They provide evidence of Wolsey's accumulation of wealth and his request to the pope to delay ruling on Queen Katherine's case, since Wolsey has been scheming to arrange a marriage between the king and the French king's sister, and a marriage with Anne would frustrate those plans.

The lords watch as Henry prompts Wolsey to declare his loyalty. "For your Highness' good I ever laboured more than mine own," says Wolsey, before Henry hands him the condemning documents. As Wolsey reads them he realizes "I have touched the highest point of all my greatness, and from that full meridian of my glory I haste now to my setting."

Two men, meeting at the same place where the Duke of Buckingham spoke on his way to the headsman, hear of the king's divorce decree and watch the coronation train of Anne Bullen ("as I have a soul, she is an angel" one notes). Shortly thereafter, a dying Katherine hears of the sickness and death of Wolsey in a Leicester Abbey.

While recalling Wolsey's faults of arrogance, greed and duplicity, she and her companions are also willing to recall his scholarship, generosity to his friends, and his founding of centers of learning at Ipswich and Oxford. A messenger from the king arrives to inquire after her health and bring the king's greetings. She gives him a letter with her last requests on behalf of their daughter Mary, and her servants and companions. "Tell him in death I blessed him," says Katherine.

As Queen Anne is in labor, Henry meets with Cranmer, Archbishop of Canterbury, and an ally of Anne. Henry tells him that he must be heard before a King's Council on a charge of heresy, but Henry gives him his ring and instructs him to show it to the Council if they try to imprison him on the charges. As Cranmer leaves Henry is informed of the birth of his daughter.

Before the entrance to the Council chamber, Cranmer is made to wait among the servants, a discourtesy brought to Henry's attention. At the hearing Cranmer is ordered to the Tower, but he forestalls the sentence by bringing forth Henry's ring. The king himself arrives, denounces the process of Cranmer's accusation, and invites Cranmer to be godfather to his new daughter, a series of events that persuades all the Council members that any proceedings against the archbishop are impolitic.

Amid the tumult of commoners who have forced their way past the outer gates and into the palace yard, a great procession opens the baptism of Elizabeth. The ceremony itself includes a long panegyric about the coming glories of Elizabeth's reign ("A pattern to all princes...in her days every man shall eat in safety under his own vine what he plants, and sing the merry songs of peace to all his neighbors").

Likely Source of the Plot

The play is drawn largely from Holinshed's *Chronicles of England*. Shakespeare, as usual, telescopes the action. In the play, Katherine's death shortly follows that of Wolsey. In fact Wolsey died in 1530, Katherine not until 1536.

Background

Shakespeare correctly notes the resentment of many nobles at the power and authority granted Wolsey, who was of common birth. "This butcher's cur is venomed-toothed," says Buckingham of the man who rose from meatcutter's son to one of the highest offices in the land (the Tudors valued ability). Wolsey's sympathetic side also has a basis in fact. He was widely respected for his learning, was a humanist of leading reputation, and while willing to imprison heretics was so reluctant to have them burned at the stake that he was criticized for it by his enemies.

Notable Features

Unlike Shakespeare's other histories, there are no battle scenes in *Henry VIII*. Nor are there clear-cut villains. Buckingham makes a noble speech before his death, but the play never disproves the charges against him. Wolsey's sins are itemized, but even the queen admits his virtues, and he is at his most human as he falls. The king's public face is one of regret that his marriage to Katherine has been called into question. He insists to Wolsey that she have the best advocates for her position, and says, "Would it not grieve an able man to leave so sweet a bedfellow? But conscience, conscience." (In one of her scenes, however, Katherine says the king "has banished me his bed already.")

Even while Katherine is treated with great sympathy, Anne is never criticized. Rather she is described as "the goodliest woman that ever lay by man," and as someone who "had all the royal makings of a Queen." (Anne, of course, as the mother of the monarch who ruled during most of Shakespeare's career, was an unlikely subject for public criticism.)

"Men's evil manners live in brass; their virtues we write in water," says the queen's servant, Griffith, at the news of Cardinal Wolsey's death. The statement echoes Marc Antony's funeral oration for Caesar, "the evil that men do live after them, / The good is oft interred with their bones."

Notable Productions and Performances

The play is believed to be the same drama as *All Is True*, a work performed in 1613 at the Globe Theatre. In one performance there, a shot from the ceremonial cannon apparently set alight the thatched roof, and the building burned to the ground (it was rebuilt the next year).

There is a substantial body of serious opinion, based on both subjective readings and textual analysis, that *Henry VIII* is not the work of Shakespeare alone. The leading candidate for co-authorship or collaboration is John Fletcher, who succeeded Shakespeare as the principal dramatist of the King's Men. Given the late dating of the play, it is possible that a semiretired Shakespeare undertook to collaborate on or even to "play doctor" a

piece by his successor that the company was relying on to fill the playhouse. Nevertheless, it is listed as Shakespeare's work in the *First Folio*.

The cast for this play is large by the standards of Shakespeare's time, and the play is written with repeated opportunities for great spectacle, including Wolsey's ball, Katherine's trial, and Elizabeth's baptism. The stage directions for these occasions are unusually explicit ("Marquess Dorset, bearing a sceptre of gold, on his head a demicoronal of gold.... A canopy borne by four of the Cinque-ports...the old Duchess of Norfolk, in a coronal of gold, wrought with flowers, bearing the Queen's train....)

It may have been written originally as part of the celebration of the marriage in 1613 of the daughter of Elizabeth's successor, James I. That princess was also named Elizabeth. It was selected more than three hundred years later (in the 1950s) by the Old Vic to celebrate the coronation of another Elizabeth—the current queen.

King Henry VIII was popular on the English stage in the 18th and 19th centuries, when many productions focused on its pageantry. Charles Laughton and Anthony Quayle played Henry in important stage productions in the 20th century. The *Time-Life*/BBC version features a memorable performance by Claire Bloom as Queen Katherine.

Notable Other Uses of the Basic Plot

There have been a number of movies made about Henry VIII (including one in which Laughton stars), but they are not generally based on Shakespeare's play.

The Music, Ho! Renaissance
Rhythms, Highbrow and Low

f a hairy Elizabethan faced a
long wait at the barbershop,
instead of browsing through
a frayed magazine, he might
look around for a musical instrument to
play. Chances are his barber had
thoughtfully placed a cittern in the corner for the customers to pluck. The cittern, a simplified lute with frets like a
guitar and only four strings, was considered vulgar, but it was easy to play and
useful for whiling away the time making
"barber's musick."

Gone were the days when music
belonged almost exclusively either in
the church and the royal courts, and
when it had been considered effeminate
for a man to sing or play an instrument
unless he was training for the priest-
hood. The Renaissance—the age of
rebirth, Reformation, and the printing
press—had changed all that.

Psalm-singing and Celibacy:
Music in the Church

Throughout the Middle Ages, the
exquisite liturgical music fostered by the
Roman Catholic Church had been performed by trained singers who sang only
in Latin, a language few could understand. The music evoked mystery and
awe, but also images of seclusion and
celibacy. In *A Midsummer Night's
Dream*, Theseus tells Hermia that, if she
chooses not to marry, she may be sent
away to a life of "chanting faint hymns
to the cold fruitless moon."

The Protestant Reformation, ignited
by Martin Luther in 1517, made literacy and collective singing gifts to the people. Men, women, and children, regardless of education or training, were
allowed to sing in their own language.
But what should they sing? German
Protestants sang lustily, especially \
Luther's "A Mighty Fortress" known as
the "battle hymn of the Reformation."
Flemish Protestants, too, fleeing persecution, raised their voices in Psalm-
singing and anthems. Shakespeare's
Falstaff in *Henry IV, Part One*, referred
to this community, dominant in the wool
trade, when he sighed "I would I were a
weaver; I could sing psalms or anything."

The English Protestants, not ready for such spiritual passion or musical freedom, were influenced by stiff-lipped extremists who argued that music itself had no place in Protestant worship. But the people wanted to sing. British Protestants proceeded with caution—allowing metrical versions of the Psalms to be "lined out," that is, read aloud by parish clerks and repeated by all the members of the congregation in simple harmonies. The queen disapproved, calling these simple Psalm-based songs "Genevan jigs." Only in cathedrals did choirs thrive, voices soaring with new anthems, in either Latin or English, by Thomas Tallis (ca.1505–85) and his pupil William Byrd (1542–1623), and his pupil Thomas Morley (ca.1557–1603).

Pop Tunes in Tudor Times

Not only was ecclesiastical music now written down and preserved, but, with the invention of printing, secular music was as well. This was an age of music, both highbrow and low. Educated ladies and gents of the Renaissance were expected to be musically literate. It was not unusual for "part-books" to be handed around for family singing after supper. Guests who could not sight-read their parts and hold onto their melody were considered unfit for polite society.

Especially popular were madrigals, unaccompanied secular songs, usually about love, in which two or more melodies wove around each other, creating harmony. In 1588, a collection of Italian madrigals with English words was published. This collection inspired a school of English madrigal composers, many of whom were employed as music-masters in the great houses.

Not all the songs were as demanding as madrigals. Canons and rounds (sometimes called *catches*), ballads and airs, ditties and carols were the music of recreation for students and working folk. According to a 1598 text, one poor London shoemaker was suspected of being an imposter because he could neither "sing, sound the trumpet, play upon the flute, nor reckon up his tools in rhyme." Each trade had its special songs.

With tinkers, milkmaids, and even beggars making music, it is odd that wandering minstrels, so popular during the Middle Ages, were rapidly growing out of favor. Henry VIII disapproved of them, but under Elizabeth's reign, regulations began to curtail the travels of these "ballad-mongers" who entertained "boyes and countrye fellowes." In 1593, an act was issued that anyone caught wandering with "minstrelsy" as his profession was to be treated as a rogue and a vagabond. Branding was the penalty for the first conviction, death for the third. Nevertheless, while minstrels were languishing, everyone else was merrily singing.

"To sing a song that old was sung"—Shakespeare's Use of Song

Shakespeare was adept at weaving snatches of popular songs into his plays. In *The Taming of the Shrew*, when Grumio calls out, "Why, 'Jack, boy! ho, boy!' and as much news as thou wilt," theatergoers of the day would have rec-

ognized the reference to an old catch they had sung since childhood:

Jack, boy, ho! boy, news;
The cat is in the well,
Let us ring now for her knell,
Ding, dong, ding, dong, bell.

In *Twelfth Night*, Feste the clown sings a love song upon request for a six- pence. Then, Sir Toby suggests to Sir Andrew and Feste that they "draw three souls out of one weaver," and sing a familiar round "Thou Knave," which has lyrics simple enough to be sung by drunken men.

Hold thy peace, and I prithee hold thy
    peace,
Thou knave, Hold thy peace thou knave,
    thou knave.

What ensues is much silly singing as the men commence with snatches of songs an Elizabethan audience would have known. "Three merry men be we" was a catch borrowed from Peele's 1595 production of *Old Wives' Tale*, and "There dwelt a man in Babylon" is the beginning of the "Ballad of Constant Susanna," popular at the time.

In *Othello*, Desdemona, perplexed by the moody Moor's brooding, weeps as she prepares for bed and complains that a certain song is going around and around in her head. She sings it for Emilia, her maid:

A poor soul sat sighing under a
    sycamore tree:
O Willow, Willow, Willow!
With his hand on his bosom, his head
    on his knee;
O Willow, Willow, Willow!

Actually, Desdemona's song is a combi- nation of two popular ballads—"A Lover's Complaint" and, "The Song of the Green Willow," from John Hey- wood's 1541 manuscript.

In *Hamlet,* as Ophelia descends into madness, she stumbles through a wild medley of songs. As fragmented as her mind, the broken bits and pieces of song spill out with words haphazardly jumbled. "How Should I Your True Love Know?" melts into "Tomorrow Is Saint Valentine's Day."

Then comes a ribald verse, by which the audience understood that only in madness would a young woman of Ophelia's social position stoop so low:

By Gis and by Saint Charity,
Alack and, fie for shame!
Young men will do 't, if they come to 't,
By Cock, they are to blame.
Quoth she, "Before you tumbled me,
You promised me to wed."
"So would I have done, by yonder sun,
An thou hadst not come to my bed."

It is clear by her choice of songs that poor Ophelia is out of her mind, but she keeps singing. "They Bore Him Barefaced on the Bier" is fused with "And Will He Not Come Again?"

In the same play, the gravedigger sings a song with lyrics that Shakespeare borrowed from Lord Vaux's "The Image of Death." This was a popular ballad of the day, sung frequently by court clowns. Shakespeare added some o's and ah's into the lyrics to convey the physical exertion it takes to sing while digging a grave.

In *Henry IV, Part Two,* Silence, a rural justice of the peace who rarely speaks, has too much wine at a garden party and uncharacteristically begins to sing some lewd ballads. The lyrics—about cheap flesh, females dear, and lusty lads who roam here and there—would have been well-known to Shakespeare's theater crowd.

Shakespeare used original songs to help establish and distinguish his characters. In *The Tempest,* Ariel's songs are unearthly, the fragile stuff of dreams. As a creature of the air, he sings more than he speaks.

Where the bee sucks, there suck I;
In a cowslip's bell I lie...
Merrily, merrily shall I live now
Under the blossom that hangs on the
bough.

Stephano's are a working-man's songs full of the crude humor often associated with sailors. He enters in act 2 with a bottle in his hand as he sings "a scurvy tune" about a woman named Kate:

She loved not the savour of tar nor of
pitch,
Yet a tailor might scratch her where'er
she did itch.

Caliban's songs give vent to the frustration and rage of the colonized and dispossessed. Drunk and howling, he sings:

Farewell, master; farewell, farewell!
No more dams I'll make for fish;
Nor fetch in firing
At requiring,
Nor scrape trenchering, nor wash dish.
'Ban 'Ban, Ca—Caliban,
Has a new master—Get a new man.

With that, he cries, "Freedom!"

Songs were also used to evoke a mood or to reinforce a play's theme. In

Village dance, from a broadside

Twelfth Night, "O Mistress Mine" is sung by the clown, Feste, to the aging Sir Toby Belch and Sir Andrew Aguecheek. Set to a familiar old tune, arranged both by Thomas Morley in his *Consort Lessons* and by William Byrd in *The Fitzwilliam Virginal Book,* scholars believe the lyrics are by Shakespeare. There is no doubt that the sentiment of the song reinforces a seize-the-day theme of the comedy, "If music be the food of love, play on, Give me excess of it.... "

What is love? 'Tis not hereafter;
Present mirth hath present laughter;
What's to come is still unsure.
In delay there lies no plenty;
Then come kiss me, sweet and twenty;
Youth's a stuff will not endure.

In some plays, Shakespeare used songs to conjure a sense of magic and mystery. Music precedes the appearance of the ghost in *Julius Caesar* and the apparitions in *Cymbeline.* In *Macbeth,* a witch calls for music, saying, "I'll charm the air to give a sound, While you perform your antic round." With that, the witches dance around a cauldron and vanish. In *The Winter's Tale,* music is used to awaken the "statue" of Hermione, while in *A Midsummer Night's Dream,* fairies gently sing their queen to sleep:

Never harm
Nor spell nor charm
Come our lovely lady nigh.
So good night, with lullaby.

Music directly influences the conduct of the characters. In *Othello,* when the duplicitous Iago wants to coax the conscientious Cassio into letting down his guard for a night of carousing and heavy drink, he does so with a carefree but cleverly calculated song.

And let me the canakin clink, clink:
And let me the canakin clink.
A soldier's a man:
A life's but a span,
Why then let a soldier drink.

In other words—eat, drink, and be merry for tomorrow you die. It is a persuasive argument to a soldier, who might easily think himself merely cannon fodder for kings. Iago's song works. The honorable Cassio gets smashed and finds his good name gone in a matter of minutes.

In *A Midsummer Night's Dream*, Bottom the weaver, newly "translated" into a donkey, sings to show that he is not afraid. Pacing in the woods, he says, "I will walk up and down here, and I will sing, that they shall hear I am not afraid." His song, about birds, not only endears him to the audience, but moves the action along, for his singing awakens Titania, the fairy queeen.

In *As You Like It*, Amiens sings "Under the greenwood tree" to the gloomy realist, Jaques. The song extols the joys of a careless existence in a place, far from civilization, where one is not likely to find a human enemy. Jaques, who boasts that he can "suck melancholy out of a song, as a weasel sucks eggs," immediately parodies the song with a version of his own which begins:

If it do come to pass
That any man turn ass....

In *The Merry Wives of Windsor*, song is used as punishment and public humiliation. The lecherous Falstaff agrees to a rendezvous at midnight in the park and is met there by revelers dressed as fairies who sing a "scornful rhyme." They dance around the rotund knight, pinching and mocking him.

Fie on sinful fantasy!
Fie on lust and luxury!...
Pinch him, fairies, mutually;
Pinch him for his villainy.

In *Love's Labour's Lost*, two songs are used as Epilogue, to clear the stage and to restore the comedic tone that has been briefly interrupted by last-minute bad news. It is a movement from the sublime images of amorous spring in "The Cuckoo Song," to the ridiculous but more realistic winter image in "The Owl Song" of greasy Joan kneeling by the pot.

"The sweet power of music!"— Shakespeare's Use of Instrumental Music

Instrumental music was a part of daily life for the whole spectrum of citizenry in Elizabethan England, from courtier to ploughman. Even Queen Elizabeth herself composed music and was accomplished on the **virginal.** This keyboard instrument had wire strings that were plucked by quills when the keys were depressed. The Virgin Queen played in private to lift her spirits and "shun melancholy." Like Edward VI before her, she played the lute as well.

The **lute** was the most popular instrument of the day, though it was difficult to play well. Shaped like a mandolin, but much larger, it was effectively used to accompany love songs. Because it was hard to tune, in the wrong hands, it was an instrument of torture. One popular song of the day derided a musically inept man who tried to pass as educated by playing the lute.

He tumbryth on a lewde lewte, Rotybulle
    Joyse,
Rumbill downe, tumbill downe, hey go,
    now now,
He fumblyth in his fyngering an ugly
    rude noise,
It seemyth the sobbying of an old sow.

Lutes were used when a calming or romantic effect was desired on stage. In *Much Ado about Nothing*, Benedick muses about the power of the instrument, saying, "Is it not strange that sheep's guts [from which the lute's strings were made] should hale souls out of men's bodies?"

In *Henry VIII*, Queen Katherine, seeking solace, commands one of her attendants, "Take thy lute, wench. My soul grows sad with troubles; Sing and disperse them, if thou canst." The song her waiting maid sings echos Shakespeare's association of the lute as the instrument of the gods which, in the right hands, could calm the sea or cure "grief of heart."

Orpheus with his lute made trees,
And the mountain tops that freeze,
Bow themselves, when he did sing;
To his music plants and flowers
Ever sprung, as sun and showers
There had made a lasting spring.

Whereas lutes calmed frayed nerves, **hautboys** (an early form of oboe) heralded doom. With its shrill, reedy sound, the instrument evoked ill winds. In *Macbeth*, the hautboy was the instrument of choice at banquet scenes in the ominous castle. In *Hamlet*, Shakespeare specified that they be used to provide background music for the provocative play-within-a-play. At the lavish banquet in *Timon of Athens*, just before the host's fortune changes and he becomes a raving misanthrope, dancing Amazons appear carrying lutes, but the music is actually played on harsh hautboys as if foretelling the coming disaster.

In the open-air theaters and curtainless stages of Shakespeare's day, fanfares played on **trumpets** or **sackbuts** (something like the trombone) generally announced the beginning of a play. A trumpeter would blow a "flourish" to accompany the actors onto the stage.

Lute builder, by Albrecht Dürer

Trumpets were also used to announce royalty or wedding parties in a play, and they were essential for battlefield scenes. "Trumpet, blow loud. Send thy brass voice through all these lazy tents," cries the Trojan commander Aeneas in *Troilus and Cressida*. Toward the end of *Henry VI, Part Two*, Warwick makes himself hoarse calling, "Now, when the angry trumpet sounds alarm, / And dead men's cries do fill the empty air, / Clifford, I say, come forth and fight with me."

From a broadside ballad

From a broadside ballad

Small **drums,** called **tabors, fifes,** and **pipes** were also called for in battle scenes. Drummers were useful for staging military marches and accompanying the dead, as in *Hamlet*. Horns made of wood covered in leather were used by hunters on stage. In *A Midsummer Night's Dream*, huntsmen's horns awaken the sleeping lovers.

The six-stringed **viol** was another important instrument in Shakespeare's day. Until 1650, the soft-toned viol was favored over the violin which was new to England and considered by the elite to be a banal and boorish instrument suited only for country folk. Educated Elizabethans were expected to be able to play the viol. In Shakespeare's *Pericles*, it is the music of the viol that restores the good and beautiful Thaisa to life after she's been buried at sea. Cerimon, working to revive Thaisa, calls out,

The rough and woeful music that we
    have,
Cause it to sound, beseech you.
The viol once more. How thou stirr'st,
    thou block!
The music there! I pray you give her air.

Recorders were popular for their sweet tones. In what is sometimes referred to as the "recorder scene" in *Hamlet*, the troubled prince carries on at length, trying to persuade Guildenstern to pick up a recorder and play. Poor Guildenstern protests, insisting that he doesn't know how. Hamlet proceeds to give instructions. He says that playing a recorder is "as easy as lying:

govern these ventages with your fingers and thumb, give it breath with your mouth, and it will discourse most eloquent music." Using the recorder as a metaphor, he warns Rosencrantz and Guildenstern not to try manipulate or conspire against him.

Why, look you now, how unworthy a thing you make of me! You would play upon me; you would seem to know my stops; you would pluck out the heart of my mystery; you would sound me from my lowest note to the top of my compass; and there is much music, excellent voice, in this little organ, yet cannot you make it speak. 'Sblood, do you think I am easier to be play'd on than a pipe? Call me what instrument you will, though you can fret me, yet you cannot play upon me.

Shakespeare has fun with more musical word-play in *The Taming of the Shrew*, when Hortensio, with his head broken, describes his attempts to teach Kate to play the lute. The double meaning of the word "fret" works well, as Kate has cleverly taken it from noun (the ridge across the fingerboard of a stringed instrument) to verb (to be vexed or worried), and from "fret" to "fume." Asked if he "canst not break her to the lute," Hortensio replies:

*Why, no, for she hath broke the
   lute to me.
I did but tell her she mistook her frets,
And bow'd her hand to teach her
   fingering,
When, with a most impatient,
   devilish spirit,
"Frets call you these?" quoth she;
   "I'll fume with them";*

*And with that word she struck me
   on the head.*

Shakespeare plays with musical metaphor and sexual double entendre in *Cymbeline* when Cloten, the crass and tacky son of the queen and a comic villain in this story, crudely describes one of his schemes for courting the charming and virtuous Imogen. "I am advised to give her music a mornings; they say it will penetrate. [Addressing the musicians] Come on, tune. If you can penetrate her with your fingering, so. We'll try with tongue too."

Most of Shakespeare's references to music, unlike the passage from *Cymbeline*, speak of its power in our lives, to move us, lift us. There is no more beautiful passage than Lorenzo's lengthy soliloquy in *The Merchant of Venice*:

*How sweet the moonlight sleeps upon
   this bank!
Here will we sit and let the sounds of
   music
Creep in our ears; soft stillness and the
   night
Become the touches of sweet harmony....
Come, ho, and wake Diana with a
   hymn;
With sweetest touches pierce your
   mistress' ear,
And draw her home with music....
The man that hath no music in himself,
Nor is not moved with concord of sweet
   sounds,
Is fit for treasons, stratagems, and spoils;
The motions of his spirit are dull as
   night,
And his affections dark as Erebus:
Let no such man be trusted.*

TROILUS
AND CRESSIDA

TROJAN WAR DRAGS
ON DESPITE LOSS OF INTEREST
ON BOTH SIDES

Period

The Trojan War

Settings

Troy and a Greek camp outside the city

War is hell: often it is pointless. Sometimes it is also boring. All of this seems to be true as the play opens. Seven long years have passed since Paris abducted Helen, the world's most beautiful woman. The Greeks have been pounding at the gates of Troy ever since to get her back but they are stuck in a stalemate with a stale cause; no one is very excited about Helen anymore.

Troilus, the brother of bad-boy Paris, wants to get on with his life and take a wife. He's sick of the war. "Fools on both sides!" he mutters. He's in love with Cressida. This being ancient times, however, he can't approach her directly, so he uses a go-between, her Uncle Pandarus (from whom we get the word

"pander"). After a bit of coaxing and cooing, Cressida says she loves Troilus too. Uncle Pandarus happily leads the young lovers to a bedroom where they spend one hot night together and profess their undying love.

The Greeks outside the city walls, meanwhile, are ready to quit and go home. They're sick of the whole thing. The famed Ulysses meets with other leaders to discuss the situation. They come to the conclusion that the core of the problem is Achilles, who just lies on his bed and laughs at his superiors.

Back in Troy, Hector voices his irritation with the war. Why not just give Helen back to the Greeks? "She is not worth what she doth cost the holding," he says. Troilus, sick of the war too, disagrees. If they quit now, many soldiers will have died in vain. And so it goes. No one believes in the cause, but the war must go on since the war must go on.

Cressida, who has pledged her undying love to Troilus, finds herself part of a bargain. Her father has defected to the Greek side and wants her there with him. In exchange, the Greeks will give back several prisoners of war. A handsome Greek lad is sent to escort Cressida outside the walls of Troy. She bids a tearful farewell to her true love, then gives her escort the once over. By the time they reach the Greek lines, she's ready to kiss half the camp. Ulysses is disgusted, saying, "Fie, fie upon her! / There's language in her eye, her cheek, her lip, / Nay, her foot speaks; her wanton spirits look out / At every joint and motive of her body."

A challenge is issued by the Trojans.

Prince Hector, Troy's most formidable warrior, will engage any Greek in hand-to-hand combat. He anticipates fighting the mighty Achilles, but the Greek commanders enlist the asinine Ajax instead, hoping to teach the insolent Achilles a lesson.

When Hector arrives at the Greek camp for his fight with Ajax, all the men, except Achilles, are on their very best knightly behavior, with pretensions of chivalry. Hector and Ajax, who, as it turns out, are cousins, take only a couple half-hearted jabs at each other

before Hector calls a truce, lays down his arms and embraces Ajax. At that, friendly introductions are made all around and the warriors sit down to a great banquet. Only Achilles keeps the war going with an insult, and Hector agrees to fight him the next day.

Troilus, who has accompanied Hector to the Greek encampment, goes off to find his sworn love, Cressida, while the others feast. He does find her—in the arms of the handsome Greek escort. Ulysses and Thersites, the camp fool, witness the rendezvous and watch Troilus watching Cressida. They try to console, or at least quiet, the jilted lover as he cries, "O Cressid! O false Cressid! False, false, false!" Troilus vows to kill the Greek escort the next day in battle.

Dawn comes with signs of impending disaster. The warriors have had enough of their short detour through the back roads of peace and are eager to renew the fighting. From the sidelines, the fool Thersites looks on, disgusted with what he calls the "clapper-clawing."

There is one fight after another, in this pageant of bloodshed. Finally, Hector, thinking he has battled and killed enough for one day, misjudges the moment when he says, "Now is my day's work done; I'll take good breath: / Rest, sword; thou hast thy fill of blood and death!" Just as he puts down his sword, however, Achilles appears with some soldiers. Ignoring all rules of fair play, Achilles orders his men to slaughter the unarmed man, then steps forward as a victor claiming his spoils, to drag Hector's body off the battlefield. There

is brief conjecturing that, perhaps now, the war will end. Troilus appears, however, to argue that Hector's death must be avenged. Violence begets violence, and so the war continues.

Likely Source of the Plot

Homer's *Iliad,* in George Chapman's translation, was one primary source for the plot of this play, although the Trojan War was described more authentically in other accounts. The story of Cressida's betrayal was inspired by Geoffrey Chaucer's *Troilus and Criseyde.*

Notable Features

Included in the 1623 *First Folio* but accidentally omitted from the table of contents, *Troilus and Cressida* is considered one of Shakespeare's bitter "problem plays." That it is satire is not disputed, but sometimes it is categorized as a comedy, sometimes tragedy.

Notable Productions and Performances

No one knows where or when this play was first performed. There was a German-language performance in Munich, in 1898, but there is no record of a performance in English until 1907, though a variation titled *Truth Found Too Late* was produced in 1679. The play finally found its audience in the nihilistic, militaristic 20th century, with its Holocaust, atomic weapons, and atrocities in Europe and southeast.

CORIOLANUS

PATRIOTIC ROMAN LEADER OFFENDS POPULACE, LOSES CHANCE AT LEADERSHIP

Period

5th century B.C.E.

Setting

Italy

Rome's commoners are unhappy. There is a shortage of grain in Rome, and they suspect that the city's nobles are hoarding it. One of their principal targets is Caius Martius, a prominent noble who has done great service to Rome, but who holds the commoners in contempt ("a very dog to the commonalty," as one citizen puts it).

Martius is sent as one of the military leaders to put down a rebellion of the Volscians, another Italian tribe, and their leader, Aufidius. At Corioli, the Volscian capital, Martius takes his own soldiers to task for their inability to capture the city ("You souls of geese that bear the shapes of men, how have you run?..."). He heartens them for a new attack, and by himself breaches the city

gates. Thought dead, he appears blood-stained on the walls, and his bravery inspires the rest of the soldiers to renew their attack and take the city. Because of the victory, Martius is given the surname Coriolanus. On his return to Rome, he becomes a candidate for the consulship. He easily wins the approval of the senate, but custom dictates that he also get the approval of the people. He is reluctant, ("Please you that I may pass this doing," he tells Mennenius, a patrician who has a good relationship with the commoners) but finally agrees. He presents himself before the people, and wins their assent.

But the commoners, put off by his obvious reluctance and encouraged by two tribunes of the people, Sicinius and Brutus, later withdraw their approval. They eventually accuse Martius of opposing the distribution of free grain to the hungry; he does not deny the charge, saying that since the people were unwilling to fight Rome's wars they do not deserve her generosity.

His verbal attacks on the people provoke the citizens to try to seize Coriolanus and charge him with treason, and Mennenius agrees to bring Coriolanus to the Forum to answer the charges against him. Coriolanus at first refuses to go, but he is persuaded by his redoubtable mother, Volumnia, to place himself again before the people ("I'll mountebank their loves...and come home belov'd of all the trades in Rome").

Forgetting his promise to be mild in the face of accusations, he reacts with fury to charges that his real desire is to become a tyrant. Amid the clamor of the citizens, he is banished on pain of death, and goes proudly ("thus I turn my back. There is a world elsewhere"). Leaving Rome, he goes in disguise to the city of Antium and finds his way to the house of his old foe, Aufidius. There he offers to become the ally of the Volscians, who are brewing a new revolt against Rome. Aufidius welcomes him into an alliance, and agrees to share the leadership of the rebellion with him.

Under the leadership of Aufidius and Coriolanus, the Volscians lay waste to the countryside and threaten Rome itself. Old allies of Coriolanus visit him to seek peace, including Mennenius, but he is deaf to their pleas. Finally his mother Volumnia, along with his wife Virgilia and their small son, come to Coriolanus in the enemy camp. They kneel before him to ask that he negotiate an honorable peace between the Volscians and the Romans. He eventually agrees.

Aufidius and Coriolanus appear before the Volscians to explain the new treaty. Aufidius accuses Coriolanus of abandoning the Volscians at the brink of victory. "He has betrayed your business,"

Aufidius tells the Volscian leadership, while Coriolanus angrily reminds Aufidius and the nobles that "like an eagle in a dovecote" he had conquered their city. His statement enrages the watchers, many of whom lost family members in Coriolanus's attack. They fall upon and murder him. Aufidius immediately regrets his death, ("My rage is gone, and I am struck with sorrow,") and orders an honorable burial for his old enemy.

Likely Source of the Plot

Plutarch's *Lives of the Noble Greeks and Romans* was the principal source for this play, the same source on which Shakespeare drew for *Julius Caesar* and *Antony and Cleopatra*.

Background

At the time of this story, Rome was just beginning to establish its hegemony over the other cities of Italy. It had also recently become a republic, having driven out the Tarquins who had ruled the city. Coriolanus is said to have played an active role in this war when he was only a youth ("At sixteen years...he fought beyond the mark of others..." says his friend and fellow soldier Cominius).

The expulsion of the Tarquins established the republic as a state ruled by an aristocratic oligarchy rather than by one man, but it was not a modern democracy by any means. Men of the leading families made up the Senate, which appointed officials to conduct the republic's business, and military leaders to conduct wars. Two leading aristocrats were appointed every year to serve as consuls, handling day-to-day administration of the state.

Additional duties of the state were performed by lower officers, known as *tribunes.* At first a designation for infantry commanders, the title was later bestowed on civilian officials, among them *tribuni plebs,* or tribunes of the people, who were charged with overseeing the interests of the lower or working classes. They could invalidate decrees of other officials, including the consuls. In this play, Shakespeare has Coriolanus saying that the plebians had been given permission to appoint five tribunes to "defend their vulgar wisdoms." Two of these tribunes, Sicinius Velutus and Junius Brutus, are the principal Roman foes of Coriolanus.

Notable Feature

The threat of the re-establishment of the monarchy ("tyranny") was a constant issue for the Roman republic. Although in this play it is the commoners who express such a fear, the same emotion guides the actions of the nobles who assassinate Julius Caesar in Shakespeare's play of that name.

Notable Productions and Performances

In the 18th century, adaptations of this play dominated its productions, and the original text version reasserted itself only in the 19th century. Twentieth century versions of the play have starred Laurence Olivier (in two notable productions), Anthony Quayle, Richard Burton, and Ralph Fiennes, while Volumnia has been played by Sybil Thorndike and Edith Evans among others. The 1984 *Time-Life*/BBC version features Alan Howard as Coriolanus, Joss Ackland as Mennenius, and Irene Worth as Volumnia.

> **A kiss long as my exile,**
> **sweet as my revenge!**
> **—*Coriolanus***

TITUS ANDRONICUS

FAMILY FEUD LEADS TO RAPE, MUTILATION, MURDER, AND WORSE

Period

Antiquity

Setting

Imperial Rome

The Roman general Titus Andronicus returns triumphant from a a decade of warfare with the Goths. In his train, along with his own daughter and sons, are the Gothic Queen Tamora, her sons, and her Moorish servant and lover, Aaron. To appease the souls of his own dead sons, Titus determines to sacrifice one of Tamora's sons ("O cruel, irreligious piety," she exclaims).

Titus walks into a contest for succession, the previous emperor having died leaving two sons, Saturninus and Bassianus. Whereas Titus's brother urges him to seek the throne himself, Titus refuses, saying, "Give me staff of honor for my age, but not a sceptre to control the world." At his urging the people confirm Saturninus, the emperor's eldest son, as the new emperor.

A grateful Saturninus offers to marry Titus's daughter, Lavinia, but she is kidnapped by the other royal son, Bassianus, with the cooperation of Titus's sons. Saturninus then chooses Tamora for his queen. The involvement of Titus's family on Lavina's kidnapping enrages Saturninus, but Tamora urges him, given Titus's popularity, to "dissemble all your griefs and discontents" while she figures out a way "to massacre them all" in revenge for Titus's execution of her son.

Her first chance to do so comes when she and her sons encounter Bassianus and Lavinia during a hunting expedition. The boys murder Bassianus and throw his body in a pit, then drag Lavinia off despite her pleas that Tamora show "a woman's pity." Remembering how Titus executed Tamora's son, she tells her remaining sons to use Lavinia "as you will."

Aaron meanwhile lures to the pit Titus's sons Quintus and Martius, and makes sure that the emperor finds them there as the body of Bassianus is discovered. The emperor immediately condemns them for murdering Bassianus.

Titus shortly thereafter discovers his daughter, alive but having been raped and with her tongue and hands cut off (so she cannot identify her attackers), two of his sons condemned for murder, and another banished for trying to rescue them. Aaron brings him word that the emperor is ready to forgive the boys if Titus agrees to cut off his hand and send it to him. With Aaron's help, Titus does so. The reply is the return of the hand, along with the heads of his two sons. Titus now laughs. "I have not another tear to shed," he says, and would not have his eyes blinded by tears from determining "which way shall I find Revenge's cave?"

Lavinia uses a copy of Ovid's *Metamorphoses* (which contains a story similar to her own) and a stick held in her mouth to write in the sand a description of what happened to her and who her attackers were. Titus sends his remaining son Lucius, already ordered banished, to raise an army among Titus's old enemies, the Goths.

Titus now feigns insanity, sending weapons as gifts to Tamora's sons, and going about the city shooting arrows into the air, including into the emperor's house. Tamora is delivered of a son, but his dark skin makes it obvious that his father was Aaron rather than the emperor. Aaron protects the child from Tamora's older sons, kills the nurse that attended at its birth, and flees with the baby, saying he will bring him up "to be a warrior and command a camp."

Aaron is captured by Lucius and the Goths, and trades the assurance of the baby's life for the true story of all the misdeeds of Tamora, her sons, and him-self, including the murder of Bassianus and the rape and mutilation of Lavinia. He is unrepentant about his own role in these and other crimes. ("I have done a thousand dreadful things...and nothing grieves me heartily indeed but that I cannot do ten thousand more.")

As Lucius brings his army of Goths closer to the city, Tamora persuades the Emperor to let her ask Titus to arrange a banquet at his home at which the emperor, Lucius, and the Gothic commanders can sit down and work out a peace agreement. She goes to Titus's house along with her sons, all in disguise, to ask him to host the banquet. Though he continues to feign insanity, he agrees, and asks her to let her two sons remain with him when she leaves. She does so, and after she has gone he abandons his performance, has them bound, and cuts their throats.

When the night of the banquet arrives Titus appears in the garb of a cook, seats everyone and sets them to their meal. He then stabs his daughter ("die, Lavinia, and thy shame with thee"), tells Tamora that she has just eaten a dish prepared with the flesh of her sons, and kills her. The Emperor Saturninus then kills him, and Saturninus is killed by Lucius. Lucius is proclaimed emperor, orders the lingering death of Aaron, the honorable burial of Saturninus, Titus and Lavinia, and has the body of "that ravenous tiger, Tamora" thrown to the beasts for "her life was beastly and devoid of pity."

Likely Source of Plot

There appears to be no single potential source for this play. Although *Titus* was a common Roman name, there is no historical record of this narrative. Its elements may have been drawn from a variety of places, including the obvious internal quote of Ovid, in whose *Metamorphoses* there was a story of Io, raped and transformed by Jupiter, and of Philomela, who reveals the identity of her attacker in a sampler, and who feeds her attacker the flesh of his son in a pie.

Notable Features

So appalling is this story that many critics, among them Samuel Johnson, refused to believe it was Shakespeare's, or theorized that he did no more than play-doctor some scenes of a work created by someone else. But there are many elements here that are found in other (and presumably later) Shakespeare plays. The Moor, portrayed more sympathetically, is Othello. The villain, written in a good deal more depth, is Richard III. Queen Margaret, in the *Henry VI* plays, is just as fierce in many ways as is Tamora, and shares with her the comparison to a tiger. However gruesome we find its details, its original audience was perfectly aware that in their own time people found guilty of

heresy were burned alive, and those who committed treason were hanged, cut down alive, disemboweled, and their bodies cut up and sent to different parts of the realm.

This is the only Shakespeare play for which we have a roughly contemporary illustration—a drawing by one Henry Peacham of Tamora's entrance, with characters in a mix of Roman and Renaissance dress.

Notable Productions

Titus was apparently very popular in the early 1590s, with repeated productions. It was cited in 1614 by Ben Jonson as a long-popular play (along with Thomas Kyd's *The Spanish Tragedy*, another revenge melodrama). A Restoration version of the play put more emphasis on the role of Aaron, and in the 19th century a well-known black American actor, Ira Aldridge, made the role famous. In the 1950s Laurence Olivier played Titus onstage, with Vivian Leigh as Lavinia. The 1985 *Time-Life*/BBC production has Trevor Peacock as Titus; Julie Taymor's 1999 big budget version stars Anthony Hopkins as Titus, with Jessica Lange as Tamora.

When "Goose-Turd Green" Was All the Rage: Elizabethan Fashions

very morning, between the hours of ten and twelve, London's fashionable young men paraded up and down the central aisle at St. Paul's Cathedral showing off their new clothes, while tailors hid in the shadows taking notes. This was an age when men's flamboyance of dress rivaled women's.

Under the security of Queen Elizabeth's steady hand, the whole country seemed to wrap itself in new fabrics and bright colors. Gone were the days of mouse brown and somber maroon. Now, the colors had amusing names like "goose-turd green" or poetic names like "flame," "pease-porridge tawny," "lusty gallant," and "maiden's blush." "Dead Spaniard" was a pale greyish tan. Archers dressed in "Lincoln Green." It was understood that black looked good when complemented by silver and gold accessories. White, too, had its place. Blue, however, was the color of loyal service and was therefore the color reserved for serving men and women and others of the lower classes. The only blue favored by aristocrats was

one with a hint of green called "watchet" or "azure" which was the color of a clear sky.

Legislating Attire

Emerging from the stylized austerity of mid-century, the English followed their queen's penchant for elaborate and impressive clothes. It was understood, however, that the queen could also be the voice of restraint, enforcing a national dress code at her whim. This was not a new idea. King Henry VIII had put his foot down, so to speak, on the outrageous design of shoes in his kingdom, and had ordered that they be limited to six-inches width across the toe.

In 1571, by an Act of Parliament, all male citizens of London over the age of six, excepting the nobility, gentry, and officeholders, were required to wear special knit caps on Sundays and holidays. "City Flat Caps," berets with narrow brims, had been worn since the 1530s. After the 1571 decree, these were called "Statute Caps." They were

made of wool manufactured in England and so were thought to benefit local industry. The statute remained in effect for six years, and essentially killed all affection for the cap.

Shoes and caps were not the only items subject to governmental dictates or royal decree. Oversized collars known as "ruffs," which were worn by both men and women, became cause for the monarch's intervention as well. After starch was introduced in England about 1560, the ruffs grew stiffer and larger than ever, sometimes measuring over nine inches wide, and often had to be supported by steel rods. The queen herself fancied the style and wore it often, but in 1580 she issued a sumptuary statute limiting the size of neckwear. Guards were stationed at London's Bishopsgate to stop anyone from entering the city with "monstrous ruffs" under penalty of arrest.

Eventually, under the reign of James I, the English were ready to relax the starch, and ruffs gave way to "whisks." In the Droeshout engraving on the title page of the *First Folio* (see page 81), William Shakespeare is depicted wearing a whisk—a standing collar supported by piccadills.

A Question of Class

Elizabeth, loving magnificent clothing as she did, sided with those who worried that the distinctions between the classes, once so clearly defined and reinforced by appearance, were becoming blurred. It seemed that everyone was dressing like nobility in the late 16th century. Laws had been used in the past to limit the degree of luxury permitted each class, and Queen Elizabeth kept some of these intact.

Lamenting that "the meanest are as richly apparelled as their betters" and worried about the "pride that such inferior persons take in their garments," the queen issued a ban on wearing satin, damask or taffeta for men whose status was lower than that of a gentleman bearing arms. Under the degree of a knight, none could wear embroideries with silk or velvet in their gowns or cloaks. A new statute issued in 1580 modified the rules to allow more finery than had previously been legal, but Elizabeth had a losing battle on her hands.

"Against Excess of Apparel," a sermon circulated by the Church of England and officially published by government authority in 1563, seemingly had had little effect. Nor did the frequent remarks by the day's satirists have much impact. In his 1583 publication, *Anatomy of Abuses*, Philip Stubbes ridiculed those who went into debt for fashion:

Everyone almost, though otherwise very poor, having scarce forty shillings of wages by the year, will be sure to have two or three pair of these silk netherstocks, or else of the finest yarn that may be got, though the price of them be a royal ten or twenty shillings, or more.

He was outraged that,

those who are neither of the nobility, gentility nor yeomanry, no, nor yet any magistrate, or officer in the commonwealth, go daily in silks, velvets, satins, damasks, taffetas and such like, notwithstanding that they be both base by birth, mean by estate and servile by calling.

A traveler from Germany, Thomas Platter, published similar observations in 1599 after a visit to London. He said of the merchant women:

They lay great store by ruffs and starch them blue, so that their complexion shall appear the whiter, and some may well wear velvet for the street— quite common with them—who cannot afford a crust of bread at home I have been told.

> **"The fashion of the time is changed."**
> **—The Two Gentlemen of Verona**

Another pamphleteer, Robert Greene, worried about the role of current fashion in undermining and unbalancing the economic and social order of Britain, published a morality tale in which a dandy, "stepping so proudly" in velvet breeches "exceeding sumptuous to the eie" was pitted against a hard-working man, "more soberly marching and with a softer pace" in simple, sturdy cloth breeches. In this battle of the breeches, the functional pragmatism of the country man's clothes were contrasted with the expense of the city man's frivolous and ostentatious display.

Even Hamlet complains that he lives in an age when the toe of the peasant is coming too near the heel of the courtier. And in *Love's Labour's Lost*, Shakespeare used the fashion debate as a metaphor in an argument about the language of love. Ardent young Berowne promises his lady love that, henceforth, he will stop using "taffeta phrases, silken terms precise"— taffeta and silk being the fabrics of pretense and pomposity—and will speak instead "russet yeas and honest kersey noes"—russet and kersey being plain-spun fabrics worn by peasants

Women's Goodly Robes and Raiment

While Puritans and pamphleteers derided the day's fashions, the rest of the country was playing dress-up and loving it. By the year 1600, it is said that the queen had an inventory of almost three hundred gowns and several hundred other complete costumes as well as special apparel for state occasions.

Exaggeration and extravagance were the themes of the age. Women of the aristocracy, following their queen, wore clothing so inflated—gigantic sleeves and collars, oversized skirts—that pamphleteer Philip Stubbes observed that,

when they have all these goodly robes upon them, women seem to be the smallest part of themselves, not natural women, but artificial women: not women of flesh and blood, but rather puppets or mommets [dolls] of rags and cloths compact together.

Women wore undergarments called **smocks** over which they put several petticoats and a boned underbodice. One popular kind of underskirt, lined with a series of hoops made of wood, wire, or whalebone, was called a **farthingale.** The Spanish style farthingales produced a cone-shaped effect, while the French style produced the cylindrical skirt effect. "Bum Rolls" were padded wheel-shaped cushions that could be tied around the waist and were so common that working women sometimes wore them.

Over all of this was worn the **kirtle** (skirt) and the **bodice**. A "stomacher" was a triangular piece joined to the bodice, with the front dipping below the natural waistline. Women dressed one piece at a time, all the independent parts being pinned together or tied. Other pieces were added to hide the hooks or pins. At the end of the sleeve were wrist ruffs or cuffs. In cold weather or on ceremonial occasions, women would put on one-piece gowns over the assembled outfit.

Necklines could be high or low, but the collar was what mattered. Both men's and women's fashions featured **ruffs,** small, medium, or large, which might circle the neck like a gauzy wheel or rise, fan-shaped, around the neck or present the head, as if on a platter. Lockets, pendants, and strings of pearls added to the effect. Sometimes strands of beads were caught up and held to one side in a brooch. Jeweled buttons competed for attention with insect-shaped pins and rings and earrings.

When a woman went outdoors, she might choose to wear a short coat called a **cassock** or a long cloak with an extra skirt called a **safeguard** to protect her kirtle from getting dirty.

Around the lower part of the bodice, women wore **girdles** (belts) made of ribbon or gold chains, from which they could hang a jewel, or a muff made of silk or fur in which to warm their hands. Sometimes they attached a *pomander*—a metal container holding a scented potpourri. Useful, as well as ornamental, pomanders might contain herbs to protect the wearer from the plague or dried flowers to sniff in the presence of unpleasant odors.

Although unmarried women sometimes went bare-headed, married women often covered their hair, both indoor and out, with decorative hoods or hair nets, or hats trimmed with feathers or jewels. Toward the end of the 16th century, wigs were popular with women who could afford them. Sometimes women painted their faces a morbid masklike white and brushed their hair upward into beehive shapes. Wired headrails or billiments were sometimes worn like haloes around the head, shimmering with jewels or pearls.

Dressing was a time-consuming process. As one observer of the day noted, "A ship is sooner rigged by far, than a gentlewoman made ready." Once assembled, women looked like geometric puzzles, their puffy funnel shapes fitting neatly against oversized concentric circles.

Codpieces and Other Secrets of Men's Fashion

Men of the day were no less preoccupied with dress, and often outshone women in the complexity of their clothing. Next to the skin, men generally wore shirts and waistcoats with padded chests over which they would put on another **doublet** (shirt) and a **jerkin** (sleeveless vest). High collars were supported with stiff tabs called **piccadills** and, as with women's outfits, the sleeves were attached separately, stiff cloth called "wings" hiding the hooks and laces.

Toward the end of the century, men began to wear a fashion borrowed from the Dutch, a **peascod belly.** The bottom of the doublet would be padded so much that it bulged over the **girdle** (belt). **Codpieces**, too, were padded, and though meant to conceal the open-

ing in the front of men's breeches, they actually exaggerated the genital area. *Bombast* (padding) materials could be horsehair, flocks, wool, cotton, flax, or various rags. For a time, codpieces served as pockets to hold a handkerchief, small purse, or bit of fruit, such as an orange. It was a strange vogue.

Points tied the doublet to the **hose, breeches** and **stockings.** Like the women's skirts, the men's breeches were usually puffed and stuffed. *Venetians* came just below the knee and were extensively padded. Other breeches were more close-fitting or cut to just above the knee. *Canions* were close-fitting cylinders of cloth worn around the thighs. *Trunk hose* either hung in panes or ballooned around the hips like an oversized onion.

Stockings came in all colors, the brighter the better—yellow, red, green, violet, blue. There were called *nether stocks* and were either tailored or knit and made from either wool (for the poor) or silk, though some were made of leather. In cold weather, men would often wear more than one pair of stockings for warmth. The stockings were generally held up by garters of ribbon or taffeta, or buckled straps.

Like the women, the men enjoyed wearing bows on their shoes and ribboned garters as well as bright colors and detailed embroidery. As the century progressed, stylized masculinity sometimes gave way to a softened romanticism, with looser doublets, worn unbuttoned over embroidered shirts. Men's hair grew longer, and they sometimes curled their locks. "Love-locks" were tresses brought forward, brushed to one side, and curled to drape over one shoulder and over the chest. Beards of many shapes were fashionable—*Vandyke* (long and pointed), *Pickdevant* (short and pointed), Forked (short and square) and *Marquisetto* (close to the chin). Mustaches were common, but never without a beard.

Men of the upper classes wore lace and jewelry and cloaks trimmed with gold braid or fur. It was not uncommon for a man to wear earrings, like the one sported by Shakespeare in the Chandos portrait. Men wore perfumed gloves of kid, suede, silk, or leather, and carried purses. Some carried fans, though swords and daggers were also worn hanging from their belts.

Men enjoyed wearing a variety of hats both indoor and out, though they were expected to doff them in deference to someone of higher rank. After the 1570s, hats with high crowns became fashionable. **Copotain** hats had high-rounded crowns, but hats with "bowler"

crowns were also popular, as were hats with flat crowns. Indoors, men often wore under-caps or night caps. These could be made of linen, velvet or silk, though country men and the poor used coarser materials.

Given the extravagance of the age, is it any wonder that, in *King Lear*, the monarch, at the height of his famous storm scene, considers the advantages of going without clothes altogether. He bellows into the wind that humans cover themselves in what they have borrowed from nature, silk from the worm, hide from the beast, wool from the sheep, perfume from the cat. Looking at a naked companion, King Lear cries, "Thou art the thing itself: unaccommodated man is no more but such a poor, bare, forked animal as thou art." Inspired, he tears off his own clothing, the stuff of pompous and false civilization, and stands naked in the storm.

Commonsense Clothing of Commoners

Though they did not go so far as the naked King Lear, the clothing worn by common men and women was not nearly as complicated or fantastical as the clothing worn by the aristocracy. Who could afford the time it took to dress, let alone the expense of fabrics that were not washable? But even the clothes of the commoners were rarely washed. Soap was coarse in Elizabethan England, and it took work to get hot water. There was a guild of professional laundresses, but, since most clothing was washed only twice a year, it's a wonder any of them made a living. For most folks, it was enough to beat their clothing with large wooden bats to get the lice out and easier to disguise body odors with perfumes and herbs.

Colors, usually limited to greens, browns, and blues, were duller for people of modest means. Fabrics worn by workers were durable, usually made of cotton or flax and wool. *Russet* was the name of a coarse wool which was often of a reddish-brown color. Coarse linen was used for shirts, *linsey-woolsey* (a mixture of wool and yarn), canvas, or sackcloth. Tradesmen and household servants might have several articles of clothing made of silk. Good clothes were valued and were often left to friends or relatives in death-bed bequests. Aristocrats sometimes donated their elegant used clothing to acting troupes for use as costumes on stage.

Knitting had been introduced to England in the early 1500s and, by mid-century, both men and women had learned to knit. By 1560 knitted clothes were worn by all classes, and by the end of the century knitting was a profit-making business in England.

For people of the lower classes, fashions changed slowly. More focused on keeping a roof over their heads and food on the table, they were not subject to the changing whims of the fashion world. For most working men of Elizabethan England, this meant that their day-to-day wardrobe centered on the simple **jerkin,** similar to the tunics worn by their medieval ancestors. **Soled stockings** could be worn without shoes. Tradesmen and craftsmen might wear paned **trunk hose** and **cloaks** and **copotain hats**. Smiths, tanners, cobblers, and carpenters wore leather aprons, butchers and cooks wore aprons

made of linen, and barbers wore checkered aprons.

Working women did not wear **farthingales** to shape their skirts. Sometimes the skirts themselves got in the way, and they tucked them in the **waist girdle** to keep them clean while they were working. Sporting no fancy ruffs or strings of pearls around their necks, these women draped simple **neckerchiefs** over their shoulders or wore waist-length aprons over their petticoats. On their heads they wore veils, kerchiefs, or flat caps. Tiny ruffs at the neck and wrists might adorn a townswoman's gown, with a bit of lace on the bodice.

Both men and women who worked for fashion-conscious aristocrats might enjoy a luxurious wardrobe in specified colors and styles. The queen, after all, wanted to see her horsemen outfitted handsomely in bright hose and lace edged cloaks.

Babies wore caps called **biggins** and long dresses with bibbed aprons. Until they were five, boys and girls wore dresses. After that, boys were dressed like their fathers and girls like their mothers, although they did not have to wear hats. The most common material for children's clothing, even among the upper classes, was the relatively inexpensive russet.

At the end of the day, the nobility went to bed in gowns so elaborate that they could have been worn in public without much ado. Most people, however, had no special garments at all, but either slept nude or in the undershirts and smocks they had worn all day. In the Elizabethan era, cleanliness was not next to godliness; appearance was.

ROMEO AND JULIET

TEEN LOVERS DEAD IN APPARENT DOUBLE SUICIDE: FEUDING FAMILIES UNITE IN MOURNING

Period

Five summer days in the 15th century

Setting

Verona, Italy

The first Elizabethan audiences to see this play had no idea what they were in for. Thwarted young love was the stuff of comedy, and everyone expected any complications to be ironed out before the inevitable wedding scene at the end. Indeed, the play begins with enough wit, bawdy dialogue and partying to hint at comedy. Imagine the surprise of the first playgoers when they watched the teen lovers die, victims— not of greed, ambition, or jealousy like characters in other tragedies—but of circumstances beyond their control.

From the start we are told how the story will end—that two "star-cross'd" lovers" will take their lives and that this tragedy will unite their two feuding families. Even with the end revealed, there

is suspense as the plot unfolds with a grim and fast-paced inevitability.

As the story opens, the Prince of Verona has had just about enough. "Two households, both alike in dignity" are trapped in an ancient grudge and are ruining his city with their endless, bloody brawls. He decrees that, henceforth, anyone from the feuding Montague or Capulet families who disturbs his quiet streets will get the death penalty. After the prince departs, young Romeo Montague wanders onto the scene. He cares nothing for his family's troubles. All he can think about is Rosaline, his one true love. Lord Capulet, meanwhile, has also tired of the ongoing bloodshed. He wants to find a suitable husband for his thirteen-year-old daughter, Juliet, and has decided on a young nobleman named Paris, kinsman of the prince. He has planned a feast for that evening and urges Paris to take the opportunity to flirt with Juliet, woo her, "get her heart."

When, Romeo hears about the banquet, he and his friend Benvolio decide to disguise themselves and crash the party at the house of their sworn enemies. Luckily for them, the other guests are wearing masks too and the lighting is poor.

At the party, Romeo sees Juliet, and forgets all about Rosaline. At that same moment, however, Romeo is recognized by Tybalt, Juliet's belligerent cousin. Seemingly oblivious to the turmoil around them, Romeo and Juliet speak to each other for the first time and, after a brief exchange of sweet teasing talk, they kiss. After she leaves, Romeo learns from the Nurse that the girl he has just fallen in love with is the daughter of Lord Capulet, his family's adversary.

That night, after the party, Romeo climbs over the wall surrounding the Capulet estate in an attempt to catch a glimpse of the girl who has stolen his heart. Juliet, unable to sleep, appears on her balcony. Though it is night, it is sunrise in Romeo's heart and soul. He says to himself,

But, soft! What light through yonder
  window breaks?
It is the east, and Juliet is the sun....
See how she leans her cheek upon her
  hand!
O that I were a glove upon that hand,
That I might touch that cheek!

Juliet, too, is musing aloud to herself. Her thoughts are anxious, however, as she ponders the dilemma of having fallen in love with a boy from the wrong family.

O Romeo, Romeo! Wherefore art thou
  Romeo?
Deny thy father and refuse thy name;

Or, if thou wilt not, be but sworn my
  love,
And I'll no longer be a Capulet.

As Juliet leans over her balcony, the two find each other. In this, theater's most famous love scene, the teenagers plan to wed secretly the next day. Romeo runs to find Friar Laurence, his friend and confessor, who imagines a great opportunity for healing in this union. He agrees to help Romeo and Juliet. Romeo sends a message to Juliet, via the Nurse, to meet him at the cell of Friar Laurence, and they are married that afternoon.

Romeo's two pleasant friends, Benvolio and Mercutio, are on the streets, enjoying the hot summer afternoon, when both Romeo and the trouble-maker, Tybalt, appear. Though taunted, Romeo refuses to fight. Tybalt is Juliet's cousin, after all, and Romeo wants them all to be friends. Mercutio, watching from the sidelines, is outraged that Tybalt is picking a fight. He jumps in to defend Romeo and is fatally stabbed. Dying, he screams "A plague a both your houses!" Romeo is now caught in the nightmare. He picks up his sword to duel Tybalt, and kills him. Reminded of the prince's execution order, Romeo runs.

The Nurse, upset about Tybalt's death, tells Juliet the bad news and hurries to find Romeo, who is hiding in the friar's cell, cursing his fate. He is relieved to hear from the Nurse that Juliet does not blame him for her cousin's death and that she wants him by her side that night. But the night passes too quickly for the young lovers and when morning comes, Romeo departs Juliet's bedroom by the window. Almost at once there is a bustle of activity. The Capulets, unaware that their daughter is already married to Romeo, have decided Juliet will marry Paris on Thursday, just three days away. Juliet cannot stop crying. She runs to Friar Laurence for help.

The friar, as it turns out, has a plan. He will give Juliet a potion to drink that will put her in a deathlike trance for forty-two hours. She will lie in the family vault, as if dead. Meanwhile, he will send word to Romeo who will come to take her where they can live happily ever after. Juliet, wary but happy, returns home and drinks the potion. The Nurse is the first to discover Juliet, and soon the parents come running. They are all wild with grief and disbelief. Now, instead of a wedding, there will be a funeral.

Far to the north, in the city of Mantua, the exiled Romeo was supposed to have gotten word of the secret plan in a letter from the friar, but that letter never arrived, so when he hears that Juliet is dead, he believes it. He buys poison from an old apothecary and hurries to Juliet's tomb in Verona. Paris has come to Juliet's tomb too, carrying flowers. He is surprised to see the banished Romeo and, misunderstanding the situation, attacks Romeo, who kills him in self-defense. Then, eager for his own death, Romeo drinks the poison, kisses Juliet, and dies.

The friar enters the tomb and discovers the bloody scene in the tomb just as Juliet awakens. He tells her that both Romeo and Paris are dead beside her, then he hurries away. Juliet takes a moment to look around. She sees the cup in Romeo's hand and laments that there is not one drop of poison left for her. She kisses him and remarks that his lips are still warm. Then she sees his dagger. Without a second thought, she stabs herself and dies.

The tomb soon fills with disbelieving relatives from both the Capulet and Montague families. The two feuding lords, now sick with grief for their dead children, clasp hands and vow to erect golden statues in memory of Romeo and Juliet. The prince has the final word:

For never was a story of more woe
Than this of Juliet and her Romeo.

Likely Source of the Plot

Shakespeare's primary source was a poem titled *The Tragicall Historye of Romeus and Juliet*, written in 1562 by Arthur Brooke, which was, in turn, a free translation of a French work by Pierre Boaistuau, published in 1559. The French poem, however, had been largely derived from a 1554 story by the Italian writer Mateo Bandello, who had gotten the story from Luigi Da Porto's version, published in 1530.

Notable Feature

This story unfolds as if someone had pushed the "fast-forward" button. Romeo meets Juliet on a Sunday. They marry the next day and are dead by Friday.

Notable Productions and Performances

At London's Haymarket Theatre,

Leonard Whiting and Olivia Hussey as Romeo and Juliet in Zeffirelli's 1968 production.
Courtesy Museum of Modern Art/Film Stills Archive

1845, the American actress Charlotte Cushman played Romeo to her sister Susan's Juliet.

John Gielgud and Laurence Olivier, 1935, alternated as Romeo and Mercutio at the New Theatre, while Peggy Ashcroft played Juliet.

Michael Arabian's 1993 production on a back lot in Studio City, Los Angeles, used contemporary symbolism, swastikas, and Stars of David, to convey the deep animosity behind the feuding families.

Directed by Ali Rafii, 2000. This *Romeo and Juliet*, staged in Tehran, played by the strict rules established during Iran's Islamic Revolution of 1979, loosened only a little when reform-minded Mohammad Khatami came to power in 1997. That the play was staged at all was the big news, signaling something of an artistic renaissance in Iran. In this production, Juliet's hair was covered with a dark brown head scarf as required by Islamic law. Touching, let alone kissing, was not allowed, although it was reported that Juliet leaned very closely over Romeo's dead body and that she brushed his cheek with the back of her fingers.

Other Use of Basic Plot

Shakespeare's story has inspired a range of musical expressions, including the opera *I Capuleti e I Montecchi* composed in 1830 by Bellini, a symphony composed in 1839 by Berlioz, an opera written in 1867 by Gounod, a "symphonic poem" composed in 1869 by Tchaikovsky, and a doomed ballet with music by Ukrainian composer Serge Prokofiev about which it was said, "Never was a story of more woe than this of Prokofiev and his Romeo."

The 1936 black-and-white film, directed by George Cukor and starring Norma Shearer and Leslie Howard, was nominated for four Academy Awards.

West Side Story, 1957, directed/choreographed by Jerome Robbins, songs and lyrics by Leonard Bernstein and Stephen Sondheim was a Broadway hit. The musical was adapted for the screen in 1961. In this retelling, rival 1950s–style New York City gangs—the Sharks (Puerto Rican) and the Jets (white)—stand in the way of the young lovers. The film, starring Natalie Wood as the Puerto Rican teen Maria, and Richard Beymer as Tony, won ten Academy Awards.

The 1968 film directed by Franco Zeffirelli, starring Leonard Whiting and Olivia Hussey, earned two Academy Awards and was a runaway hit with moviegoers. Filmed on location in Italy, the stars were both unknown and young—just seventeen and fifteen.

Film directed by Baz Luhrmann, 1996, starring Leonardo DiCaprio and Claire Danes. This time, the tale of love, sex, and violence is set in Verona Beach, a surrealistic, futuristic city plagued by gang warfare. Dubbed "Shakespeare for the MTV generation," a rock soundtrack throbs under fast camera cuts of car chases and shoot outs.

The Boxer, 1998 film, directed by James Sheridan. This "Romeo and Juliet in Belfast" stars Daniel Day-Lewis and Emily Watson as Danny and Maggie, teenage lovers in Northern Ireland, separated when Danny is imprisoned. After his release fourteen years later, Danny tries to use the sport of boxing as a way to bring Catholics and Protestants together. Maggie's love for Danny is viewed as treason and his love for her is forbidden by tribe and tradition.

Hip hop opera *Rome & Jewels*, 2000, choreographed by Rennie Harris for the "PureMovement" dance troupe. Combining acrobatics, moon walking, martial arts, jazz, and break dancing, in this fusion of Shakespeare and African cultural forms, the text is spoken in street jive. Here, the Montagues become the "Monster Qs," a hip-hop rival gang to the break-dancing Caps.

Romeo Must Die, 2000 film, directed by Andrzej Bartkowiak, starring martial-arts legend Jet Li. Set in present-day Oakland, Jet Li plays an ex-cop, ex-con from Hong Kong who is in love with African American R&B star Aaliyah.

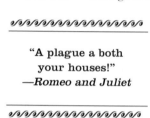

"A plague a both your houses!"
—Romeo and Juliet

The Moons of Uranus

n *Romeo and Juliet*, the star-crossed lovers have a moment of tension around the use of the moon as an appropriate object on which to swear one's faithful intentions. Romeo means well as he innocently begins his flowery speech, saying, "Lady, by yonder blessed moon, I swear, / That tips with silver all these fruit-tree tops—" Juliet, with all the brash self-confidence of her thirteen years, interrupts him saying, "O, swear not by the moon, the inconstant moon, / That monthly changes in her circled orb, / Lest that thy love prove likewise variable."

There was but one pale moon in the lovers' sky. Imagine our moonstruck teens gazing up at the sky over the planet Uranus, where there is not one moon, but twenty.

Fifteen of the twenty moons of Uranus are named after characters in Shakespeare's plays. Four take their names from *The Tempest*: **Ariel**, airy sprite attending Prospero, and **Caliban**, Prospero's earthy slave, as well as Caliban's mother, the witch **Sycorax**, and **Miranda**, Prospero's awe-filled daughter. Three moons are named after characters in *A Midsummer Night's Dream*: **Oberon**, the Fairy King, **Titania**, the Fairy Queen, and **Puck**, the mischievous elfin creature who delights in chaos. Except for some moons named after characters from the poems of Alexandar Pope, the rest are named after Shakespearean heroines. There is **Desdemona**, the faithful but fated wife in *Othello* and **Bianca**, Cassio's courtesan from the same play. One moon is named after **Portia**, the rich and wise heiress of the *Merchant of Venice*, and there is one for **Rosalind**, cross-dressing kidder from *As You Like It*. There is a moon named for **Juliet**, but not for Romeo, and one for **Cressida**, but not for Troilus.

In 1986, Voyager II discovered two tiny "shepherding moons" hidden in the rings of Uranus. They were named for **Ophelia**, who killed herself in *Hamlet,* and **Cordelia**, the beloved but rejected daughter of *King Lear*. Once discovered, however, the little moons disappeared from sight. Even the Hubble Space Telescope had a hard time finding them. Eventually, scientists followed some ripples in the rings, and the lost moons were found.

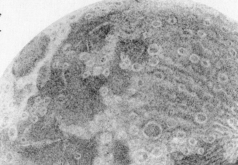

TIMON OF ATHENS

EMBITTERED BANKRUPT BENEFACTOR FINDS GOLD IN WILDERNESS, CURSES HUMANITY

Period

4th century B.C.E.

Settings

Athens and environs

Step into an allegory, a pageant of sorts, in which one-dimensional characters representing abstract concepts will teach us all a lesson. When we first meet Timon, he is the generous, big-hearted center of attention, surrounded by a wide circle of friends who feast at his table and fawn at his feet. He is altruism personified, and his is a world of abundance, sensuous delight, luxury. He shares all of it freely, believing himself blessed, rich in friends. He cares little for gold, except that it allows him to treat his friends and help them in their time of need. He sees the best in everyone. Enjoying the opulent excess are Poet, Painter, Jeweler, Merchant, Alcibiades (a military leader), and several others.

Two men remain on the sidelines of all the festivities, unconvinced. Flavius, Timon's devoted servant, worries what will happen when the gold runs out. He frets, "Ah, when the means are gone that buy this praise, / The breath is gone whereof this praise is made: / Feast-won, fast-lost."

The other who remains an observer is Apemantus, a cynic. He respects Timon for his childlike faith and pities him for his foolish philanthropy. He also recognizes Timon's friends to be flatterers and parasites. Apemantus offers up a prayer of mistrust to the gods:

Grant I may never prove so fond
To trust man on his oath or bond,
Or a harlot for her weeping,
Or a dog that seems a-sleeping,
Or a keeper with my freedom,
Or my friends, if I should need'em.
Amen.

When the money does, inevitably, run out, Timon is not worried. He is sure his friends will help him through his hard times, as he has helped them through theirs. He sends his servants through the city to ask for help, but each is turned away, empty-handed.

There is no measured transformation here. When next we meet Timon he is a changed man. Once wholly loving, now he wholly hates. With the abruptness that is possible in allegory, Timon now names himself Misanthrope. He throws one last party. All his old friends come, sheepishly, out of curiosity, thinking he must have been testing them and is not bankrupt after all. Each is seated at the banquet table and served a covered dish. When the lids are removed, the would-be diners find nothing but lukewarm water. Timon offers a long prayer, far angrier and darker than the cynic's earlier one. As he prays, his words turn from sarcastic blessings to heartfelt curses. He begins to splash water from the serving bowls on his guests. It is a baptism of bitterness. "For these, my present friends, as they are to me nothing, so in nothing bless them, and to nothing are they welcome." With that, the dishes begin to fly and the guests flee. "Let confusion live!" he bellows to his gods, begging plagues, itches, and leprosy to torment the Athenians. "Breath infect breath, / That their society, as their friendship, may / Be merely poison!" He proclaims his intention, to live in the wilderness, as far from fellow humans as possible. And with that he cries, "Amen."

Preferring the cruelty of nature to that of false friends, he finds a remote cave in the woods near the seashore. His old steward weeps, "Poor honest lord, brought low by his own heart, / Undone by goodness!" The world has been turned upside-down. Where once Timon was surrounded by music, food, rich colors, and friends, he is now a hermit in a loin cloth, shunning all beauty, all love.

Hungry, he begins to dig for roots. As luck would have it, he finds gold instead. There will soon be a line of spongers outside his cave, and he knows it. When the procession of unwanted visitors begins, none go away empty-handed. Each is given coins and curses. Alcibiades, the military man, is on his way to attack Athens because ungrateful senators there have carelessly dismissed his pleas of mercy for a friend sentenced to death. Timon is glad to fund the invasion and gives him gold with which he is instructed to "make large confusion." Alcibiades' soldiers are to kill babies, virgin girls, pregnant women, priests, and, finally, all who live in Athens.

Apemantus, the cynic, comes too. He and Timon each try to out-do the other in bitterness. The cynic thrives on his hatred. Timon, on the other hand, takes no delight in hatred. With the passion of a new convert, he describes, not only humanity, but all of Nature and the universe itself, to be based on greed, distrust, and cruelty. The men exchange insults—"Beast!" "Slave!" "Toad!" "Rogue!" Others come, and are met with the same excess of bitterness and rage. Only the faithful old steward, Flavius, affects the now hardened misanthrope. He momentarily brings tears to Timon's eyes with his sincerity, but is eventually pushed away like the others, with the admonition to "Hate all, curse all, show charity to none."

Timon's contempt for life is not softened at play's end. He wills his own

Timon as played by British actor Edmund Kean in 1816. Shakespeare Birthplace Trust

death, while still steeped in hatred. The note of redemption, limp as it is, belongs, not to the protagonist, but to the man of war, who is so appalled by Timon's wrath, that he seeks a gesture of mercy. He vows not to slay everyone in the decadent city of Athens, but to spare the innocent.

Likely Source of the Plot

The story of Timon dates back to a 2nd century Greek "comic dialogue" by Lucian, *Timon the Misanthrope*. In Elizabethan England this story existed in Latin, French, and Italian translations, but not in English. The story of

Timon was also told by Plutarch in the *Life of Marcus Antonius*, translated into English in 1579.

Notable Feature

More pageant than play, this allegorical drama has been categorized as tragedy, comedy, tragicomedy, social satire, morality play, all of the above, none of the above. It is one of the least popular of Shakespeare's plays, not only because of its unremitting bitterness, but because it seems to be a rough draft, in need of editing.

Notable Productions and Performances

Timon of Athens, the Man-Hater, 1678, an adaptation by Thomas Shadwell, was staged with the addition of a love interest.

The first known staging with the original Shakespearean text in England, 1851, directed by Samuel Phelps.

In Thick Description's production in San Francisco, 1993, directed by Tony Kelly, adapted by Karen Amano, Apemantus, a hellfire-and-brimstone black Baptist preacher, watches as Timon and his false friends drink Evian water and gorge themselves on roast pig. When an accountant pulls out a computer printout of Timon's debts, the bootlicking freeloaders disappear. In a rage, Timon rips down the plush purple curtains to reveal the theater's bare brick walls and windows that look out on the street. As he delivers his fierce soliloquy of hate, Timon heads into the wilderness, but returns to madly pound on the windows from outside the theater, looking in at the startled audience.

The Teatro Stabile of Turin's production in Florence, Italy, directed by Walter Pagliao, 1995, in what the director viewed as a proto-Marxist Shakespearean text about the bewilderment of a society devastated by money, Timon, like Italian capitalists in the credit-card age, is portrayed as addicted to immediate gratification.

In a production by Sacred Fools Theater in Los Angeles, 1998, directed by Scott Rabinowitz, the opening scene is set in Hollywood, a world that thrives on insincerity and schmoozing. Timon's friends are screenwriters, casting directors, crooked cops, and burned-out movie stars, all entertained by lascivious lap dancers. A female Apemantus is the angry, sometime lover dressed all in black, who can't wait to say "I told you so." The wilderness is a Las Vegas casino.

Other

A musical score was written by the legendary Duke Ellington in 1963 for a production in Stratford, Ontario. It was later adapted by Stanley Silverman when the show was remounted in 1991. It was used again by the Royal Shakespeare Theatre, under the direction of Gregory Doran, in 1999. In addition to Duke Ellington, other composers have been inspired to write music based on the play, including Henry Purcell in 1694.

Poems of the Bard

A "bard" is a poet. The Bard—capital T, capital B—is, specifically, Shakespeare. The nickname honors the exquisite poetry of his plays and sonnets, but it is also a reminder that, in his own day, when literary folk heard the name Shakespeare they did not think of *Hamlet* or *Macbeth*, but of the two long poems he had contributed to the Top-Ten list of Elizabethan favorites—"Venus and Adonis" and "The Rape of Lucrece."

"Venus and Adonis"

Shakespeare's funny and erotic narrative poem, published in 1593, was loosely drawn from Ovid's *Metamorphoses*, but is about 1,125 lines longer. It describes the unrequited infatuation of Venus, the Roman goddess of love and beauty, for "rose-cheek'd" Adonis, a disinterested golden boy. He is engrossed in his hunt and annoyed at any distraction, but the goddess is determined and relentless as she pursues him. She plucks him from his horse, kisses him all over, aggressively chases him over hill and dale.

*Now quick desire hath caught the yield-
    ing prey,*
*And glutton-like she feeds, yet never fill-
    eth;*
Her lips are conquerors, his lips obey,
Paying what ransom the insulter willeth.

The hunter becomes the hunted, and he's not happy about it. The lusty goddess works up a sweat of desire, and the balky boy blushes; "She red and hot as coals of glowing fire, / He red for shame, but frosty in desire." She does her bawdy best to seduce him with imagery, and is close to vulgar when she describes herself as landscape:

I'll be a park, and thou shalt be my deer;
*Feed where thou wilt, on mountain
    or in dale;*
Graze on my lips; and if those hills be dry,
*Stray lower, where the pleasant
    fountains lie.*

Within this limit is relief enough,
Sweet bottom-grass, and high delightful
    plain,
Round rising hillocks, brakes obscure
    and rough,
To shelter thee from tempest and from
    rain;
Then be my deer, since I am such a park;
No dog shall rouse thee, though a thou-
    sand bark.

Venus is lovesick and feverish with desire, but all this sex talk does nothing for Adonis. "No, lady, no; my heart longs not to groan, / But soundly sleeps, while now it sleeps alone," he says. She is sensuous and earthy; he is abstract and cerebral.

In the end, he returns to the hunt, but is killed by a wild boar. In her grief, Venus puts a curse on love for all eternity, a curse that any who have known love are sure to recognize:

Sorrow on love hereafter shall attend:
It shall be waited on with jealousy,
Find sweet beginning but unsavory end,
Ne'er settled equally, but high or low,
That all love's pleasure shall not match
    his woe....
It shall be raging mad and silly mild,
Make the young old, the old become a
    child.
It shall suspect where is no cause of fear;
It shall not fear where it should most
    mistrust.

Sound familiar?

Venus, now weary of the world and needing solitude for her mourning, turns the dead Adonis into a purple and white flower, a memorial to her beloved's pale, blood-stained cheeks.

She vows to wear this nosegay in the "hollow cradle" of her bosom where "My throbbing heart shall rock thee day and night."

Published by Richard Field, with great attention to detail by the author, "Venus and Adonis" was enormously popular. It was reprinted several times in the poet's lifetime and was frequently quoted by other poets and writers in various anthologies of the day. The poem was prefaced with a fawning dedication to the Earl of Southampton, a wealthy and influential patron of the arts, in which Shakespeare called this work the "first heir of my invention" and promised "some graver labor" to come.

"The Rape of Lucrece"

That graver labor was another narrative poem, published just one year later, longer and far more serious in tone and theme than the first. Based on an ancient legend, it was a retelling of the rape of Lucretia, an aristocratic Roman matron, by Tarquin, the son of a Roman king.

As Tarquin, in the grip of sexual desire, moves in on his victim, Shakespeare paints a picture of foreboding:

Now stole upon the time the dead of
    night,
When heavy sleep had clos'd up mortal
    eyes;
No comfortable star did lend his light,
No noise but owls' and wolves'
    death-boding cries;
Now serves the season that they
    may surprise
The silly lambs. Pure thoughts are dead
    and still,

While lust and murder wake to
stain and kill.

Tarquin knows he is about to do wrong, and he frets that it will bring shame on his name and his family. "Yea, though I die, the scandal will survive."

Creeping into her bedroom, Tarquin awakens Lucrece when he grabs her breast, and, seeing her terror, is angered by it. She spends the first half of the poem begging to be spared, but she pleads "in a wilderness where are no laws." She reminds him that her husband is his friend, and she tries for pity, saying, "If ever man were mov'd with woman's moans, / Be moved with my tears, my sighs, my groans."

Nothing works. Tarquin says simply, "this night I must enjoy thee. / If thou deny, then force must work my way, / For in thy bed I purpose to destroy thee."

After the rape, the poem becomes a "Complaint," a popular genre in the 16th century. While the first half of the poem focused most of the attention on the rapist's mind, intention, drive, desperation, and reactions to his victim, the second half belongs to Lucrece. She curses the night:

O comfort-killing Night, image of hell!
Dim register and notary of shame!
Black stage for tragedies and murders fell!
Vast sin-concealing chaos! nurse of blame!

She curses Tarquin, too, and condemns his memory.

The nurse, to still her child, will tell my
story,
And fright her crying babe with
Tarquin's name;

The orator, to deck his oratory,
Will couple my reproach to Tarquin's
shame.

She prays that he will be cursed with time:

Let him have time to tear his curled hair,
Let him have time against himself to
rave...
Let him have time to see his friends his
foes,
And merry fools to mock at him resort;
Let him have time to mark how slow
time goes
In time of sorrow, and how swift and short
His time of folly and his time of sport.

Though she cannot stop weeping, she bravely proclaims, "I am the mistress of my fate," and sets about reclaiming control of her life. She makes the decision to kill herself and to tell everything that has happened before she does. She summons her family. When her husband comes home, he finds her dressed in mourning. Then Lucrece, "this pale swan in her wat'ry nest / Begins the sad dirge of her certain ending." After telling all, she urges revenge for the violence done to her. Her father, her husband, and his lords have no trouble swearing an oath of vengence.

Lucrece now imagines her defiled body a "blemish'd fort" from which she longs to free her tormented soul. In a gesture parallel to the penetration of rape, she penetrates her own heart with a knife to make a hole for her soul's escape. Though it is a tragic ending, Lucrece has determined how the story ends. Her dead and bloody body is paraded through the streets of Rome.

Tarquin's crime is reported and he is banished forever. According to legend, the removal of the prince led to the establishment of the Roman Republic and the rule by consuls, not kings.

Like his first poem, Shakespeare also dedicated this one to the Earl of Southampton, but the formal tone used in the earlier preface was replaced by a noticeably more intimate one. "The Rape of Lucrece," based largely on works by Fasti and Livy and written in a seven-line rhyme stanza called "royal rhyme," was published in May 1594 to great acclaim, unlike two other poems ascribed to him, "A Lover's Complaint" and "The Phoenix and the Turtle," which received little attention, though the latter poem in particular has some haunting images.

JULIUS CAESAR

AMBITION PROVES FATAL: THE MAN WHO WOULD BE KING

Period

1st century B.C.E.

Setting

Rome

The play begins with two Roman officials berating a group of artisans in the streets of Rome for neglecting their work. The officials are appalled to learn that the rabble are celebrating Julius Caesar's triumphant return from battle. "What captives brings he home?" asks Marullus, one of the officials. There are no prisoners since the war in which Caesar triumphed was not a defense of the empire from its enemies, but a civil conflict with the sons of Pompey.

In the streets of Rome, Caesar, on his way to a ceremonial race in which his protégé Marc Antony is to run, is stopped by a soothsayer. The man warns him to "beware the ides of March" (the ides were the midpoint in each Roman month). Two other noblemen, Brutus

and Cassius, discuss the threat to Rome's republican government posed by the combination of Caesar's ambition and the widespread—but not universal—desire to crown him a king, a form of government fervently opposed by many members of the ruling oligarchy.

As they talk they hear, but cannot see, several loud public shouts. When Caesar and his party reappear, Casca tells Brutus and Cassius that Marc Antony three times offered Caesar a crown in front of the assembled crowd, and Caesar "put it by thrice, each time gentler than the other." As Caesar and Marc Antony walk past the two men, Caesar tells Marc Antony that Cassius has "a lean and hungry look...such men as he be never at heart's ease whiles they behold a greater than themselves." Brutus agrees to talk later with Cassius and his friends.

At night seeming portents overwhelm the sky—thunder, lightning, meteor showers. Casca discovers Cassius stalking the troubled streets, interpreting the signs as a heavenly reaction to Caesar's growing power. Casca tells him that he has heard that the next day the Senate will offer Caesar a crown to govern all the empire except for Italy, and joins Cassius's conspiracy against Caesar. Brutus, sleepless in his garden thanks to his earlier conversation, finds Cassius at his door with other Romans unhappy with the situation—Casca, Decius, Cinna, Metellus Cimber and Trebonius. Together they make a fateful decision—to assassinate Caesar to prevent his acquiring the crown, but to spare Marc Antony.

As the plotters depart, Brutus is joined by his wife, Portia, who has noted his recent anxiety and preoccupation. She demands to be "acquainted with your cause of grief," not to mention what has brought men hiding their faces to her house in the middle of the night. "By and by thy bosom shall partake of the secrets of my heart," Brutus tells her.

The omens of the night have also troubled Calpurnia, the wife of Caesar, who as morning breaks urges him not to leave their house. He is unmoved, saying "these same predictions are to the world in general as to Caesar," while she notes that "when beggars die there are no comets seen. The heavens themselves blaze forth the deaths of princes."

Caesar's resolve softens when Calpurnia tells him she dreamed his statue ran with blood "and many lusty Romans came smiling and did bathe their hands in it." His decision to avoid the Senate that day is overcome, however, when Decius (who boasted to the plotters that he had mastered the ability to flatter Caesar by seeming not to do so), arrives and reinterprets the dream to mean that Rome relies on him for sustenance. He adds that the Senate is to offer Caesar that day a crown—an offer that may not be extended again if Caesar fails to appear.

His mind changing again, Caesar dismisses Calpurnia's fears and makes ready to go to the capitol, along with the other conspirators, who have come to his house to escort him to the Senate. On the way there he ignores one petitioner with a scroll warning him of the plot, and he observes—to the soothsayer who had warned him of the ides of March—that the ides have come. "Ay, Caesar, but not gone," the man replies.

In the Senate chamber the plotters surround him, ostensibly to plead for the return from banishment of Metellus Cimber's brother. After a high-minded lecture in which Caesar refuses to change his mind on the basis of obsequiousness and flattery ("I am as constant as the Northern Star") Casca stabs him and the rest join in, including, at the last, Brutus, giving the famous line, "Et tu, Brute?" When he is dead, the conspirators bathe their hands in Caesar's blood and prepare to announce to the people that "tyranny is dead."

The conspirators grant Antony—over the objections of Cassius—the chance to give Caesar's funeral oration. In an aside to the audience after the conspirators have left him alone with Caesar's body, Antony makes it clear that he will use the occasion of his

> **"Beware the ides of March."**
> —*Julius Caesar*

The suicide of Brutus

speech to "cry 'Havoc' and let slip the dogs of war" on the conspirators. Brutus's oration is short, to the point ("As Caesar loved me, I weep for him; as he was fortunate, I rejoice at it; as he was valiant, I honor him; but, as he was ambitious, I slew him") and well-received by the crowd in the Forum, roaring their approval of Caesar's demise. Antony's answering oration starts slowly ("He was my friend, faithful and just to me..."), and repeatedly cites the "honorable" qualities of Brutus and the other conspirators. But Antony reminds the crowd of Caesar's triumphs, his contributions to the general welfare, and his refusal to accept the crown that he was offered.

The sight of Caesar's dead body, the itemization of his wounds ("See what a rent the envious Casca made...through this the well-beloved Brutus stabbed..."), and finally the reading of the will (it leaves an inheritance for every citizen and the use of his estate for a public park) is enough to stir the crowd to a frenzy of revenge. Antony now allies himself with Caesar's adopted heir Octavius and another powerful Roman, Lepidus, and raises forces to oppose Caesar's assassins, who have fled the city.

Near the city of Sardis, Brutus and Cassius quarrel bitterly over accusations that Cassius has turned a blind eye to bribery and his failure to raise money to pay Brutus's legions. They nearly come to blows before they manage to patch up their differences, and it becomes clear that Brutus, "sick of many griefs," is also very upset over the death of his wife. The two and their generals agree to go forth to meet the forces of Antony and Octavius, though Cassius prefers to stand their ground. The ghost of Caesar visits Brutus later that night in his tent, promising to see him at Philippi, and at Philippi the armies meet.

At one point Cassius sends his friend Titinius for a closer look at the battle, and Titinius is captured. Despairing of victory and unwilling to be captured as well as led through Rome in triumph, Cassius has a servant kill him with the sword he had used to kill Caesar. But Titinius, rather than being captured, was actually surrounded by allies, and when he finds Cassius dead he too kills himself.

The battle continues. Although Brutus's forces at first were winning their contest with those of Octavius, eventually they too are worn down, and as his enemies close in Brutus has one of his officers hold his sword while he impales himself on it and dies. Both Antony and Octavius demonstrate their respect for him in death. "This was the noblest Roman of them all. All the conspirators save only he did that they did in envy of great Caesar," says Antony, while Octavius offers, "Within my tent his bones tonight shall lie, most like a soldier ordered honorably."

Likely Source of the Plot

Plutarch's *Lives of the Noble Greeks and Romans* was Shakespeare's source, in an English version of a French translation.

Background

For centuries before the time of Julius Caesar, Rome was ruled as a republic, with the Senate the official governing body and individuals rotating service in judicial and executive posts such as tribune, quaestor, praetor, and consul. A growing empire, associated wars, and civil unrest built the pressure for a single leader. In 49 B.C.E., Julius Caesar, a successful general in the Gallic Wars, brought his legions across the Rubicon (the boundary of the province) in defiance of the Senate, ostensibly to bring order out of chaos. Pompey, a successful and popular leader who had served with Caesar and Crassus in the governing alliance later known as the *First Triumvirate*, opposed him. Their war ranged across the Mediterranean and after Pompey died in Egypt, his sons continued the fight. It was from a victory against them at the battle of Munda in Spain in 46 B.C.E. that Caesar returned at the beginning of this play. While the play telescopes the celebration of the Lupercal and Caesar's assassination, in fact these events were months apart.

Octavius, Julius Caesar's adopted heir, eventually joined Marc Antony and Lepidus in the ruling coalition known as the *Second Triumvirate*. By 31 B.C.E., Lepidus and Antony were dead (a story told in Shakespeare's *Antony and Cleopatra*). Octavius, eventually known as Augustus Caesar, then became the leading figure in Rome. Most historians credit him with maintaining and even reviving the outward trappings of republican government, while making sure that in reality all power remained concentrated in his hands. He died in 14 C.E.

Notable Features

The words Brutus uses to actually join the conspiracy are never said in front of the audience. When he leaves Cassius after Caesar refuses the crown at the Lupercal, Brutus promises to speak again on the subject. He is alone when he reaches the decision that only Caesar's death will halt his ambition. When the plotters arrive in his garden he has a few offstage words with Cassius, after which he proceeds as if his participation were never in doubt.

The play is full of familiar lines: *There is a tide in the affairs of men, which, taken at the flood, leads on to fortune....Yond Cassius has a lean and hungry look....Cowards die many times before their deaths, the valiant never taste of death but once....not that I loved Caesar less, but that I loved Rome more....I come to bury Caesar, not to praise him....The noblest Roman of them all.*

Marlon Brando as Marc Antony in Julius Caesar. Courtesy Museum of Modern Art/Film Stills Archive

Notable Productions and Performances

The American actor Edwin Booth was a famous 19th century Brutus on the stage. Orson Welles played Brutus in a modern-dress version in New York City in 1938.

The 1953 film version was directed by Joseph Mankiewicz and received five Oscar nominations, including Best Picture and Best Actor (for Marlon Brando, an unconventional but compelling Marc Antony). James Mason and John Gielgud as Brutus and Cassius give excellent performances, and Greer Garson and Deborah Kerr appear as Calpurnia and Portia, respectively.

The ever-reliable Gielgud appears in the 1970 film remake as Julius Caesar, with Charlton Heston as Marc Antony and a horribly miscast Jason Robards as Brutus (critics described his performance as "zombie-like"). The 1979 *Time-Life*/BBC version has a first-rate Richard Pasco as Brutus, with David Collings as Cassius and Charles Gray as Caesar.

MACBETH

SCOTLAND IN TURMOIL AS AMBITIOUS KING AND QUEEN FORCE FULFILLMENT OF PROPHECY

Period

11th century

Setting

Scotland

Prepare to descend into a dark and bloody nightmare, an Elizabethan horror movie like an early Chainsaw Massacre—only, instead of Texas, it's Scotland and instead of your standard dumbed-down dialogue, it is Shakespeare. If only those three witches hadn't appeared on the "blasted heath," cackling their prophecy that Macbeth would be king. If only. But they did, and once the idea has been introduced, Macbeth can't stop it from seeping into his consciousness, staining his every thought.

Macbeth and Banquo, generals of the Scottish king's army, have successfully quelled a rebel uprising. The king is so impressed with stories of Macbeth's valor that he decides to promote him from Thane of Glamis to Thane of Cawdor. Before word of the title change reaches Macbeth by conventional means, however, he hears it from three bearded witches, midnight hags, who appear in the filthy air muttering that "fair is foul and foul is fair," and cackling, "All hail, Macbeth, that shalt be King hereafter!" Banquo sees the witches too. He is told he will beget kings.

The two men are ready to shrug off the encounter with these "weird sisters," but, just then, word comes from the king about Macbeth's promotion. Later, when Macbeth is told to expect a visit from the king, a disturbing thought flickers through his mind. He puts the thought aside and writes a note to Lady Macbeth. If only Macbeth hadn't told his wife about his encounter with the witches and their prophecy. If only. But he did and now a thought seeps into her mind, too.

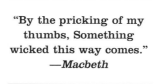

> "By the pricking of my thumbs, Something wicked this way comes."
> —*Macbeth*

While she's reading her husband's letter, a messenger arrives with word that the king is coming to Macbeth's castle at Inverness that very night. Lady Macbeth, worried that her husband's

Macbeth tells her husband to screw his courage to the sticking place and their plan will succeed.

If only Macbeth had screwed his sense of honor and ethics to the sticking

nature has too much of "the milk of human kindness" in it, utters aloud a prayer—that she be filled with cruelty.

When the king and his sons arrive, Macbeth and his lady are both charming and generous hosts. Macbeth knows that Duncan, the king, is a good man and there is no reason, other than raw ambition, to murder him. Lady Macbeth sees nothing wrong with raw ambition. She argues her case and Macbeth backs down, agreeing to the plan his lady has devised: that night, when the king is asleep, she will get the guards drunk and borrow their daggers. Then, she'll give an all-clear signal and Macbeth will murder the king and plant the bloody daggers on the drunken men. Lady

place instead. If only. That night, as he wanders the courtyard, awaiting the signal, he sees a vision—a bloody knife floating through the air. This is the first hint of blood. There will be more. Much more.

When he hears the all-clear signal, he goes in to kill the king. Lady Macbeth has prepared everything very well, the daggers laid just so, but Macbeth is shaken and distressed after he murders the king. Lady Macbeth has to retrieve the daggers and plant them on the guards. She returns from this task with her hands covered in the blood she's smeared on the guards. "A little water clears us of this deed," she says. Right.

Suddenly, there's knocking at the south gate. A drunken porter, who imagines himself the gatekeeper to hell, admits two noblemen, Macduff and Lennox, who have arrived early to visit the king. Macbeth is again the gracious host, but when Macduff discovers that the king is dead, alarm spreads through the castle. In the confusion that follows, Macbeth kills the guards, telling everyone that they were obviously the murderers. The dead king's sons, seeing "daggers in men's smiles," realize they can trust no one and they bolt. With fingers of blame wagging in various directions, no one points at the Macbeths. On the contrary, it is decided that Macbeth will be crowned king.

Mission accomplished, or so one would think. Macbeth remembers that Banquo heard the witches' prophecies and may put two and two together. Macbeth orders the murder of both Banquo (who is killed) and his son (who is not). But the new king can no longer feign nerves of steel, when Banquo's ghost shows up at a feast. "Blood will have blood," mumbles Macbeth as his guests run away.

Macbeth begs words of reassurance from the three witches who started all this trouble. They comply, chanting their famous "Double, double, toil and trouble," and conjure three apparitions from the foul air to give Macbeth three warnings and riddles. First, he is warned to beware Macduff. Second, he's told he'll never be harmed by any man born of a woman. Third, he's told he'll not be conquered until Birnam Wood comes to the hill of Dunsinane. Hearing this, Macbeth heaves a sigh of relief. He's never heard of a man not born of a woman, nor of a forest moving from one place to another.

As for Macduff, however, Macbeth decides to act swiftly. The nobleman has defected to London and is voicing his suspicions about what's happening in Scotland. Macbeth gives his most brutal order yet, that Macduff's family is to be massacred. When Macduff hears that his children are dead, he vows revenge.

Now the Macbeths are quite over the edge. Macbeth can't sleep for all the nightmares. He goes off to organize his dwindling forces to fight the army of English and Scottish soldiers amassing against him.

Lady Macbeth has lost her mind, sleepwalking and muttering and moving her hands as if she's constantly washing them. When she commits suicide, the women of the castle wail, but Macbeth is so emotionally shut down that he barely blinks at the news. He ponders life's futility in his soliloquy of despair:

Tomorrow and tomorrow and tomorrow,
Creeps in this petty pace from day to day
To the last syllable of recorded time,
And all our yesterdays have lighted fools
The way to dusty death. Out, out, brief
   candle!
Life's but a walking shadow, a poor
   player,
That struts and frets his hour upon the
   stage,
And then is heard no more; it is a tale
Told by an idiot, full of sound and fury,
Signifying nothing.

Macbeth doesn't begin to worry about his own well-being until he is told that Birnam Wood seems to be on the move. In fact, the advancing soldiers have put on tree branches as camouflage; the prophecy is being fulfilled.

With his life in ruins, Macbeth vows to keep fighting. After all, wasn't it also foretold that no man born of a woman would harm him?

If only Macbeth had asked the witches' apparition to be more specific and explain what it had meant by these words. If only. But he hadn't asked, and so, for a brief while, Macbeth continues to imagine himself invulnerable, immune to death on the battlefield.

Suddenly, he is in hand-to-hand combat with Macduff, but he's still not worried. He boasts that his is "a charmed life, which must not yield / To one of woman born." Hearing this, Macduff realizes his advantage. He cries, "Despair thy charm" and blurts out that he was "from his mother's womb / Untimely ripp'd"—another way of saying he was born by Ceasarean section. At this, Macbeth's bubble of imagined invincibility bursts, and he is slain by Macduff. Duncan's son Malcolm is named King of Scotland, while the Macbeths are damned as the "dead butcher, and his fiend-like queen."

Likely Source of the Plot

The character of Macbeth is loosely based on an historic figure of the same name, who lived from 1005 to 1057 and who launched a civil war and seized the Scottish throne from his cousin Duncan. There is no evidence that the real Macbeth was ever prompted by his wife, Gruoch, nor that his actions led to the turmoil depicted in Shakespeare's play. In fact, the real Macbeth ruled in peace for fifteen years. The primary source for *Macbeth* was Holinshed's *Chronicles*, second edition, published in 1587.

Notable Features

Macbeth is the shortest of the major tragedies. Nearly one third of the lines belong to the blood-stained Scot himself. In theater-lore, this play is associated with bad luck and disaster (see "The Curse of the 'M' Word," pages 250–51).

Notable Productions and Performances

Popular from its first performance at the court of James I, the witches were reduced to comic characters in the late 17th century and early 18th century. The role of Lady Macbeth has brought fame to a number of transcendent tragedians, including Sarah Siddons (1755–1831) about whose sleepwalking scene one audience member raved, "I smelt blood! I swear that I smelt blood!" Vivien Leigh played the part in 1955 opposite Laurence Olivier at the Royal Shakespeare Theatre, and Judi Dench played opposite Ian McKellen at Stratford-upon-Avon in Trevor Nunn's 1976 production, later filmed for television.

Other Uses of Basic Plot

A production by the Federal Theater Project's Negro Unit, 1936, directed by Orson Welles, made news when it opened in depression-era Harlem. With an all-black cast, the play was dubbed "Voodoo Macbeth" because it was set in 19th century Haiti and utilized voodoo drummers.

Film directed by Orson Welles, 1948, who also played the lead role.

A haunted Orson Welles as Macbeth. Courtesy Museum of Modern Art/Film Stills Archive

Joe Macbeth, 1955, a film adaptation about a mobster and his nagging wife who reach for power after arranging to have their Mafia kingpin rubbed out.

Throne of Blood, 1957, Japanese film directed by Akira Kurosawa, an adaptation of Shakespeare's play, influenced by traditional Noh drama.

MacBird!, 1966, by Barbara Garson. Celebrated as anti-establishment literature, this is Shakespearean English with a Texas drawl. Here, America's First Lady, "Ladybird" Johnson, was depicted as Lady MacBird whose husband is contemptuous of the young and handsome John Ken O'Dunc, ahead in the race for king. As the 1960 Presidential Convention draws to a close, three witches tell MacBird that he is destined to rule. Later, when the popular king visits the MacBirds, he is assassinated during a grand procession through their streets.

British film directed by Roman Polanski, 1971, notable for its graphic depictions of violence inflicted by a repressive regime, like the one Polanski experienced as a child in Poland.

Resistance Theater's 1999 production in Brooklyn of an adaptation by Heiner Müller. With a techno soundtrack blaring in the background, the medieval Scots and witches dress in their heavy-metal best, with thick black boots, metal studs and chains, on a harsh landscape of industrial props, while Lady Macbeth perches atop a mountain of bloodless mannequin limbs hauntingly reminiscent of bodies piled high at Nazi death camps.

Film directed by Quentin Tarantino, 1999. Set in crime-ridden New Yorkshire, Lady Macbeth is a prostitute and Macbeth her pimp who is influenced by three jive-rhyming rappers.

The Curse of the "M" Word

ost actors know better than to utter the name "Macbeth" backstage. The name itself is synonymous with bad luck, and the one who makes a slip is likely to be cast out of the dressing room in a ritual exorcism. To get back in, the actor must turn around three times, spit, recite a line from *The Merchant of Venice*—"Fair thoughts and happy hours attend on you"— then knock on the door and beg permission to reenter.

Why all the superstition? There's good reason. Consider this laundry list of historic disasters:

1606: The Premature Death of Lady Macbeth

At the very first performance of the play, in the court of James I (a descendant of the real life Duncan), Hal Berridge, the boy actor playing the part of Lady Macbeth, collapsed from a fever and died. Legend has it that Shakespeare himself, obeying the dictate that the show must go on, stepped in to replace the young actor.

1703: Show Blamed for Stormy Weather

On the afternoon *Macbeth* opened in London, the city was hit with one of the most severe storms ever recorded in England. Blaming the play, Queen Anne ordered all the theaters to be closed for a week of prayer and repentance.

1849: Theatergoers Killed in Riot

Handsome, hearty Edwin Forrest was an American-born actor with a big following in New York City. His working-class fans got a little upset when they heard that he would not be playing the part of Macbeth at the Astor Place Opera House. Instead, the part would be played by Charles Macready, a British actor favored by the city's elite. On opening night, May 10th, a crowd of ten thousand gathered outside the theater, including members of two gangs, the Bowery Boys and the Dead Rabbits. When they began to pelt the theater windows with stones, the city sent in two hundred militia from the Seventh Regiment and four cavalry companies. Instead of restoring order, the soldiers overreacted and began shooting. Over twenty unarmed theatergoers were killed in the streets that night (some accounts put the number at thirty-one) and another three dozen were seriously injured.

Edwin Forrest (1806–72)

1865: Abraham Lincoln Entertains Guests

It is well known that *Macbeth* was President Lincoln's favorite play. The story goes that he spent the afternoon of April 9th (the day Lee surrendered) reading passages of the play aloud to friends as they sailed down the Potomac on board the *River Queen*. Five days later, he was assassinated by John Wilkes Booth, an actor whose father, Junius Brutus Booth (1796–1852) had been an English tragedian, famous for his performances in *Macbeth*.

1936: A Drama Critic's Last Quibble

Thousands of theatergoers celebrated opening night in Harlem when, at the height of the depression, an all-black cast put on a government-sponsored production of the play which was directed by Orson Welles. Dubbed the "Voodoo *Macbeth*" because it was set in Haiti instead of Scotland, it got rave reviews from audience members and mixed reviews from critics. Percy Hammond, a conservative critic for the anti-New Deal *Herald Tribune*, wrote a scathing attack, calling the production a waste of taxpayer dollars and denouncing it as "an exhibition of deluxe boondoggling." Several days after his review appeared, he suddenly became ill and tragically died.

1937: Adversity at the Old Vic

During rehearsals for a production starring Laurence Olivier and Judith Anderson, there were a number of near disasters and several genuine misfortunes. First, a sandbag fell from above the stage and missed Olivier by only a hair. Then, the director and the actress playing Lady Macduff were involved in a car accident on their way to the theater. Worst of all was what happened to Lilian Baylis. She had been the sole manager of London's Old Vic since 1912 and, under her guidance, the theater had managed to stage all of William Shakespeare's plays. (Baylis, a one-woman visionary and powerhouse, had also taken on Sadler's Wells Theatre and made it a thriving center of opera and ballet.) In what might have been an odd foreshadowing of tragedy to come, Baylis's little dog, Snoo, died just before *Macbeth* was to open. Then, the grande dame herself died of a heart attack on the day of the final dress rehearsal. Several years later, during another production of *Macbeth* at the Old Vic, a portrait of Lilian Baylis fell off the lobby wall and crashed to the floor.

Accidents and illnesses continue to plague those involved in productions of *Macbeth*. Is it any wonder, then, that actors go to great lengths to avoid saying the "M" word? Instead, they euphemistically call it the "Scottish Play," the "Scottish Business," the "Unmentionable," and sometimes simply "*That* Play."

The Ten Best Movies
Ever Made of Shakespeare's Plays

ARRANGED BY YEAR OF RELEASE

thello (1999), starring Laurence Fishburne as the tragic Moor and Kenneth Branagh as the definitive Iago, charming and utterly sinister.

Hamlet (1996), starring Kenneth Branagh, Kate Winslet, Derek Jacobi, Julie Christie; uncut, visually arresting, a full-throttle version of what is arguably the best known of Shakespeare's dramas.

Romeo and Juliet (1996), starring Leonardo DiCaprio and Claire Danes; set in a gang-ridden postmodern Los Angeles; heavily cut, but Danes gives a luminous performance.

Much Ado about Nothing (1993), starring Kenneth Branagh, Emma Thompson, Denzel Washington, and Keanu Reeves romping through the lush landscape of Tuscany.

Henry V (1989), starring Kenneth Branagh, Brian Blessed, Emma Thompson; bravura moviemaking, and the most convincing cinematic rendering of the classic St. Crispin's Day speech before the battle of Agincourt.

Richard II (1978), with Derek Jacobi, John Gielgud, Wendy Hiller; the *Time-Life*/BBC production hangs together on the basis of Jacobi's performance.

Romeo and Juliet (1968), directed by Franco Zeffirelli. The movie starred a very young Olivia Hussey and Leonard Whiting, whose chemistry was convincing to teen moviegoers even if their Shakespearean dialogue was awkward at times.

Othello (1965), with Laurence Olivier and Maggie Smith; all four leading roles, including Frank Finlay and Joyce Redman as Iago and Emilia, were nominated for Academy Awards.

Richard III (1956), with Laurence Olivier, John Gielgud, Ralph Richardson, Claire Bloom; the script bears the marks of 19th century edits of the text, but Olivier is suitably venomous in the title role.

Julius Caesar (1953), starring John Gielgud as Cassius, Marlon Brando as Marc Antony; the best of the three major versions of this film.

The Ten Best Movies
Inspired By Shakespeare

ARRANGED BY YEAR OF RELEASE

hakespeare in Love (1998), written by Marc Norman and Tom Stoppard, a love story involving a young Will Shakespeare set against the first performance of *Romeo and Juliet;* Joseph Fiennes as Will, Gwyneth Paltrow as his love interest, with Geoffrey Rush as the theater impresario Philip Henslowe; fabulously entertaining.

Looking for Richard (1996), documentary directed by Al Pacino of his own attempt to direct and produce a movie version of *Richard III;* fascinating interviews with actors (Penelope Allen, Harris Yulin, Kevin Spacey, et al.) about their roles; great footage of them performing, including Pacino himself as Richard.

Rosencrantz and Guildenstern Are Dead (1990), written and directed by Tom Stoppard, starring Richard Dreyfuss. This retelling of *Hamlet* from the point of view of two minor characters won Best Picture at the 1991 Venice Film Festival.

Ran (1985), Akiro Kurosawa's retelling of *King Lear*, with Lord Hidetora dividing his kingdom among his sons rather than his daughters.

The Dresser (1983), Tom Courtenay as the backstage aide propping up his own King Lear (Albert Finney), actually the fading star of an acting company in wartime Britain.

The Goodbye Girl (1977), charming Neil Simon romance, with Richard Dreyfuss as a young actor struggling to bring to life a director's vision of *Richard III* as a lisping drag queen. Drey-fuss won an Oscar for best actor and the film was nominated for four more.

Chimes at Midnight (1965), one of Orson Welles's last works, it is a conflation of parts of several plays involving

> **"Love looks not with the eyes, but with the mind; And therefore is winged Cupid painted blind."**
> —*A Midsummer-Night's Dream*

Gwyneth Paltrow and Joseph Fiennes in "Shakespeare in Love." Courtesy Museum of Modern Art/Film Stills Archive

Falstaff; interesting take on one of Shakespeare's most memorable characters.

West Side Story (1961), starring Natalie Wood and Richard Beymer, with music by Leonard Bernstein and choreography by Jerome Robbins; this retelling of *Romeo and Juliet* takes place in 1950s New York City with warring gangs and prejudice keeping the young lovers apart.

Throne of Blood (1957), Akiro Kurosawa's Japanese version of *Macbeth,* starring Toshiro Mifune.

A Double Life (1948), film noir directed by George Cukor, starring Ronald Colman (who won an Academy Award for his performance), Signe Hasso, and Shelley Winters (in her first film role) about an actor who begins to confuse his life with his stage role of Othello.

HAMLET

YOUNG PRINCE TAKES REVENGE ON MURDEROUS UNCLE

Period

Renaissance

Setting

Denmark

Hamlet tells the story of a young Prince of Denmark who returns from his studies abroad to discover that his father, the King of Denmark, is dead, and that his uncle Claudius has not only replaced him as king, but has married Gertrude, the king's widow and Hamlet's mother. As if this weren't enough, soldiers bring Hamlet to the battlements, where he sees the ghost of his father, who eventually relates the story of his murder by Claudius ("murder most foul...by a brother's hand of life, of crown, of queen at once dispatched,") and lays upon his son the duty of revenging his death. Hamlet swears his

~~~~~~~~~~~~~~~~~~~
**"A rhapsody of words....
The rest is silence."
—Hamlet**
~~~~~~~~~~~~~~~~~~~

companions to secrecy, and makes them promise that they will not betray him as he decides "to put an antic disposition on," or to act unbalanced. Meanwhile, the young woman he loves, Ophelia, daughter of the king's chamberlain, has promised her brother and her father that she will resist Hamlet's advances.

At the news that a troupe of actors is coming to the castle, Hamlet determines to use them to "catch the conscience of the king," by inserting in their performance a play—"The Mousetrap" —a minidrama that replicates the circumstances of his father's death. The players act out the death of the king in his garden with poison poured in his ear. The play-within-a-play, in rhymed couplets, contains a scene in which the queen promises the king she will not remarry after his death. "Methinks the lady doth protest too much," the real Queen Gertrude allows, while Claudius leaves in a rage.

The king and Ophelia's father, the chamberlain Polonius, contrive to examine Hamlet's apparent madness by setting up a meeting with Ophelia, which they watch unseen. On Hamlet's entrance he utters the soliloquy that summarizes his quandary ("To be or not to be...") His ravings to Ophelia ("get thee to a nunnery") persuade the king and Polonius that he is mad, and they determine to send him to England or confine him.

In a soliloquy, Claudius regrets the ambition that caused him to murder his brother, but he is unwilling to seek complete forgiveness by giving up what his crime produced—"my crown, mine own ambition and my Queen." Hamlet, even more sure of Claudius's guilt, and determined to avenge himself, finds his uncle kneeling at his prayers. The idea of sending Claudius to heaven deters him. "When he is drunk asleep, or in his rage, or in th' incestuous pleasure of his bed," will be the time to kill him, Hamlet tells himself, to ensure "that his soul be as damned and black as hell, whereto it goes."

In a confrontation with his mother, Hamlet, surprised by a noise behind the curtain, stabs the person standing there, thinking it is the king. It is instead Polonius. The ghost of his father reappears, and tells Hamlet his visit "is but to whet thy almost blunted purpose" of revenge on Claudius. Claudius then dispatches Hamlet for England, accompanied by two friends, Rosencrantz and Guildenstern. The messages they carry include a request to the King of England that Hamlet be killed.

Back at the royal castle, Ophelia, in grief for her father's death and Hamlet's rejection, has gone insane. Her brother

Sarah Bernhardt as Hamlet, 1899

Laertes arrives, enraged at his father's death and leading a mob. Claudius calms him down and—having received word that Hamlet is returning—persuades him to join in a plot to see to Hamlet's demise "and for his death no wind of blame shall breathe." Laertes' conviction is confirmed by Gertrude's news that Ophelia has drowned herself in her madness.

Hamlet and his friend Horatio, returning to the castle, pass the graveyard and encounter two gravediggers. One skull they unearth in digging a grave for Ophelia is that of Yorick, the old king's jester ("Alas, poor Yorick, I knew him, Horatio," says Hamlet). When the king and queen and their party arrive with Ophelia's body, Hamlet gets into a fight with Laertes. At a fencing exhibition between the two that Claudius has arranged, Hamlet asks Laertes' pardon. Laertes appears to accept his apology, but his sword has been treated with a poison that will kill anyone who receives the slightest wound. He scratches Hamlet, but in the fray they exchange swords and Hamlet in turns draws blood from him. Meanwhile, the king had plotted to ensure Hamlet's death by giving him poisoned wine—which instead Gertrude drinks and dies. Hamlet forces the poison on Claudius before he himself dies. The play ends with the arrival of the Norwegian Prince Fortinbras, who finds the Danish royal family dead and claims the kingship.

Likely Source of the Plot

The revenge drama, or melodrama, was something of a staple of the Elizabethan theater. Another famous contemporary play on a similar theme was Thomas Kyd's *The Spanish Tragedy*. Hamlet may owe some debt to Kyd, but much of the story was apparently taken from a French translation of a 13th century Danish history. The version in the *First Folio* is actually somewhat shorter than a quarto edition that appeared in 1605. There is speculation that the play existed in some earlier version, known to critics as the "Ur-Hamlet," perhaps written by Shakespeare, perhaps by someone else.

Notable Features

Many of the treasured and oft-repeated quotes from this play are uttered by the duplicitous, pompous, and ultimately foolish Polonius ("to thine own self be true... neither a borrower nor a lender be"). Even Hamlet's "What a piece of work is a man! How noble in reason, how infinite in faculties... " is delivered to Rosencrantz and Guildenstern in a speech meant to deceive them about his sanity.

At the same time, surely no other single work in English has contributed so many memorable phrases to the language. Besides those already mentioned, even a partial list would include: *Not a mouse stirring...How weary, stale, flat and unprofitable seem to me all the uses of this world...A custom more honored in the breach than the observance...Though this be madness, yet there is method in 't...What a noble mind is here o'erthrown...I must be cruel only to be kind...There's a divinity that shapes our ends...Good-night, sweet prince....*

Notable Productions and Performances

Hamlet was apparently written and performed in the form we know around 1600, with Richard Burbage, the leading actor of Shakespeare's company, in the title role (tradition holds that Shakespeare himself took the role of the Ghost). The title role has traditionally represented the summit of an actor's ambition, and major English and American players ever since the 17th century have seen it as their ultimate career goal. Indeed, although the part is written for a young man not even out of university, actors have played it into middle age and even until their retirements. The renowned English actor and

Laurence Olivier as Hamlet and Eileen Herlie as Gertrude in the 1948 film.
Courtesy Museum of Modern Art/Film Stills Archive

Kenneth Branagh as Hamlet and Julie Christie as Gertrude in the 1996 version.
Courtesy Museum of Modern Art/Film Stills Archive

impresario David Garrick played it almost annually from 1742 until his retirement in 1776. Edwin Booth played it on the American stage from 1853 to 1891. In the early 20th century, John Barrymore was a very successful Hamlet in America, while memorable English Hamlets included John Gielgud ("I had no idea I was going to be good," he said in his memoir), Laurence Olivier, Alec Guiness, Richard Burton, Nicol Williamson, Derek Jacobi, and Kenneth Branagh.

Prominent actresses of their day have taken the role of Ophelia—Ellen Terry and Lillian Gish in the early 20th century, and in later years Jean Simmons, Vivien Leigh, Marianne Faithful, Helen Mirren, Helena Bon-ham Carter, and Kate Winslet. The play itself has also appealed to actresses such as Sarah Bernhardt in the 19th century and Siobhan McKenna in 1953, who fashioned productions with themselves as Hamlet.

> "To be, or not to be: that is the question."
> —*Hamlet*

The play in its full form can take up to four hours to perform, leading many directors to cut it substantially. Some delete all references to Fortinbras and the Norwegian forces; others truncate or eliminate the roles of Rosencrantz and Guildenstern, much of the stage business around the discovery of the body of Polonius, or even the graveyard scene.

A number of video versions are available. The most critically praised are Laurence Olivier's 1948 film, with Jean Simmons as Ophelia; the *Time-Life*/BBC 1980 production, with Derek Jacobi as Hamlet, Claire Bloom as Gertrude, and Patrick Stewart as Claudius; and Kenneth Branagh's visually stunning 1996 version, virtually uncut, with Branagh in the title role, Derek Jacobi as Claudius, Julie Christie as Gertrude, and cameos by Shakespearean stalwarts Judi Dench, Rosemary Harris, Charlton Heston, and Brian Blessed.

The Elizabethan Oscars

illiam Shakespeare has come down to us as the premier theatrical figure of Elizabethan England. But during his own time Shakespeare as a dramatist (and as an actor) had a number of important competitors. If members of the Elizabethan dramatic world had had their own Oscar election, the winners might well have been....

Best Play 1580–1600

Tamburlaine, epic drama based loosely on the life of a conqueror of Central Asia; probably the most popular of the works of Marlowe. (Other nominees: Marlowe's *Dr. Faustus,* Thomas Kyd's *The Spanish Tragedy,* Shakespeare's *Richard III.*)

Best Actor

Edward Alleyn, the star of *Tamburlaine, Doctor Faustus, The Jew of Malta,* and other popular works. First married to the stepdaughter of the theatrical impresario Philip Henslowe, after her death he married the daughter of John Donne. In 1619 he founded a college. (Other nominee: Richard Burbage, leading tragedian of Shakespeare's company).

Best Actress

Given the Elizabethan insistence on having boys and young men play all female parts, there could have been no award in this category until later in the 17th century (women took the stage officially after the Restoration in 1660).

Best Comic

Will Kempe, the clown of Shakespeare's company, and creator of roles such as Dogberry in *Much Ado about Nothing* and Falstaff. He was famous for a stunt—dancing all the way from London to the town of Norwich, a distance of about 100 miles. (Other nominee: Richard Tarlton, actor and the queen's jester).

Best Writer

Before his premature death, Christopher Marlowe was probably the most highly regarded Elizabethan dramatist; later honors would probably have gone to Ben Jonson, author of *Every Man in His Humour* and other plays, though Shakespeare would certainly have been a contender.

KING LEAR

AGING KING FACES
STORMY WEATHER AFTER
BANISHING FAVORITE DAUGHTER,
LOSES EVERYTHING

Period

1st century B.C.E.

Setting

Britain

Here is a Cinderella story in which the cruel sisters get their way, at least for a time, and the good daughter suffers. There is no fairy godmother to save the day, nor a prince charming, only a fairy-tale father-king caught in a storm of regret and bewilderment. There will be no happy ending.

As the play opens, the king, ready to retire, has decided it is time to divide his land between his three daughters. First, however, he plays a foolish game, demanding from each child a few words of flattery. Goneril and Regan, two greedy, selfish, and ultimately cruel daughters (later aptly named by their father "unnatural hags") have no trouble exaggerating their declarations of love with flowery phrases and ridiculous claims. But Cordelia, the youngest and Lear's favorite of the three, refuses to play the game. She has consistently shown her love through action and is offended at being asked to spew forth meaningless adulation.

In the mistake of a lifetime, the king disowns the one child whose love is genuine saying, "we / Have no such daughter nor shall ever see / That face of hers again." It is the beginning of the end for King Lear and for just about everyone else. Cordelia, devastated and in shock, accompanies the King of France to his country where they plan to wed. Her mind is not on matrimony, however. Ever the faithful daughter, she will soon make the decision to assemble an army of French soldiers and return to England to defend her father when he needs help.

Now at the mercy of two wicked daughters, Lear is abruptly stripped of all authority and his royal retinue is downsized. The wheel of fortune has been given a powerful turn and now the whole world seems to be spinning into chaos. In short order, Lear is banished by his daughters, with his Fool beside him. Deprived of home, family, power and status, the naked King Lear endures a great raging storm on the barren heath crying, "Is man no more than this?" The greater storm is wracking his heart and soul as the king, realizing his mistake, sinks into despair and madness. There is a glimmer of growth when Lear suddenly worries over the comfort of his shivering Fool. "How dost my boy? Art cold?"

Meanwhile, back in the subplot, Edmund, the Earl of Gloucester's bastard son, has played a few tricks and won the favor of his foolish father at the expense of his good brother Edgar. Forced into exile, Edgar hides in the stormy wilderness disguised as the lunatic "Tom of Bedlam." Lear finds him there and recognizes a kindred spirit. Then Gloucester, too, comes by, hoping to find and help his old friend Lear. As if already sightless, he fails to recognize his own son, disguised in rags, and is unable to do much for Lear. When Gloucester returns to the castle, Lear's demonic daughters are outraged that he tried to help their father. In one of Shakespeare's most violent scenes, Gloucester is sadistically blinded (on stage) and sent packing by Regan who sneers, "Go thrust him out at gates, and let him smell / His way to Dover." Now there are two aging fathers, regretting their mistakes as they stumble in an unforgiving wilderness.

As this play of reversals nears its end, the two evil sisters die in a murder-suicide while the children who loved most sincerely, Lear's Cordelia and Gloucester's Edgar, are reunited and reconciled with their fathers. There is

not to be a happy ending, however. The shock of recognizing Edgar kills Gloucester.

As for Lear, he is reborn to sanity, emerging from a coma in the arms of his forgiving daughter, but his happiness is brief. Cordelia is soon hanged in a prison cell. Lear, carrying the dead body of the child he wronged, cries, "Thou'lt come no more, / Never, never, never, never, never," and dies of a broken heart.

Likely Source of the Plot

This storyline was a popular one in Elizabethan England. There are at least forty known versions from which Shakespeare could have taken his main plot. It is likely that he drew most heavily from an anonymously written play titled *The True Chronicle History of King Lear and His Three Daughters*, which was in circulation ca. 1590. In that version, however, as in most others of the day as well as in many of the later adaptations of Shakespeare's play, the king and his beloved daughter were happily reconciled at the end. The likely source of the subplot involving Gloucester, betrayed by one son, saved by another, was Sir Philip Sidney's *Arcadia*, also in circulation in 1590. This may have been the source of the idea for the great storm that engulfs the despairing King Lear.

Notable Feature

Lear's Fool, a truth-teller dressed in motley (see page 265), disappears right after the storm scene and is never mentioned again. This has puzzled scholars through the years, but most conjecture

Paul Scofield, right, as King Lear, and Alan Webb as Gloucester.
Courtesy Museum of Modern Art/Film Stills Archive

that the reason is a practical one. On Shakespeare's stage, one actor, Robert Armin, played both the part of the Fool and of Cordelia. The two characters are never on the stage at the same time. Shakespeare may have given a knowing nod in this direction when he wrote the line Lear says at the end of the play over Cordelia's lifeless body, "And my poor fool is hanged!"

Notable Productions and Performances

1606, earliest known performance of the play, starring Richard Burbage as the original Lear, at the court of King James I. It is believed that the play was not well received. During the 1760–1820 reign of King George III, who was thought to be insane, this play about a mad king was suppressed by the British government. The play, as written by Shakespeare, became popular in the 20th century.

Other Uses of Basic Plot

1818 poem by John Keats (1795–1821): "On Sitting down to Read King Lear Once Again," a 14-line sonnet in which Keats says he must once more "burn through" the "fierce dispute Betwixt damnation and impassion'd clay."

Orchestral work, 1831, *King Lear Overture*, by Hector Berlioz.

Made in the United States and directed by Harry Thomashefsky (1935): *The Yiddish King Lear (Der Yidisher Kenig Lir)*. In Yiddish with English subtitles. Based on an 1892 play by Jacob Gordin. At a seder, an aging patriarch announces his plans to divide his fortune among three daughters and retire to Jerusalem. Disaster follows.

The story crystallizes the conflicts between immigrant parents and their Americanized children.

U.S. release of Soviet film 1970, directed by Grigori Kozintsev. In response to Peter Brook's heartless stage version of *Lear*, Kozintsev emphasized the power of love to transform the human experience of desolation and grief. Influenced by Yiddish-theater productions, Kozintsev's optimistic closing shot is of the Fool playing the flute as workers remove battlefield debris.

Film directed by Peter Brook, 1971, starring Paul Scofield as Lear. Filmed in Lapland on bleak, barren terrain, this is Lear stripped of compassion or any hint of redemption.

Opera by Aribert Reimann, 1978.

The Dresser, 1983, film directed by Peter Yates, written by Ronald Harwood. World War II is raging as a troupe of aging Shakespearean actors travel throughout England, doing the best that they can to keep drama alive. Central to the film is the complex relationship between Sir (played by Albert Finney) and the unsung backstage hero, his dresser, Norman (Tom Courtenay). Devoted, if campy, Norman tends, coaxes, and coddles Sir just as the Fool tended, coaxed, and coddled King Lear. Stormlike bombing raids shake the the-

ater but do not deter the brave Britons from attending the plays. The storm on the *King Lear* stage and on Sir's internal landscape, however, prove to be too much, and the broken actor suffers a nervous breakdown.

Made for Granada Television, 1984, directed by Michael Elliot. An aged Laurence Olivier, in his last Shakespearean role, played a heartbroken and heartbreaking Lear. Diana Rigg was Regan.

Ran, 1985, film by Akira Kurosawa. An epic tale set in 16th century Samurai Japan, *Ran* (which means "chaos" in Japanese), is about Hidetora and his three sons.

A Thousand Acres, 1991, novel by Jane Smiley. Winner of the Pulitzer Prize, this is a retelling of *King Lear*, set in 1970s Iowa. *A Thousand Acres*, 1997, film directed by Jocelyn Moorhouse, starring Jessica Lange, Michelle Pfeiffer, and Jennifer Jason Leigh as the three daughters and Jason Robards as the lecherous, fumbling farmer father.

King Lear has inspired musical works including operas by Gobatti (1881), Reynaud (1888), Cottrau (1913), Frazzi (1939), and Reimann (1978), as well as a ballet choreographed in 1994 by Bejart to the music of Henry Purcell.

> "Break heart;
> I prithee break."
> —*King Lear*

"Wise Enough to Play the Fool"

n the hierarchy of Elizabethan society, fools held a special place, although all fools were not created equal. On the one hand, there were the natural born fools, the simpletons and sweet-natured lunatics. Dwarfs and people with physical disabilities might also be made fools, kept as pets for the privileged, laughed at, mocked. They provided crude and cruel humor, at best, as they shuffled and sang for their room and board.

The other fools were professionals, adept at word games and verbal sparring. They were free to comment on the world around them, providing comic relief and philosophical insights, bitter sarcasm and biting derision. Not that everything they said and did was highbrow. Sometimes, when words failed, they would whistle and fart for a laugh. Vulgar ballads and scatological jokes were their forte.

Fools are not to be confused with clowns. Clowns were more country than city. They did tricks, tumbled, and danced, and left most of the wordplay to others.

A fool might be a court jester, dressed in the colors of those they served, or in multicolor "motley" with a cap and bells. They usually shaved their heads and often carried some sort of phallic object—a baton or a stick with a pig's bladder tied to the end—about which they would make endless crude jokes or with which they would hit members of the audience. (This is where we get the word "slapstick.")

There were famous fools. Henry VIII had Will Somers whose epitaph reads, "He that beneath this Tombstone lies / Some called Fool, some held him wise." Queen Elizabeth's fool was Richard Tarlton who was also a comic actor with the Queen's Men. He wrote several plays and developed the character of the stage clown. Known for his ability to improvise, he may have inspired Shakespeare to pen Hamlet's complaint:

Let those that play your clowns speak no more than is set down for them; for there be of them that will themselves laugh, to set on some quantity of barren spectators to laugh too, though in the meantime some necessary question of the play be then to be considered. That's villainous, and shows a most pitiful ambition in the fool that uses it.

Despite Shakespeare's jab, Tarlton was popular and became a cult figure after his death in 1588, and was the subject of numerous ballads.

Tarlton's successor was William Kempe, jester to the Earl of Leicester and an actor with the Chamberlain's Men. His great claim to fame was a publicity stunt in 1600, noted earlier, when he danced from London to Norwich, approximately one hundred miles, and then wrote a book about it. A large man, he was one of the principal actors in Shakespeare's plays for a number of years. He is believed to have originated the roles of Bottom, Costard, and possibly Falstaff before being replaced by the diminutive and musically talented Robert Armin who is thought to have developed Feste,

Will Kempe, dancing from London to Norwich

Touchstone, and Lear's Fool. Viola's remark in *Twelfth Night*, upon meeting Feste, may have been a hidden compliment to Armin—"This fellow is wise enough to play the fool."

Queen Mary had the only known female fool whose no-nonsense name was Jane the Fool. She had a fondness for shoes and, according to the records of the day, was granted thirty-six pair one year.

> **"Love's not Time's fool."**
> **—Sonnet 116**

Some of Shakespeare's most wonderful lines are spoken by his fools and clowns. When they speak, sometimes we laugh, sometimes we cry.

Touchstone, the fool in *As You Like It*—follows Rosalind and Celia to the Forest of Arden. He parodies the romances blossoming around him by wooing the charming goatherd, Audrey. The generally pessimistic Jaques says of Touchstone:

A fool, a fool! I met a fool i' th' forest,
A motley fool. A miserable world!
As I do live by food, I met a fool,
Who laid him down and bask'd him in
*   the sun,*
And rail'd on Lady Fortune in good terms,
In good set terms—and yet a motley fool.

Jaques has been especially amused by a bit of philosophizing he heard from Touchstone. As he reports it, the fool commented on the time of day saying, "And so, from hour to hour, we ripe and ripe, / And then, from hour to hour, we rot and rot; / And thereby hangs a tale."

Feste, the singing fool in *Twelfth Night*—proclaims, "Better a witty fool than a foolish wit," and observes,

"Foolery...doth walk about the orb like the sun, it shines everywhere."

The **Fool** in *King Lear*—accompanies his master into the storm but speaks hard truths along the way, such as, "Thou should'st not have been old till thou hadst been wise."

Trinculo in *The Tempest*—more clown than fool, is drunk most of the time and is more the butt of humor than the source of it. His funniest line is the observation he makes after being washed ashore to awaken beside Stephano and Caliban: "The folly of this island! They say there's but five upon this isle: we are three of them; if th' other two be brain'd like us, the state totters."

Lavatch, melancholy clown/jester of *All's Well That Ends Well*—is a cynic who enjoys ridiculing the royal court.

Clown, in *The Winter's Tale*—son of the kind shepherd who finds the abandoned infant princess. He is none too bright, but sweet and lovable neverthe-less. Toward the end of the play, when his circumstances change, he describes this scene:

The King's son took me by the hand and call'd me brother; and then the two kings call'd my father brother; and then the Prince, my brother, and the Princess, my sister, call'd my father father. And so we wept; and there was the first gentle-manlike tears that ever we shed.

Clown, in *Titus Andronicus*—not surprisingly, winds up being executed like just about everyone else in the play.

Clown, in *Antony and Cleopatra*—pretends to be a fig seller and brings the poisonous snake for Cleopatra's suicide. Seeing him, the queen muses, "What poor an instrument / May do a noble deed! He brings me liberty." The clown provides comic relief, warning the queen not to touch the snake, "for his biting is immortal; those that do die of it do seldom or never recover."

OTHELLO, THE MOOR OF VENICE

MOORISH GENERAL KILLS WIFE IN JEALOUS RAGE OVER MISPLACED HANDKERCHIEF

Period

Early 16th century

Settings

Venice and Cyprus

Refined but spirited Desdemona, the beautiful daughter of a Venetian Senator, has secretly married the exotic Moor, Othello, commander of the armed forces of Venice. Her father, Brabantio, is told of this in the crudest language—"an old black ram / Is tupping your white ewe." The image leaves the father trembling, which was the intention of the villainous Iago. This is but his first attempt to provoke trouble for Othello. Iago hates Othello, in part, because, though they were old friends, he was passed over for promotion. Othello named Cassio his lieutenant, instead. From the opening lines of this play to the bitter end, the audience will watch Iago's hatred cause havoc.

When Othello and Desdemona are given the opportunity to profess their deep and profound love for each other before the duke and all the senators, the father is forced to back down. As he does, however, he mutters a warning to Othello, "She has deceiv'd her father, and may thee." Othello is sent to Cypress to fight the Turks, and Desdemona leaves the security of hearth and home to follow him. As luck would have it, a great storm destroys the Turkish fleet. Freed from the larger battlefield, Othello will find himself the unwitting warrior on the homefront.

Skillfully, the clever Iago drops hints of Desdemona's infidelity. With clever and patient manipulation of people and events, he leads Othello to doubt her love and to suspect that she is cheating on him with Cassio. On the edge of every scuffle stands sneaky and charming Iago. He is the proverbial snake in the grass. Others are prompted to speak his insults and fight his fights while he stays hidden, only to appear when the tension is abating, as if to defuse the situation. He is always there with a word of comfort or chastisement. Suave and disarming, "honest" Iago is anything but. He is the instigator, a psychopath who delights in sowing seeds of distrust, until friend turns against friend.

Iago talks Cassio into drinking too much and then provokes him into a drunken brawl with Roderigo. Cassio is promptly demoted. When Desdemona urges her husband to forgive Cassio's uncharacteristic slip-up, Iago uses this too, to fuel suspicions of a liaison.

Finally, there is the mystery of the precious handkerchief, a gift from Othello to Desdemona. When it is inadvertently dropped, Emilia, Iago's wife and Desdemona's maid, picks it up. Iago takes the handkerchief and hides it in Cassio's room. Later, Othello is set up to see Cassio holding the handkerchief.

Now, Othello is beside himself. Iago, in his goal of revenge and destruction, has remained consistent throughout the drama. On the opposite end of the spectrum, Desdemona has remained consistent too, blameless, innocent, faithful; she utterly loves her husband. Only Othello has changed. From the steady and self-possessed general of the battlefield, a man of noble bearing, he has deteriorated into a raging bull of a jealous man. Long before she is smothered in her bed, Desdemona is smothered by the confinement she experiences as her husband grows increasingly jealous and angry with her. She is baffled and at a loss to explain why and how her world is closing in on her. The audience, too, feels almost claustrophobic, as if we too are caught in a bad dream.

Inevitably, one night, as Cassio is set upon in the streets by Roderigo and Iago, Desdemona is attacked in her bed by Othello. Cassio does not die, but Desdemona does. When Emilia tells Othello that Iago has manipulated him into this rage, and that his wife was faithful and pure, Emilia is stabbed by her husband. She collapses on the bed beside her dead mistress. Before he kills himself and collapses on the crowded bed, Othello, mad with grief and shame, speaks in his own defense.

I pray you in your letters,
When you shall these unlucky
*   deeds relate,*
Speak of me, as I am. Nothing
*   extenuate,*
Nor set down aught in malice.
*   Then must you speak*
Of one that loved not wisely,
*   but too well.*

Likely Source of the Plot

In 1565, the Italian author Giraldi Cinthio told the story of the jealous Moor in his collection *Hecatommithi*. There was no English translation at the time Shakespeare reshaped the story into *Othello*.

Notable Productions and Performances

The first known performance of the play was at the court of King James I in 1604. The great Richard Burbage played Othello. In 1660, Margaret Hughes, playing Desdemona, became the first woman permitted to perform on an English stage. In the late 17th century, there were reports of audience members rushing the stage to prevent Othello's murder of Desdemona.

Paul Robeson on stage as Othello with Jose Ferrer as Iago. Courtesy of the New York Public Library

Edmund Kean (1787–1833) collapsed playing Othello opposite his son who played Iago. He died several weeks later. Some believe he was the greatest Othello of all time.

Ira Aldridge (ca.1807–67), an African American born when slavery was legal, moved to Europe where he became famous as a Shakespearean actor. Although Othello, Shakespeare's most celebrated black character, was a prime role for Aldridge, he was also acclaimed for his Lear, Hamlet, Richard III, and Macbeth.

Margaret Webster's production of *Othello* on Broadway in 1943, starred the legendary black actor Paul Robeson opposite Uta Hagen as Desdemona.

Robeson, known not only for his resonant bass voice but also for his outspoken views on socialism and civil rights, had played the part in London in 1930, when American audiences were thought to be averse to seeing a black man touch a white woman, on stage or off. In 1943, however, the play was a hit in New York, running for almost three hundred performances, breaking all records for a Shakespearean play in America.

Directed by John Dexter, 1964: Laurence Olivier in blackface played Othello to Maggie Smith's Desdemona.

An *Othello* adaptation by avant-garde writer/director Charles Marowitz, 1972, was staged during the London race riots and incorporated material from Malcolm X. In this production Iago is a black-power activist and Othello is an Uncle Tom.

The Royal Shakespeare Theatre at Stratford-on-Avon, 1986, directed by Terry Hands, with Ben Kingsley, wearing a turban, as Othello.

Other Use of Basic Plot

Othello, 1922, silent film directed by Dimitri Buchowetzki. Avant-garde of the German Expressionist school.

A Double Life, 1948, film noir directed by George Cukor, script by Ruth Gordon and Garson Kanin. Tony John, played by Ronald Colman who won the Academy Award for this performance, is a popular stage actor whose ex-wife, Brita (Signe Hasso), often co-stars with him. She knows from experience that dramatic roles tend to send him over the edge. "We married during Kaufmann and Hart and were divorced during Chekhov." When he plays Othello to her Desdemona, Tony John's green-eyed monster grows off-stage as well as on, and he begins to confuse his life with his stage role. A vampy waitress, played by Shelley Winters in her first film role, has the misfortune to invite him up to her place. We watch in fascinated horror as the suave actor loses touch with reality and the murderous Moor takes over.

The Tragedy of Othello, the Moor of Venice, 1952, film directed by Orson Welles who also played the lead role. Completed in 1952, released in 1955, rereleased in 1992, the movie incorporates some text from Shakespeare's story source, Cinthio's *Hecatommithi*.

Catch My Soul (a.k.a. *Santa Fe Satan*), 1974, a rock-musical film adaptation directed by Patrick McGoohan. The story is set in a commune in the New Mexico desert and stars Richie Havens as a hippie Othello. It bombed at the box office.

BBC-TV production, 1981, directed by Jonathan Miller: Anthony Hopkins played Othello as a light-skinned Arab.

Othello, 1999, directed by Oliver Parker, starring Laurence Fishburne (self-described as "a black kid from Brooklyn") opposite Kenneth Branagh ("an Irish kid from Belfast"). It was a hit.

Both Rossini (in 1816) and Verdi (in 1887) wrote operas titled *Otello*. Many other composers have been inspired by this play, including contemporary masters. The American-born contemporary jazz composer George Russell composed the *Othello Ballet Suite for Electronic Organ* in 1968, and the Italian pianist-composer Giorgio Gaslini wrote *Mister O: A Jazz Opera* in 1996.

ANTONY AND CLEOPATRA

ROMAN LEADER
LOSES EVERYTHING FOR LOVE
OF EGYPTIAN QUEEN

Period

1st century, B.C.E.

Settings

Egypt, Italy, and elsewhere in the Mediterranean

As the play begins, Marc Antony is one of the three most powerful men in the Roman world. He and his two compatriots in the Triumvirate—Octavius Caesar and Lepidus—hold the supreme military power in the Roman Empire, the most powerful civilization in the West. But Antony, instead of extending Roman power among the barbarians or consolidating his place in the empire's politics, is spending his time in the decadent court of Egypt, besotted with the charms of Queen Cleopatra.

The empire, meanwhile, is not quiet. Young Pompeii, whose father died leading a rebellion, is gathering new forces, and there is other civil unrest that needs to be attended to, some of it fomented by Antony's wife, Fulvia, back in Rome. The torrent of news persuades Antony ("These strong Egyptian fetters I must break...I must from this enchanting Queen break off,") to go back to Rome and his duties.

In Rome, after some sharp words between himself and his fellow Triumvirate member Octavius Caesar, the two mend their fences, and as an indication of their new accord, Antony agrees to marry Octavius's sister, Octavia. The leaders then meet with Pompeii to negotiate their differences, an event concluded by a drunken revel abroad one of Pompeii's ships.

During the party Pompeii declines, with some reluctance, the suggestion of one of his followers that his new allies could easily be dispatched, leaving Pompeii as effective ruler of the Roman world. ("This thou shouldst have done and not spoken on't," he tells the aide, "in me 'tis villainy, in thee 't would have been good service.")

Cleopatra, meanwhile, is less than pleased with the news that Mark Antony has married Octavia, though she is somewhat mollified by the report that the lady is unattractive ("dull of tongue and dwarfish"). Antony and Octavia go to Athens, while one of Antony's lieutenants subdues a local revolt in the eastern empire. When Octavius renews the war against Pompeii without consulting Antony, Octavia goes back to Rome to try to sort out the new difficulties. But as she does so, Antony returns to Egypt, taking up again with Cleopatra. The dishonor to his sister is enough for Octavius to declare war against Antony.

The rival forces meet at Actium, where Antony forgoes his advantage by land to press the battle by sea, despite Octavius's superior navy. The battle goes well for Antony until Cleopatra, in command of her fleet, turns back at a crucial moment, and Antony follows her, leading to the defeat of all their forces.

Antony, as loser of the battle of Actium, attempts to win a concession from Octavius that he be allowed to live in Egypt or in Athens. He also forgives Cleopatra for her strategic failure, and even for negotiating later with the representatives of Octavius, who had sought to win her from Antony's side by promising to leave her to rule her kingdom if she exiles Antony or has him killed.

Although Antony determines to maintain the fight, his followers begin to desert him. In a second battle with the forces of Octavius, he is at first successful, but at last loses, in part because the Egyptian fleet for a second time flees the battle scene. Enraged at Cleopatra, he learns that she has killed herself, with his name on her lips.

In despair at his loss of her and the empire, he is determined not to end up "behind the wheeled seat of fortunate Caesar," a prisoner following the chariot of Octavius in his triumphal procession in Rome. He eventually falls on his own sword. Mortally wounded, he discovers that Cleopatra is still alive, is taken to her, and reconciles with her before he dies.

Caesar, victorious, sends assurances that Cleopatra will be treated kindly, but she assumes that he is merely keeping her alive so that she, rather than Antony, can adorn his triumphal procession where "mechanic slaves with greasy

Cleopatra at the Battle of Actium.
Drawing by H. Vogel

aprons, rules and hammers shall uplift us to their view." Despite being kept under guard, she has a poisonous snake smuggled in to her. Dressed in robe and crown, she applies the snake to her breast and dies.

Likely Source of the Plot

Shakespeare's principal source for *Antony and Cleopatra*, (and for *Julius Caesar* and other plays) was Plutarch's *Lives of the Noble Greeks and Romans*, in an English translation by Thomas North, drawn from a French translation of the original.

Background

This play in effect continues the story told in *Julius Caesar*. In that play Marc Antony, Octavius, and Lepidus joined forces to defeat the conspirators—Brutus, Cassius, et. al.—who assassinated Julius Caesar (Octavius's father by adoption) in 44 B.C.E. The story told in this play about the Triumvirate of Antony, Octavius, and Lepidus somewhat telescopes the action. The alliance fell apart about 36 B.C.E., but the Battle of Actium, the turning point of this drama, occurred in 31 B.C.E. Octavius eventually ruled Rome alone under the title of Augustus Caesar, dying in 14 C.E.

~~~~~~~~~~~~

"Age cannot wither her, nor custom stale Her infinite variety."
—Antony and Cleopatra

~~~~~~~~~~~~

Notable Features

Julius Caesar had been, before the action of this play begins, one of Cleopatra's lovers. Their son Caesarion is mentioned in the play, but has no lines. Cleopatra tells one of her companions that her relationship with Julius Caesar was "In my salad days, when I was green in judgement."

In her reluctance to be part of Octavius's triumph in Rome, Cleopatra says she does not want to have to watch, "some squeaking Cleopatra boy my greatness" during a dramatization of her story. Of course, the person proclaiming these lines in the productions of Shakespeare's time was himself a boy.

Other Notable Uses of the Plot

Dozens of films have told this story, most of them not in Shakespeare's words. Notable among them was the 1963 big-budget film *Cleopatra*, starring Elizabeth Taylor and Richard Burton in a real-life love triangle that paralleled the original plot. Charlton Heston directed himself in the title role, with Hildegarde Neil as Cleopatra, in a less-noticed 1973 version of the Shakespeare play. Trevor Nunn directed a 1974 version with Richard Johnson and Janet Suzman in the title roles, while a 1981 production by *Time-Life*/BBC featured Jane Lapotaire as Cleopatra and Colin Blakely as Antony.

The story of Octavius as Augustus Caesar is continued in many forms, including the award-winning miniseries "I, Claudius" based on the work of Robert Graves.

CYMBELINE

EARLY BRITISH KING FIGHTS ROMAN RULE WHILE DAUGHTER SUFFERS IN WEB OF JEALOUSY AND LIES

Period

1st century B.C.E

Settings

Britain and Italy

Cymbeline tells three connected stories: the mythic resistance of early Britons to Roman rule; the story of two lovers driven apart by the lies of a cunning villain; and the saga of two young princes kidnapped from the royal household and reared in the wild, who return to claim their legacy.

The British king is Cymbeline, a quasi-historical figure from Britain's Roman period, who determines that his kingdom will no longer pay the tribute to Rome that has been imposed since Julius Caesar invaded and subdued the island. His decision prompts a renewed Roman invasion. At the same time the king has banished Leonatus Posthumus, a respectable but poor young man who has had the temerity to fall in love with

and marry the king's daughter, Imogen. The king's decision is supported by his queen, although she pretends to be supportive of the lovers. In fact, the queen has a son, Cloten, by her first husband, whom she would prefer to see married to the king's daughter, thus strengthening his claim to the throne.

The exiled Posthumus finds himself in Rome, where he boasts of the fidelity of his wife. Iachimo, an Italian gentleman, wagers 10,000 ducats that he can bed Imogen. So confident is Leonatus that he gives Iachimo a letter of introduction to his wife. In England Iachimo first tries to persuade Imogen that Leonatus has been unfaithful to her; when this fails, he tells her that the story was merely designed to test her affections, and begs her forgiveness. When she does so, he asks that he be permitted to put a trunk of valuables in her room for safeguarding before his return trip.

That night he emerges from the trunk when Imogen is asleep, takes note of the furnishings of her chamber, slips from her wrist a bracelet given to her by Leonatus, and notices a mole on her breast, before returning to the trunk for the night. Even while the trunk is being carried out the next morning, the cloddish Cloten, accompanied by musicians, is before the door of Imogen's chamber, wooing her while he makes vulgar asides to the musicians. She rejects his suit in no uncertain terms.

Iachimo returns to Italy, and his phony evidence persuades Posthumus that he has won the bet. Shattered, Posthumus sends word to his servant, Pisanio, to kill Imogen for betraying him. But Pisanio, after luring her out of the castle, shows her Posthumus's letter demanding her death.

Now *she* is outraged, and Pisanio suggests she confront her husband in Rome. He recommends that she attach herself to the embassy of Caius Lucius, a Roman general. Imogen disguises herself as a young man, and wandering the Welsh countryside falls in with Belarius and his two sons. Belarius is a former British general who was unjustly exiled by Cymbeline. He is rearing two boys he claims to be his own, but who are really Cymbeline's sons, kidnapped from his household years before.

Imogen, now calling herself Fidele, makes a strong connection with Belarius and the two young men, who are of course her brothers. But overcome by the sadness at what has befallen her, Imogen takes a drug innocently given her by Pisanio ("a dram of this will drive away distemper") a dose that leaves her apparently dead. Meanwhile Cloten, taking to heart Imogen's statement that her husband's "meanest garment" is dearer to her than Cloten himself, dresses in Posthumus's clothes and sets out to find Imogen. Instead he finds and fights with one of Belarius's sons, who cuts off his head. Imogen awakes in her grave to find herself beside a headless body she takes to be that of Posthumus.

Believing herself to be a widow, she now joins the service of Caius Lucius, on his way to a battle with the forces of Cymbeline. Also joining the battle, but on the other side, are Belarius and his two charges, and eventually Posthumus himself, returned from Italy. These four are decisive in the British victory.

Posthumus, though he fought on the side of his countrymen, is captured as a Roman. In prison he sees a vision of Jupiter promising a great future for Britain.

There is a remarkable final scene of mass reconciliation. Cymbeline learns that the queen is dead, having confessed her lack of love for him and her plot to murder him to put her son on the throne. Iachimo admits to his deception. Imogen's identity is revealed. One of Belarius's boys confesses that he killed Cloten; faced with the boy's arrest, Belarius reveals that both boys are the king's sons. Posthumus reveals and regrets his attempt to have Imogen killed.

Husband and wife are thus reunited, as are father and sons; and a soothsayer reveals that the prediction of Jupiter means that Britain will have peace and prosperity based on the reuniting of these families, along with Cymbeline's decision to resume tribute to Rome to maintain that alliance, despite his victory in the recent battle.

Likely Source of the Plot

The stories are derived from three principal sources. The half-mythical story of Cymbeline was probably taken from Holinshed's *Chronicles of England*; the wager over the fidelity of Imogen was a variation of a story in *The Decameron* of Bocaccio; the story involving the kidnapped sons of the king may have come from an earlier Elizabethan drama.

Notable Features

In *Romeo and Juliet*, the heroine takes a poison whose effects mimic death. Here the substantial subplot involving such a poison begins with the queen getting the physician Cornelius to prepare for her a poison that she says she will use to get rid of animals. Suspecting her motives, Cornelius instead prepares a potion that will put the victim in a deathlike sleep. The doctor's action thus resonates through the play, as the queen gives the potion to Pisanio, Posthumus's servant, telling him it is a remedy; Pisanio gives it to Imogen; Imogen takes it to relieve her melancholy, only to be thought dead. In her final confession, the queen admits to killing Imogen, though of course she is still alive, and Cornelius's statement that the potion in fact is harmless is yet another revelation in the busy final scene.

Although dream sequences are not unusual in Shakespeare, the dream visit and prediction from the god Jupiter is very uncharacteristic of his work. Many experts believe it to be an interpolation by another writer. The play was listed by the editors of the *First Folio* as a tragedy, but its upbeat ending makes it more of a romantic drama by modern standards.

One of the most beautiful lyrics in Shakespeare is the song, "Hark, hark the lark." It is here performed by (or under the direction of) the play's least likable character, Cloten.

Notable Productions and Performances

The play was apparently first produced early in the 1600s, perhaps for the company's newly acquired Blackfriars Theatre. Although it takes for its title the name of the king, he is in fact a minor character. Most readers see *Cymbeline* as Imogen's play. Noted actresses such as Sarah Siddons, Ellen Terry, Peggy Ashcroft, and Vanessa Redgrave have played her over the years. Helen Mirren plays the role in the 1983 *Time-Life*/BBC version, while Claire Bloom plays the Queen.

Cymbeline's thematic and stylistic problems (Dr. Johnson noted "the absurdity of the conduct...the impossibility of the events") have meant that it has often been reworked. A revised version by Thomas D'Urfey supplanted Shakespeare's for decades in the 17th and 18th centuries; in the 20th, Bernard Shaw rewrote the last act and labeled the play *Cymbeline Refinished*.

The Shakespeare Industry

hakespeare is unique among English writers in having created a body of work that not only lives after four centuries, but lives to two different audiences—the playgoer and the literary scholar. In addition to the continual restaging (and refilming) of his work, Shakespeare has spawned through the years an army of commentators, critics, biographers, and academicians whose observations on the Works (and each others' works) continue to fill thousands of volumes. *Books in Print* lists more than a thousand works with Shakespeare in the title.

So large has Shakespeare loomed over English letters that virtually all serious writers *about* English literature—and almost all serious writers *of* it—have left us with public commentaries on the plays and poems. Not all of these have been adulatory. In the first centuries after his death, Shakespeare was generally regarded as a "natural" or untutored genius whose works would have been improved by a better grasp of classical learning, particularly classical dramatic forms. By the 19th century, the popular view had come around to the belief that Shakespeare was a universal genius, and the cult of Shakespeare increasingly took hold. In the 20th century Shakespeare commentators have found in the plays endless subjects for elaboration, and justification for every imaginable political and social view.

At the same time, the continual re-editing of the plays has been both a cause and a result of this critical obsession. In the usual Elizabethan theatrical practice, individual roles and complete scripts were collected and collated in a very haphazard manner, if at all. Combined with unauthorized printings, the lack of uniform proofreading standards and Shakespeare's own neglect of the texts, such re-editing promises to engage the time and effort of scholars and commentators for centuries to come.

"Wanted Art"

Ben Jonson was an Elizabethan playwright, both a friend and an occasional

A Restoration illustration of famous characters on the English Stage, including Falstaff.
British Library

competitor with Shakespeare. Though he described Shakespeare as a poet "for all time," he is also the author of the statement that Shakespeare had "small Latin and less Greek" (a charge only partly true and mostly misleading) and that his plays "wanted art."

Though, like Shakespeare, Jonson never attended university, he was very widely read and cherished a reputation for being one of the best-educated men of his time. The "art" he found wanting in Shakespeare was the classical learning Jonson had so faithfully acquired and had tried to demonstrate in his dramas, which were widely regarded at the time as equal or even superior to Shakespeare's. Later in the 17th century, John Milton echoed that analysis of Shakespeare, citing his "native wood-notes wild." So did the poet John Dryden, who in 1672 lauded him for having, of all ancient and modern poets, "the largest and most comprehensive soul," yet found much to criticize in his lack of refinement in language and dramatic style. In the early 18th century, Alexander Pope defended Shakespeare against charges that he ignored the rules of dramatic structure, saying that to judge him under such circumstances was the equivalent of "trying a man under the laws of one country who acted under the laws of another." But Pope also observed that Shakespeare had written for money rather than for literary glory, "and grew immortal in his own despite."

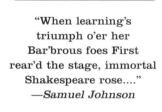

"When learning's triumph o'er her Bar'brous foes First rear'd the stage, immortal Shakespeare rose...."
—*Samuel Johnson*

The Views of Dr. Johnson

Samuel Johnson, lexicographer, critic and wit, rose to the Bard's defense in 1785 in his Preface and commentaries to an edition of Shakespeare's works. Johnson took pointed exception to much of Shakespeare, criticizing him for being "more careful to please than to instruct," and for lacking "moral purpose." He accused him of sloppy plotting, and of letting commercial interests rush him in the completion of his plays, to the damage of their dramatic effect. But overall he found Shakespeare's works to be "the mirror of life," and his characters "the genuine progeny of common humanity." The plays, he said, rather than having heroes in the dramatic sense, are occupied by characters "who act and speak as the reader thinks that he himself should have spoken or acted on the same occasion."

The 19th century saw further defense of the literary Shakespeare by writers such as Thomas De Quincey and Samuel Taylor Coleridge, even while the popular view had gone past defense or explanation and had begun to reach the level of veneration. Some of the impetus for this veneration came from the Continent. The French had a mixed view of Shakespeare (Voltaire described his plays as *farces monstreuses*), but in Germany Shakespeare was taken up with a vengeance by a number of major writers, including Goethe. (Karl Marx makes a number of references to Shakespeare in his later works.)

It was partly in reaction to the Shakespeare cult in the late 19th century that Bernard Shaw once opined, contradicting Ben Jonson ("He was not of an age, but for all time!"), that "Shakespeare is for an afternoon, but not for all time," although he had the good grace to point out that it did not follow that "the right to criticize Shakespeare involves the power of writing better plays."

20th Century Thinking

Scholarly work on Shakespeare in the 20th century often focused on narrow issues, and as *The Reader's Encyclopedia of Shakespeare* (Campbell and Quinn, eds.) dryly noted, those who turn to such criticism "because of their first-hand enthusiasm for the dramatist himself and his incomparable works, may decide that the trend toward intricacy and difficulty has gone further than they would wish." Nevertheless, major elements in Shakespeare scholarship in the 20th century include works by A. C. Bradley, L. C. Knight, Harold Goddard, and Helen Vendler. Although critical views vary, the cult of Shakespeare remains alive in many hearts, such as that of Harold Bloom, who, in *Shakespeare: The Invention of the Human*, says of the Bard, "He extensively informs the language that we speak, his principal characters have become our mythology, and he, rather than his involuntary follower Freud, is our psychologist."

The Editions

The seminal collection of Shakespeare's plays was the *First Folio* (see pages 10, 45, 68, 81-83), published in 1623. It consisted of 36 plays brought together by two of the actors in Shakespeare's company, John Heminges and Henry Condell. They published a number of plays that had never been printed, correcting and expanding those that had been printed from purloined scripts and prompt books, actor's reminiscences, and other sources. As noted earlier, *Second* and *Third Folios* followed in later years (though the new material in the later editions was often of doubtful provenance). In 1709, Nicholas Rowe published a new multivolume edition of the plays. It is to Rowe (and others) that we owe many act and scene divisions, lists of characters, and descriptions of place. Alexander Pope issued his own edition in 1725. Dr. Johnson's edition later in the 18th century was valued more for his commentaries than any careful editing of the texts.

Cum Notis Variorum

In the late 18th century editions "cum notis variorum," or containing notes from a variety of sources and editors, emerged (one was edited in part by James Boswell, son of the biographer of Dr. Johnson). In 1863, *The Cambridge Shakespeare* appeared and became a standard edition, including its line-numbering of the plays, which remains in wide use. Many publishing houses have editions of the plays in print, in single or multivolume formats, with some variations in text, layout and accompanying notes. A partial list of these imprints includes Applause, Arden, Bantam, Dover, the New Folger Library, Oxford, Pelican, Penguin, and Riverside.

The Folger Shakespeare Library in Washington, D.C.

The Lives

Nicholas Rowe included a good deal of biographical material in his 1709 edition, as did Edmund Malone in the edition completed by James Boswell. The limited information we have of Shakespeare's life has not restrained the efforts of other biographers, most of whose books attempt to re-create his life through the prism either of his time or of the works themselves. Popular modern biographies/commentaries include those of Samuel Schoenbaum, E. K. Chambers, M. M. Reese, A. L. Rowse, Russell Fraser, and more recently Peter Alexander and Park Honan.

The Industry

The great repository in the United States of Shakespeareana is the Folger Shakespeare Library in Washington, D.C., which has a collection of nearly 300,000 books and manuscripts on Shakespeare. The more than a thousand current listings in *Books in Print*, as noted, include, in addition to the works themselves, treatments of Shakespeare's life and works by prominent names (Anthony Burgess, Germaine Greer, Mark Van Doren), studies of aspects of his writings (*Shakespeare's Imagery, Shakespeare's Language*), along with the role of various subjects or

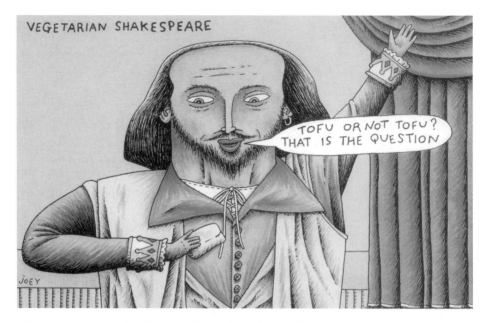

Shakespeare—a man for all seasons. Maine Line Co., Rockport, Maine 04856 © Joey Waldon

issues in his work (*Shakespeare and Gender, Shakespeare and Race, Shakespeare and the Arts, Shakespeare and Religion*).

In recent years, a subgenre has emerged that looks at the plays as models of nondramatic commercial success (*Shakespeare in Charge—How to Lead and Succeed on the Business Stage,* *Shakespeare on Management*). And among the 8,000 or more volumes available through the online bookseller amazon.com are a bewildering variety on other matters Shakespearean— *Shakespearean Detectives, Shakespeare's Clowns, Shakespeare's Villains, Shakespeare's Landlord, Shakespeare's Trollop,* and *Shakespeare's Dog.*

∽∽∽∽∽∽∽∽∽∽∽∽

"Brush up your Shakespeare."
—*Kiss Me Kate*

∽∽∽∽∽∽∽∽∽∽∽∽

Thou Knave! Thou Plague-Sore!
Shakespearean Insults

hink Shakespeare is all "prithee" and "forsooth"? Think again. Will's fingers were ink-stained from penning clever curses and juicy insults.

Probably Timon of Athens would take the prize for most venom. When he discovered that his "friends" were little more than blood-sucking parasites, he cursed them. "Live loath'd and long," he screamed. Then he got specific, calling forth plagues, massacres, and a variety of horrendous miseries to befall one and all.

Name-calling is an art form in Shakespeare's plays. Some of the best invective is reserved for family members who put the "fun" in dysfunctional, Elizabethan style. "Thou art a boil, A plague-sore," cries King Lear to his daughter, Goneril. "Thou toad, thou toad!" screams the Duchess of York to her murderous son, King Richard.

Drinking with his buddies at the Boar's Head Tavern, Falstaff is a dictionary of diatribe in *Henry IV, Part One*. Provoked after being called "clay-brain'd" and "greasy" and a "huge hill of flesh," he lashes back with his own invective. "'Sblood, you starveling, you eel-skin, you dried neat's-tongue, you bull's pizzle..." Bull's pizzle! Zounds!

Young students of Shakespearean drama, in classrooms and summer camps around the English-speaking world, take great delight in making a game of verbal dueling, using the insults found in the plays. Offered selections from three columns, as illustrated below, they are instructed to assemble their most creative combinations, prefaced with the word "Thou," and try them on a partner —varying their pacing and volume, from sarcastic whispers to shocking shouts. In a frenzy of Renaissance ranting, the students hurl their insults —"Thou peevish, swag-bellied hag!" "Thou blubbering whey-faced weasel!"

Try your own combinations from the short list on the next page. Mix and match. When these run out, look up "Shakespearean Insults" on the Internet, or do your own research and delve for more in the plays themselves. Shakespeare penned them in abundance.

Column I	Column II	Column III
artless	beetle-headed	ape
detested	brazen-faced	barnacle
droning	boil-brained	beast
faithless	common-kissing	canker-blossom
fobbing	dizzy-eyed	codpiece
gleeking	flap-mouthed	coward
lumpish	fly-bitten	dewberry
mammering	fool-born	foot-licker
mewling	lily-livered	maggot-pie
monstrous	mad-headed	malt-worm
puny	plume-plucked	pagan
puking	rump-fed	rascal
tottering	tickle-brained	rogue
wretched	toad-spotted	strumpet
yeasty	urchin-snouted	viper

"Knock, Knock. Who's There?" Shakespeare's Famous Phrases

Name That Source!

ho first said, "The game is afoot"? Was it Arthur Conan Doyle's famous sleuth, Sherlock Holmes? No. It was Shakespeare's Earl of Northumberland in *Henry IV, Part One*.

Shakespeare gave us countless other famous phrases —"pomp and circumstance" (*Othello*), "into thin air" (*The Tempest*), "star-crossed lovers" (*Romeo and Juliet*) and "the naked truth" (*Love's Labour's Lost*).

Shakespeare penned so many familiar phrases and common sayings that he is often credited with ones he didn't write.

He may have given us "All that glisters is not gold" (*Merchant of Venice*), but not "The love of money is the root of all evil," which was penned by St. Paul. (I Timothy 6:10).

He gave us "strange bedfellows" (*The Tempest*), but not "stranger in a strange land," said by Moses (Exodus 2:22).

"Neither a borrower nor a lender be" is from *Hamlet,* but "A house divided against itself cannot stand," is credited to Jesus (Matthew 12:25) and later made famous by Abraham Lincoln.

Shakespeare gave us "short shrift" (*Richard III*), "wild-goose chase" (*Romeo and Juliet*), and "one fell swoop" (*Macbeth*), but not "drop in the bucket" (Isaiah 40:15), "twinkling of an eye" (I Corinthians 15:52), or "thorn in the flesh" (II Corinthians 12:7).

"To thine own self be true" is from *Hamlet,* but "Eat, drink and be merry," believe it or not, is from the Hebrew Scriptures (Ecclesiastes 8:15 and Isaiah 22:13) and later quoted by Jesus (Luke 12:19).

"No man is an island" is from neither Shakespeare nor the Bible. It is John Donne's alone.

Though Shakespeare wrote about Helen of Troy, it was his literary rival, Christopher Marlowe (1564-93), who described her as "the face that launched a thousand ships." Marlowe also authored the oft-used phrase, "love at first sight."

In *Twelfth Night*, Shakespeare gave us, "If music be the food of love, play on," but it was William Congreve (1670-1729) who wrote "Music hath charms to soothe the savage breast."

Shakespeare's mischievous Puck lamented, "Lord, what fools these mortals be," but it was Alexander Pope (1688-1747) who wrote,"Fools rush in where angels fear to tread." Pope also gave us, "A little learning is a dangerous thing."

Aldous Huxley borrowed from Shakespeare's *The Tempest* for the title of his 1932 novel, *Brave New World*, and Ray Bradbury found his 1962 title, *Something Wicked This Way Comes*, in *Macbeth*.

Shakespeare penned "It's Greek to me" (*Julius Caesar*) and "neither rhyme nor reason" (*As You Like It*), but not "out of the mouths of babes." That was Jesus (Matthew 12:25) quoting the Old Testament (Psalm 8:2).

"Knock, knock! Who's there?" Shakespeare, again. This line from *Macbeth* might lead one to sigh, "There's nothing new under the sun," but that is a line from the Bible (Ecclesiastes 1:9). Alas.

Household Words

Of the almost 900,000 words penned by Shakespeare, it is estimated that the total vocabulary used was around 25,000 words. (By contrast, the King James Bible uses only six thousand *different* words.) He almost wore out certain adjectives. "Sweet," for example, appears 876 times, as in Juliet's musing, "Parting is such sweet sorrow." Nearly half of

his 25,000 words, however, were ones he used only once.

Even more astonishing, over two thousand of the words in his plays were either ones he coined or put into print for the first time. Many of these are now so common as to be called household words. In fact, he gave us the term "household words." It comes from *Henry V*. He also gave us "eyesore," "sea-change" and "salad days," "bated breath" and "bag and baggage."

His writings are the first authority for *amazement, assassination, auspicious, barefaced, birthplace, bloodstained, cold-blooded, countless, dauntless, distrustful, employer, eventful, eyeball, fairyland, farmhouse, fashionable, hostile, hot-blooded, ill-tempered, laughable, leaky, love letter, madcap, moonbeam, priceless, puppy-dog, remorseless, schoolboy, scuffle, shooting star, silk stocking, stillborn, time-honored, tranquil, unearthly, unmitigated, unreal, upstairs, varied, vulnerable, watchdog, well-behaved, well-bred, well-read*, and hundreds of other words and phrases.